TAKE HER DEEP!

TAKE HER DEEP!

A

Submarine

Against

Japan

in

World War II

BY ADMIRAL I. J. GALANTIN U.S.N. (RET.)

with an introduction by
Edward L. Beach

BLUEJACKET BOOKS

NAVAL INSTITUTE PRESS
Annapolis, Maryland

Naval Institute Press
291 Wood Road
Annapolis, MD 21402

Published by arrangement with Algonquin Books of Chapel Hill (a division
of Workman Publishing).

First Bluejacket Books edition, 2007
ISBN-10: 1-59114-299-7
ISBN-13: 978-1-59114-299-7

Library of Congress Cataloging-in-Publication Data

Galantin, I. J., 1910☐
  Take her deep! : a submarine against Japan in World War II / by Admiral I. J.
Galantin, USN (Ret.). ☐ 1st Bluejacket Books ed., 2007.
    p. cm. ☐ (Bluejacket books)
  Orig.ed.: Algonquin Books of Chapel Hill, Chapel Hill, N.C.,1987.
  ISBN-13: 978-1-59114-299-7 (alk. paper)
  1. Galantin, I. J., 1910☐ 2. Halibut (Submarine) 3. World War, 1939☐1945☐
Naval operations☐Submarine. 4. World War, 1939☐1945☐Naval operations,
American. 5. World War, 1939☐1945☐Campaigns☐Pacific Area. 6. World
War, 1939☐1945☐Personal narratives, American. 7. Admirals☐United
States☐Biography. 8. United States. Navy.☐Officers☐Biography. I. Title.
D783.5.H26G35 2007
940.54☐51092☐dc22
[B]

                                                            2006028531

Printed in the United States of America on acid-free paper ∞

14 13 12 11 10 09   9 8 7 6 5 4 3

for Virginia
and all other submarine wives

Contents

Illustrations

Author's Note

The record of each United States submarine's World War II exploits is available to anyone in the now-declassified war patrol reports on file at the Submarine Force Library & Museum, Groton, Conn. Those official, stereotypical reports provide the factual data of a submarine's wartime action but little in the way of human activity and behavior.

For many years the now-dwindling ranks of *Halibut* shipmates have met in biennial reunion. For the conception and continuity of these gatherings we are all greatly indebted to Clayton Rantz and Silvio Gardella. On those occasions each officer and every enlisted men had his own tale to tell, his own memory of wartime events that we had shared but had experienced individually. Each man was hungry for a more comprehensive view of *Halibut's* action than he had at his battle station in engine room, torpedo room, or wherever.

To satisfy that craving I chose to cover the story of *Halibut* for the time she was under my command—August, 1943, to December, 1944. With no personal involvement in her earlier days, I could not reconstruct adequately the actions of ship and crew, bold and successful though they were, in the period from her commissioning on April 10, 1942, until August 11, 1943.

The names of many men who contributed importantly to *Halibut's* success and survival do not appear in my story. They performed their essential tasks in various parts of the ship, often isolated from supportive shipmates. Their duties were no less important and were frequently more dependent on personal knowledge and initiative than were those which were carried out in my sight on the bridge, in conning tower or control room.

I have tried to put the cumulative personal memories of attack and counterattack, of tension and release, of sorrow and humor, in the context of our ship's part in the overall submarine war in the Pacific. All events are true; all persons are real. We were collectively one with our ship; with her we constituted a weapon. I hope all hands will find this account of their ship and their shipmates a rewarding reminder of the way it was.

I am grateful to the many shipmates whose oral and written comments contributed so much to this effort. Especially valuable were Bob Black's loan of the Watch, Quarter and Station Bill from our tenth and last patrol, and Jack Perkins' loan of certain issues of the *Hali-bastard Herald*.

My thanks are due Norman Polmar who, in the more than thirty years of our acquaintance, has grown from avid student of submarine warfare to astute, internationally recognized analyst of naval affairs in general and submarines in particular. His constructive criticism of my first, rough manuscript encouraged my continued effort.

Of great importance to me were the encouragement and suggestions given by that most sagacious of editors, himself a "former naval person," Vermont Royster.

Finally, I am greatly indebted to my editor, Louis D. Rubin, Jr., for his professional guidance, and to Marjorie Corbett for her review of the final manuscript.

Pinehurst, North Carolina   I. J. GALANTIN
January 30, 1987

Introduction

BY EDWARD L. BEACH

Much was written during the World War II years about the exploits of our aviators and submariners, most of it by persons far better qualified in the use of the written word than in the navy they were trying to describe. By consequence much of the war literature of that time is, to those who actually served in the ships or aircraft, quite unperceptive of what was really going on. Some of it deserved harsher criticism: superficial, inaccurate, self-serving, shallow in real content.

Following the war, the true memoirs began to come out: stories, articles, novels, even histories, written by individuals who participated in the events and campaigns that were their subjects. The authors of these tomes, however, while eminently qualified in the martial arts they were describing, frequently were more adept at using the machines and weapons, or at writing reports and operation orders, than in what they were now trying to do, and the quality of their product was not as good as it should have been. Most frequently, sad to say, although these postwar writers had been so often directly involved in the events and combat of which they wrote, they did not really understand how to describe what they had seen and done. Thus, for example, a complicated torpedo attack might be dismissed in a paragraph or less, simply because the person describing it did not understand what it was that his audience thirsted to hear. For that matter, too often the reading audience itself did not understand what it wanted to hear, nor why.

Submariners in particular seemed loath to tell the details of their own very special art. perhaps it was because of the sobriquet, "silent service," bestowed by a long-forgotten reporter, or some ingrained idea about classified information to which other branches of our armed forces were less sensitive. Conceivably, submariners were not convinced that others could share their inherent deep interest in the inner workings of their ships, those poetically shaped combinations of massive machinery and complicated mechanisms, on which their lives depended or the details had become so routine to them that they could not grasp how nonroutine they might be to others.

Whatever the reasons, one would have thought they might at least have wanted the public to have a clear picture of what they were, and what they had done. But submariners did not write much, despite the early proliferation of poorly conceived novels written about them and their extraordinary ships by persons unfamiliar with the navy. (Some later writings have been much better, especially those by individuals forced to postpone completion of their formal education until after the war.)

However, there were observant, thoughtful, caring people out there, doing their bit, risking their lives, getting involved in the technical intricacies of submarine and torpedo performance, who also knew how to tell a story so that it speaks the truth to all who remember how it was. Such a man was Ignatius Joseph Galantin, known as Pete, who skippered the *Halibut* during the last half of her life, and lately promised the surviving members of his old crew that he would memorialize the history of their sub. This promise, and the shared memories it evoked, were the genesis of *Take Her Deep.*

Admiral Galantin (he earned four admiral's stars in postwar service), began his career, as so many did, as a midshipman at Annapolis. Within a decade after graduation he was given his own submarine, and even today probably feels that his highest purpose in life was achieved when he took command of the *Halibut.* A so-called fleet submarine, *Halibut* was magnificent, virtually brand-new, launched in early 1942, just in time to have a decisive influence on the war. As all submariners are wont to say, however, it is not only the ship and her equipment, but also the personalities and drive of her crew that make the thing go. So has it always been, with a ship built for battle. Most specifically, the personality and capability of her skipper is what makes a ship into a true man-of-war. (There were some submarine captains who could not bring themselves to fight, but we won the war because we had enough of those who could.)

The individuals who failed can not always be faulted for only their own inadequacies. The saga of our submarine torpedo fiasco has been told and retold, but it should never be untold. The real heroes of our submarine war were those who somehow rose above the dreadful realization that our country had sent them to war with a primary weapon that would not work: a torpedo so faulty that it might have been deliberately designed by someone in the pay of the enemy. Pete Galantin experienced it all, and was one of those who rose above it.

In this book he describes in minute detail his first attack on an enemy ship, a destroyer of the *Shigure* class, which he got dead to rights in a perfect firing position. A new submarine commander's first attack on the enemy, regardless of how many torpedoes he may have fired in exercises, is the most important of his career. It set the stage for how he performs thereafter. Galantin's was perfectly planned and executed. *Shigure*'s first intimation of danger was the bubble track headed toward her, and the sonar whine of approaching torpedoes— which passed beneath her keel and (almost predictably, at that period of the war) failed to function. Her counterattack was instant, professional, and almost successful, but *Halibut* survived, and then began the inevitable analysis of what had gone wrong. Many skippers, especially in the early days, tortured themselves with self-doubt when seemingly well-managed attacks brought only failure and depth charges. Some completely lost confidence in their training and their crews. Galantin simply redoubled his efforts.

It is here, however, that *Take Her Deep* does more for us than most books. Galantin gives not only the immediate postattack assessment but also the revision, made months after the end of the war, in which our survey teams reconciled our combat reports with those of the enemy. Thus, at this point in the *Halibut*'s story we learn what was reported to him at the time as having been heard and seen (which determined his immediately resulting actions), what his later best estimate of what took place was, and what the postwar analysis determined had actually happened. Now, of course, we know beyond all guessing. In peacetime exercises, his attack would have been scored "four-oh," perfect. But in this life and death confrontation the actual score was zero. *Halibut*'s torpedoes ran some twenty to thirty feet deeper than the depth at which they had been set, far beneath *Shigure*'s keel, far below the depth at which their top-secret "influence" exploders could function. There was no way they could have performed their task, unless, in direct disobedience of many times reiterated orders, their running depth had been set to zero. In desperation, some skippers did exactly that, only to see them still run under the target.

Much later, the trouble with the torpedoes finally repaired, Galantin fired a salvo of them at what he thought was a battleship, heard hits, surfaced, and saw the capsized bottom of a great ship slowly sinking before his eyes. But he could not convince the intelligence analysts that he had actually sunk a battleship, and it turned out that they were right and he was wrong. It was a cruiser, not a battleship, and the reader is treated to a dispassionate analysis of his own mistakes of deduction, as well as those of a Japanese enemy and our intelligence experts, in finally arriving at the true account of those fateful hours.

The high point of the story of the *Halibut* is her final action during the war. I was at sea myself in a sister submarine at the time, and well remember the story we heard that *Halibut* had nearly been sunk, that her pressure hull, heavily dented by depth charges, had bulged inward, but had not quite opened to the sea. Somehow, with desperate skill and hurried but carefully choreographed repairs, Galantin and his crew waited out the expected attacks, brought their badly damaged sub to the surface when it was at last safe to do so, and finally rendezvoused with another U.S. submarine for escort into the recently captured island of Saipan.

Halibut was sent back to the States as beyond repair, but the account of her near brush with "buying the farm" (yes, we submariners sometimes used that term also, despite its inappropriateness) preceded her into Pearl Harbor and San Francisco. The story had gotten better: a wake had been held for her at the little local bar in San Francisco preempted by her crewmen for off-hours during the overhaul of only a few months before—and great was their pleasure at explaining that the wake had been premature, her death in action "greatly exaggerated."

Halibut served the U.S. Navy only four years, until late 1945, and was sold for scrap in 1946. Yet the ship was a bargain for any who cared to match results against cost. She contributed mightily to the war effort, won decorations for her crew and a commendation for herself, was always an ornament to a demanding service.

But there's much more to *Halibut*'s story than only this, for in setting it down, Pete Galantin shows himself as a skipper who had regard and respect for his crew members as fellow men—and although he does not dwell on this or even mention it, it's evident they reciprocated the feeling toward him. Every crew has its humorists, its dogmatists, its religious buffs, its "eager beavers" and its nonperformers who in a few cases turn out to be daredevils in disguise (but in most cases not). In the beginning, Galantin states clearly that he could not hope to name all the members of his crews but wishes them to know that he had them all in his mind and in his heart as he wrote about the old days. In spite of this modest disclaimer, he does very well with them, recounting their strengths and inspiration (only a few of their weaknesses), and proves that he was both aware of and amused by the personal foibles that helped them keep their sanity.

Prominent in this book are some of the escapades of an improbable backcountry character who came as a replacement ship's cook. Unaware of the traditional way to report on board, he told the Executive Officer that his name was "Mr. Mosley,"—and this he was joyously called by the entire crew forever after. Obviously they liked him, but they also delighted in the heavy-handed ribbing which accompanies most such situations. In this instance, Mr. Mosley may have been more clever than anyone gave him credit for, and the reader shares in the skipper/author's own enjoyment of the somewhat unorthodox situation. One thing is sure: his shipmates loved it.

When we come to the end of *Take Her Deep* there are both sad and glad notes. The moment of sadness came at the war's end, when Pete Galantin returned aboard the ship he had commanded, where she lay forlornly at New London, Connecticut, in the row of decommissioned subs awaiting disposition. He sat in the wardroom in the same seat where he had sat so many times, tried to remember her as she was, listened for the sequential play of the ship's mechanisms and systems; the passage of feet; the subdued, distant orders and responses; the murmur of her engines or motors; and the sibilant hum of the water swishing by. Of course, he could not awaken any of these, but he describes his poignant feelings as he listened for them. It was only a sentimental journey and perhaps he should not have gone, because at that low moment there could be no recapturing the life that had existed before. But, of course, he had to.

There was a joyous other ending, the return home, safe after the war, to the wife and little girls so happily awaiting him. Nearly every one of her crew experienced this, in one form or another. This was something against which the inanimate steel of a once but no longer vibrant ship could not hope to compete, and should not have to try. Her spirit was of a different sort, and will last forever in the minds of those who once served it. Pete Galantin went on to a long and richly rewarded career in the U.S. Navy, but once in a while the old crew members get together, and he's no longer a four-star admiral but their

"Captain Pete." Sometimes just his nickname, quietly spoken, is used by some of the men who, in years past, earned the right. There is no disrespect here; only a fond memory of days now long ago, rich in nostalgia, when they feared the enemy together and put their faith the only place they could, in their boat and in their skipper. These brought them through against the toughest ASW measures, and the greatest damage reported by any submarine of our side. It was the nearest of near misses, and it remains the truest, and strongest, of all possible bonds.

1

Hot and Straight

At 1300 on the afternoon of Friday, August 20, 1943, the fleet submarine U.S.S. *Halibut* (SS 232) sailed from Midway Island in the Central Pacific. She was bound for the sea lanes of the Empire of Japan.

The 312-foot-long submarine, powered by four 1,500 horsepower Fairbanks-Morse diesel engines and armed with twenty-four Mark XIV torpedoes, had completed five previous war patrols. This would be my first aboard her, and my first combat command in the Pacific theater.

We left Midway's reef-encircled harbor in company with two other boats,[1] *Searaven* and *Pompano*. Overhead two Navy F4U Corsairs flew escort. Three hours after we turned westward from Midway's sea buoy, our escorting planes dipped their wings, swooped low over us, and departed for their base. Not long after, the three submarines parted company, each to go her own way. Alone, separate from every friendly force, *Halibut* was now no more than a miniature marker inching westward on the huge, magnetized wall chart of the Pacific in ComSubPac's (Commander Submarine Force, Pacific Fleet) operations center back at Pearl Harbor. Not until we were well clear of enemy waters on our way back and broke radio silence would an anxious Rear Admiral Charles A. Lockwood, Jr., and his brilliant operations officer, Captain Richard Voge, know that *Halibut* still lived.

By sunset we were alone on the immensity of the Pacific, settled into the grim routine of the silent, wet war we fought. Our navigator, Lieut. Comdr. Ovid M. (Mack) Butler, took his evening star sights with the meticulous care that was his hallmark. Ceasing zigzagging, we set course for our patrol station.

---

1. Submarines of any size, then as now, were called "boats" rather than "ships." This custom derives from the early designs of submarines; they were so small that they could carry only a handful of men and were not capable of extensive cruising. In fact, for some transocean voyages they were, like boats, simply hoisted on board a transport ship and carried to their destination.

Day after day we held our course westward over the generally calm, blue Pacific, proceeding on diesel power at fifteen knots on the surface. Each dawn the sun rose astern, climbed into the sky, overtook us and plunged each night below the horizon, beyond which lay Japan. With nightfall came the still greater immensity of the heavens as the private planet of our ship throbbed its way among the constellations mirrored on the smooth, black surface of the sea. How easily Kipling's lines came to mind:

The steady forefoot snored
Through planet powdered floors.

And yet, how deceptive was our solitude! Day or night we lived with the lurking danger that an enemy sub might be concealed, hidden beneath the surface, awaiting our noisy approach, or a Jap plane flying from Marcus Island might swoop down to spew its deadly load of bombs. These were thoughts each man resolved in his own way as the 2,250 miles to our patrol area poured steadily under our keel and out *Halibut*'s foaming wake. Every turn of our screws drove us farther from our base, from our own forces, and closer to the enemy it was our duty and desire to destroy.

It was my custom to study each day a chapter of the Bible. On the morning of August 29, as we crept toward the coast of Honshu near Kuro Saki, I was absorbed in the Book of Job. The fifteenth chapter, twenty-first verse reads: "A dreadful sound is in his ears: in prosperity the destroyer shall come upon him."

Shortly before 0800, with the green hills of Honshu looming high in the field of our periscope, Ensign Ray Stewart, at his watch station in the conning tower, sighted a loaded freighter proceeding northward close inshore, escorted by a *Shigure*-class destroyer.

With the order "Battle stations, torpedo" passed over the general announcing system, word of the contact flashed through the ship like an electric spark. The general alarm in a submarine is melodious, almost like musical door chimes. Someone must have reasoned that there were enough raucous, harsh noises coming from diving alarm, collision alarm, and other sources, and that the happy event of going to battle stations deserved a more pleasant announcement.

Dashing to the conning tower, I found our carefully drilled torpedo fire control party already at work. Ensign Jack Barrett had energized

the Torpedo Data Computer (TDC) and was cranking in the first estimates of target data. Ensign Si Lake was setting up his manual plot in
the control room, where Lieut. (junior grade) Jack Hinchey had taken
over the dive. Quartermaster Bill Henderson was recording events in
his log. Others were aligning and checking instruments, testing battle
telephone circuits, or receiving reports from throughout the ship.

I was aware that all hands in the conning tower were studying the
new skipper, silently wondering, loyally supporting, instantly responsive to speed, depth, and course orders as I commenced closing the
target to where we "couldn't miss." In every compartment, old hands
who had made several war patrols and had felt the jarring concussion
of depth charges, and new men who were going into action for the
first time, gazed thoughtfully at the gray-enamelled loudspeaker from
which came the description of our target and its escort.

Our battle stations telephone talker in the conning tower was our
savvy yeoman, John T. Dempster, a tall, slim, good-looking man from
New Jersey. Mack Butler or I would tell him what orders or data to
pass, but during lulls in our action he would surreptitiously pass his
own observations of conning tower activity. My right eye, pressed to
the rubber cup of the periscope, was our link with the enemy; my
comments and reactions, even my tone of voice and appearance, were
critical to the state of mind of all those, anxious and unseeing, throughout the boat.

It was a clear, sparkling morning with a fresh breeze laying a pattern
of whitecaps on the dark blue water, an ideal day for periscope work.
In such conditions, up-sun from the destroyer, there was almost no
chance that her lookouts could sight the slender, 1.4″-diameter tip of
our attack scope, which was exposed above the wave tops just the few
inches necessary for brief looks.

With the *Shigure* destroyer about 2,000 yards to seaward of the
freighter, hence between us and the maru[2] that was our intended
victim, it was soon apparent that we could not get close enough for a
good shot at the freighter. But pressing on, it was clear that we could
attack the destroyer at a favorable range. Looking up a *Shigure's*
masthead height in our book of Japanese warship recognition data,
we used that for ranging with the periscope stadimeter.

---

2. *Maru* is the Japanese word meaning a merchant ship. The term is appended to each
ship's name.

We had to work fast to reach the best firing position. Pulling the scope down, speeding up to gain bearing on the unsuspecting destroyer, we relied on sonar to tell us what the target was doing. Looking over Jack Barrett's shoulder, on the dials of the TDC I could see the relative positions of sub and target, the gyro angles being generated for the torpedoes, and the distance the fish would have to run. Speaking to Jack, but loud enough for all in the conning tower to hear, I said, "We'll fire three bow tubes at the destroyer. I'll aim the first at her foremast. Spread the others to bow and stern."

Via John Dempster, Mack ordered, "Make ready tubes one, two, and three."

Soon the word came. "Tubes one, two, and three ready. Outer doors closed."

I sense a bit of extra tension in the boat. Could men be thinking, Why must our first attack with a new skipper be against a destroyer? Tin cans are built to find and destroy submarines.

"Let's have a look. What should he bear?"

"Three one eight, sir."

To save precious seconds during a torpedo approach, the periscope is not lowered all the way to the stops between looks, just enough to get it safely below the surface. Now, as the knurled handles come clear of the well, Quartermaster Henderson, on the opposite side of the scope from me, sets the scope to the proper bearing. There'll be no time lost searching for the target.

"Good! He doesn't see us. Angle-on-the-bow, starboard thirty-five. Mark the range! Down periscope! All ahead two-thirds!" The words and orders come fast. "Jack, what's the course for an eighty-degree starboard track, zero gyros?"

"Two six five, captain."

"Steer two six five."

Mack orders the forward torpedo room to open the torpedo tube outer doors. Emil Ade, torpedoman 1c in charge of the room, supervises intently, checks sea and impulse air pressures as Ed Bertheau, torpedoman 3c, and Jack Perkins, torpedoman 2c, turn the heavy cranks which open the outer doors. Bertheau is a powerful, stocky man, Perkins slight and wiry, but their two doors open almost simultaneously. Breathing hard, they share turns on the third.

As soon as the doors are open I tell Mack, "I'll give a final bearing, then shoot."

"Torpedo room, Control, stand by!"
"Up scope. Final bearing. Mark!"
Mack calls out, "Three three six."
Jack makes a slight adjustment on the TDC. "Set. Checking nicely."
"Shoot!"
"Fire one!" and Chief Quartermaster Robert M. Robison presses his palm firmly on the plunger of the firing switch mounted on the bulkhead to port.

At six-second intervals it's "Fire two! . . . Fire three!" All we can feel in the conning tower is a slight shudder as the fish are blown clear of their tubes, and a slight increase of pressure on our ears as the tubes are vented inboard to prevent a bubble from revealing our location.

Jack Hinchey, at his diving station in the control room, eyes his depth gauge and inclinometer carefully. The bubble which indicates a small up-angle is moving forward a little more than he likes. He asks for a little more speed, and I order, "All ahead standard." Bow and stern planesmen concentrate grimly on depth gauge and plane indicators.

"How long will it take the fish to get there?"
"Sixty-seven seconds, sir."
"All ahead one-third." There is time for "a look all around," which Mack reminds me to do as we slow down.

"Up scope!" Sweeping the horizon with the periscope set in low power (1.5 magnification), I can see no intruders, surface or air. "All clear."

I am utterly calm. I feel no elation, only the satisfaction of a job done in competent, professional fashion. It is as if all my years of training and practice have focused on this one, climactic occasion.

Twenty-four minutes after making our initial contact we have fired our torpedoes at the destroyer at a range of 1,900 yards. With the fish set to run at a depth of six feet with very small gyro angles on a favorable track angle, I have every reason to expect a kill on a man-of-war on my very first attack. There need be no concern about faulty magnetic exploders. By this time ComSubPac has had enough evidence of their malfunction to order them inactivated. We use only contact exploders.

Returning my scope to watch the destroyer as the fish near her, I remark on her smart appearance, "She's a fine-looking ship; nothing sloppy about her. I can see a lot of lookouts. They're wearing whites. Some are on her bridge. A lot more are spread along her rails."

I think, Here's a captain who knows what he wants, and give him my grudging respect.

Suddenly some of the lookouts are waving their arms, pointing in our direction, shouting to the bridge. "They see the wakes of the fish, but they're going right at her."

Just then, timing the distance run by stopwatch, Robison sings out, "Torpedoes should be there now, captain."

I am following the bubbles of the torpedo tracks as they speed to their convergence with the doomed target, and sonar is reporting steadily, "All fish running, hot, straight, and normal."

Instinctively I grip more tightly the knurled handles of the attack periscope, and brace for the expected explosions. They do not come! I watch with horrified fascination as the torpedo tracks run right to the target, but can see or hear no explosions.

Betrayed by our own weapons, all surprise lost, we are suddenly in a deadly duel—the fast, maneuverable destroyer with its potent depth charges pitted against the slow, stealthy submarine with its torpedoes that don't work! Close to the enemy shore, in water only 240 feet deep, with twelve hours of daylight before we dare surface, we are in for a busy day!

2

Before Pearl Harbor

In the words of Fleet Admiral Chester W. Nimitz, "submarine personnel filled the breach after Pearl Harbor, and can claim credit, not only for holding the line, but also for carrying the war to the enemy while our shattered forces repaired damages following the treacherous initial attack of the Japanese. . . ."

This tribute from one of our greatest naval officers, himself one of our earliest submariners, emphasizes that it was people, enlisted men and officers, not brilliant planning, superior training, or excellent weapons, who held the line. We had none of those advantages to start with.

The submarine force has always been a compact, cohesive segment of the United States Navy. It attracts officers who welcome the greater responsibilities which are promptly assigned, and the opportunity for earlier command. Similarly, enlisted men, all volunteers, seek the camaraderie and more personal involvement they can have in the workings of a smaller, less formal team. The smaller individual ships, the smaller total force, and the interdependence of every man in the crew, officer and enlisted man alike, have, since the navy's acceptance of its first submarine in 1900, led to a force with a special esprit de corps. The conditions of operation in the early, uncomfortable, often foul-smelling, small ships, and the unique hazards of submarine duty, have generated a system of leadership and discipline that is relaxed and informal but effective.

In a submarine there is no need for the trappings of rank or seniority. Once under way, officers stow their caps and neckties. Uniform caps won't last long on the open, windswept bridge; below decks they are useless. Depending on the season, baseball caps or watch caps are the fashion topside. With the first change of shirt on war patrol, even the collar marks of rank are dispensed with. Officers wear khaki shirt and trousers, enlisted men blue denim dungarees. In the tropics, or when sweating under prolonged counterattack, we peel down to shorts and sandals. We know each other, and what each man's job is. Instant response cannot wait for credentials of authority.

With a submarine force in the 1930s that averaged some eighty boats, there were only about 500 officers serving in them at any one time. All of them had the same background of training at the Submarine School in New London, Connecticut, and virtually every one was a graduate of the Naval Academy at Annapolis, Maryland. This shared experience of a small group led to a closer comradeship than existed in the much larger surface and air communities of the navy. The network of friendships interlaced the entire force.

The records and reputations of skippers were easily followed throughout the widely dispersed submarine force. One captain might be devil-may-care, another meticulous and plodding, one a wizard at estimating angles-on-the-bow,[1] another daring in torpedo attacks; no matter whether he was in New London or Panama, he could be spoken of in submarine wardrooms from San Diego to Pearl Harbor to the Asiatic station.

My own entry into the submarine service came in 1936. Following graduation from the Naval Academy in 1933 I had served my first two probationary years (with marriage banned) in the battleship *New York*. I became increasingly restive. In our operations we were encountering more and more new ships as President Roosevelt's naval augmentation program gathered momentum. In addition, naval aviation was making great progress, attracting many of my peers. I wanted to be free of the dull, repetitious, institutionalized life of the battleship navy, and to be part of a more personalized, more modern and flexible sea arm.

In 1934 the Fleet sailed from the Pacific to the East Coast for Roosevelt's Presidential Review off Sandy Hook, New Jersey. This was a fine opportunity to see all elements of our fleet—air, surface, submarine—in action in the countless exercises conducted en route. It would help many of us make up our minds as to which course to steer in our future careers. However, certain prejudices had to be overcome. When we reached New York we would read:

> The most impressive and important maneuvers ever conducted by the U.S. battle fleet have demonstrated that the Panama Canal can be captured or destroyed by an enemy fleet and that a

---

1. The angle measured to port or starboard from the bow of the target to the line of sight of the attacker.

Japanese-American naval war under present conditions is virtually impossible. In demonstrating that the canal could be taken, it was proven also that the cost would be so terrible as to make it actually impracticable, because the attacking nation would be left crippled. It was demonstrated again, also, that the battleship remains the Gibraltar of naval warfare.[2]

This was the view transmitted by the United Press correspondent who rode the battleship *Pennsylvania*, flagship of Rear Admiral D. F. Sellars, Commander in Chief, U.S. Fleet.

At any rate, I chose submarines.

The cruise led to another, even more critical decision. In New York I met for the first time Virginia Jaeckel. She was the young sister of a friend who had been captain of Princeton's fencing team (as I had been of Navy's). A mutual attraction was evident from the start, but only a fortuitous circumstance gave us the opportunity and time to develop that fact. Since my ship bore the name of the Empire State, following brief visits to other East Coast cities, she was designated to return to New York. Moored in the Hudson off Seventy-ninth Street, it was a quick and easy boat trip to midtown Manhattan, where Ginny would await me. An ensign's pay could not sustain many nights on the beach in New York City, but my pretty companion, with a family background of seven generations there, was able to guide us to the more reasonable, sometimes free, entertainments the big city offered. As the hot August days and nights sped by and the time came to sail for the West Coast, our plans were made to meet in California, where we were married in 1935.

In years to come, armed with such firsthand evidence, I would teasingly and unconvincingly argue to Ginny and our three daughters that "Marriages aren't made in heaven; they're made in BuPers." (The Bureau of Naval Personnel determined the ships or stations to which we were ordered for duty.)

Ours was a most improbable, very American marriage, joining a Mayflower descendant with a first generation American. There was no professional military background in Ginny's family. Her forebears included a colonial governor, Mary Murray who detained Lord Howe, a senator, educators, merchants, and lawyers, one of whom, Benjamin Tracy, was a Secretary of the Navy. Neither was there a military

2. *Time* magazine, June 4, 1934.

tradition in my family. My paternal ancestors, apparently Huguenots, left northern France and emigrated to Hungary. From there, in 1905 my parents came to New York City, where I was born in 1910.

My boyhood in Des Plaines, Illinois, brought no exposure to the world beyond the oceans. Only occasional vistas of Lake Michigan, its ore carriers rising slowly above the horizon or slipping gradually hull-down as they sailed away, hinted of the larger, oceanic world. There were no seafaring men in my family's poorly recorded history; only one ancestor was connected with ships. Father sometimes spoke of an uncle who was captain of a river steamer on the Danube, a man who yearned to go to sea but who was constrained to pilot the shoals and narrows of one of Europe's mightiest rivers. Somehow the lure of the sea was revived in me.

There was no Naval Academy appointment available when I graduated from high school in 1927, but I turned down the offer of a scholarship to Swarthmore and a chance to compete for West Point. I followed my next chosen path, architecture, by working as office boy–draftsman by day and attending Armour Institute of Technology in the evening. In the second year there was an uncommitted Naval Academy appointment available. Through the intercession of Dr. Clarence M. Earle, our town's senior and highly respected physician, I was assured the chance to enter the competition through which Senator Charles S. Deneen would make the award. I expected strong competition, so I quit my job in order to devote two months to full-time study at home. On the appointed day in November, 1928, I joined thirty-one other aspirants in the Federal Office Building in Chicago to take the lengthy, written examination that would determine the future for one of us. I won the appointment, took the anticlimactic entrance exam in February, and entered the Naval Academy in June, 1929. The four years that followed were among the happiest, most fulfilling of my life.

In spite of our differing heritage, Ginny and I both took easily to service life. We enjoyed the changing scenes of duty at home or overseas, the ever-widening circle of friendships, and accepted with good grace the inevitable separations of sea duty. The passionate reunions of early years were succeeded by the joys of homecoming to a house filled with love and the problems of three growing daughters.

But all that was ahead of me as I set off with my bride for sub school in December, 1935. The transfer gave us the first of seven transcontinental family journeys. Most of the subsequent ones would be enlivened by the problems and paraphernalia incident to traveling with babies or small children, but this first cross-country drive was sheer holiday. It went a long way toward overcoming the trauma of severing ties with one's first ship, one which had been home for two and a half years, and leaving familiar surroundings in which we were comfortable and secure, with shipmates who filled our days with fellowship. But as we drove away from San Pedro, California, and headed eastward, there was submerged in the excitement of the long trip the vaguely uneasy realization that I was now a mature naval officer, that I had made a critical choice, and that this was but the first of many new assignments, the start of an unforeseeable succession of ships and stations around the world.

On completion of submarine school in June, 1936, I was ordered to Pearl Harbor for duty in *Argonaut* (SS 166). She was our largest submarine, 381 feet in length with a submerged displacement of 4,164 tons. In all the world, she was second in size only to the French *Surcouf*. *Argonaut* was a hybrid, a complex, overdesigned, underpowered monster. She was the only submarine minelayer we would ever build. In her bow she had four 21″ torpedo tubes from which to fire her twelve Mark XIII, three-speed torpedoes, but the after third of the ship was given over to the stowage and launching of sixty Mark XI mines. The two mine launching tubes were 40″ in diameter; each could hold four mines at a time. The mine handling and launching mechanisms were ingenious, but crude and very noisy. Topside she mounted two 6″ 53 caliber guns such as were the normal armament of a light cruiser!

Graduation from sub school was only the first step in a submarine career. To earn the designation "Qualified in submarines," which gave the right to wear the gold dolphins insignia, would require a year of satisfactory service in an operating sub, completion of a notebook in which all ship's systems were sketched and described, demonstration of proficiency in diving the ship and in operating its machinery, as well as the ability to make a successful torpedo attack. To earn their silver dolphins, enlisted men went through a similar but less rigorous procedure.

A year or two after qualification, subject to the C.O.'s recommendation, would come the designation "Qualified to command submarines." Four years' duty in *Argonaut* brought me both designations.

The annual highlight of duty in the "Pineapple Navy," as less fortunate sailors referred to our Hawaiian contingent, came when the forces based on the West Coast of the United States steamed to the Hawaiian area to conduct a fleet problem. Generally this took the form of searching for and destroying a hostile force approaching from the north or west with the objective of seizing a base in the island chain. Thus there was reasonable similarity to the actual events we would face in just a few years. What was lacking was the element of surprise, and the bold, imaginative way our adversary would employ airplanes and submarines.

Slow, clumsy *Argonaut* was generally deployed alone in advance of other units to act as a scout, to shell "enemy" seaplanes anchored in a lagoon, or to lay simulated minefields. We were not a very reliable scout. Submarine radio equipment of the time was very poor; we had to wait for nightfall to have any hope of transmitting a signal even 650 miles. With the Hawaiian archipelago stretching almost 1,500 miles from the 13,800-foot-high "Big Island" of Hawaii northwest to Midway and tiny Kure, which barely keep their heads above water, we were frequently out of touch with headquarters in Pearl Harbor.

Meanwhile, in 1939 another step was taken in extending the reach of sea-based airpower. *Nautilus*, our sibling submarine, had part of her main ballast tanks fitted to carry aviation gas, which she uneasily transported to French Frigate Shoals. About 550 miles northwest of Pearl Harbor, this cluster of tiny, windswept islets surrounding a large lagoon was entirely unlike the lush, lofty islands of the main Hawaiian group. The dominant feature is a rocky pinnacle 135 feet high, covered with guano. Glistening white in the hot, tropic sunlight, it had seemed to the French naval explorer, La Perouse, like the sail of a distant frigate rising gradually above the horizon when he discovered it in 1787.

Argonaut had deployed with *Nautilus*, and as we lay-to on the surface of the shallow lagoon near La Perouse Rock, we watched countless seabirds wheel and dart about the pinnacle while we awaited birds of another feather. Soon PBY (Catalina) seaplanes based at Pearl Harbor swooped down and carved white wakes on the brilliant green surface. One by one they taxied to the mooring buoy where *Nautilus* headed into the wind, and took aboard the refueling hose she passed.

Perhaps the Japanese had observed or followed this test. In March, 1942, two of their submarines, *I-15* and *I-19*, refueled two "Emily" seaplanes at French Frigate Shoals. The planes then flew on to a nighttime, unsuccessful bombing of Oahu.

The navy's pre–World War II leaders did not foresee the great impact which submarines would have on war at sea, not only on seaborne commerce, but on naval forces as well. Who could imagine that a force which started with fifty-one U.S. submarines widely dispersed across the Pacific, and whose peak personnel strength would be only 1.6 percent of our total navy, would become the "most decisive single factor in the collapse of the Japanese economy and logistic support of Japanese military and naval power"?[3] The submarine force sank more enemy warships and more enemy cargo ships than did any other agent. It destroyed more than half the total tonnage lost by Japan to all causes, Allied included.

This record was all the more astonishing for a force which started with a misguided strategic concept, ineffective weapons, and unrealistic training. Our pre–World War II submarine warfare doctrine specified: "The primary task of the submarine is to attack enemy heavy ships. A heavy ship is defined as a battleship, battle cruiser, or an aircraft carrier. On occasions, the primary task may, by special order, be made to include heavy cruisers, light cruisers, or other types of ships." Consistent with this doctrine, the Navy General Board had emphasized to our submarine designers the sub's role in accompanying the battle fleet and supporting it by scouting reports and torpedo attacks on enemy fleet units.

Although it was Germany's resort to unrestricted submarine warfare in World War I that had brought the United States into that conflict, in both the United States and the United Kingdom there was reluctance to face up to the fact that only in that way could the submarine make its most meaningful contribution to war at sea. Both these sea powers still viewed the submarine as the enemy of their power afloat, not as a purposeful extension of that power. In fact, by the London Agreement of 1930, the United States, Britain, and Japan had reaffirmed the restrictions on submarine warfare first imposed by the Washington Naval Arms Limitation Treaty of 1922: "with regard to

3. *U.S. Strategic Bombing Survey* (Washington, D.C.: Government Printing Office, 1947).

merchant ships, submarines must conform to the rules of International Law to which surface vessels are subject."

This position ignored the fact that if it surfaced to halt, examine, or attack shipping by gunfire, the submarine became extremely vulnerable. Its opponent could generally deliver heavier, more accurate fire from a more stable platform. Further, it did not have the means to place crew and passengers in positions of safety, as the wishful morality of the major maritime nations decreed. Neither could it provide search teams or prize crews for ships it intercepted. Like the other new attack vehicle which was rapidly coming to the fore in the thirties—the airplane—the submarine could sink or destroy, but could not capture or control.

The weapons which were able to exploit the submarine's stealth by delivering surprise attack on targets in areas not tenable by surface forces were the torpedo and the mine. They permitted carrying the offensive into the enemy's home waters or other critical areas denied to surface or air penetration. Surprise attack by torpedo was considered barbarous and inhumane, but the surreptitious and accurate placement of minefields was considered a legitimate application of submarine warfare. Still, the perceived international morality of the time required announcement of that action. Indeed, proclamation of a mine field did not have to be followed by the fact of existence. An enemy could be led to believe that one existed, with profound military, political, and psychological consequences.

With so pervasive a mindset concerning submarines, it is not surprising that as late as 1938 the Commander-in-Chief, U.S. Fleet, concluded that "based on their employment in direct support of Fleet operations," and to "provide for other needs that might arise," a total of seventy-eight modern, long-range boats would be required.[4] This figure was absurdly low for the kind of submarine war that would actually be fought.

Although the highest echelons of the navy seemed preoccupied with the use of the submarine in direct Fleet support, the submarine operators themselves were becoming more articulate in advancing a more independent role for their craft. Addressing the same problem in 1938, the Commander Submarine Force went on record with the

4. Commander-in-Chief, United States Fleet, letter A16/0636 dated May 11, 1938.

following opinions as to the functions and necessary characteristics of future submarines:

(a) The primary purpose of the submarine is conceived to be to operate offensively in distant waters generally controlled by the enemy and consequently denied to all other types of naval vessels or aircraft. Whether operating from peacetime bases advanced as far as possible towards probable employment areas or from advanced bases established after the declaration of war, submarines of long radius and as nearly self-supporting as practicable are required for these duties.

(b) The secondary purpose of the submarine is to operate strategically or tactically with our own fleet, either in distant scouting areas or disposed to cover areas through which an enemy fleet may be expected or drawn. These duties require submarines with surface ability, sea endurance, large radius of action, and as much speed as can be reliably installed in the designed hull.[5]

As we drifted inexorably toward war with Japan, it was fortunate that the latter view was prevailing in the design and construction of *Porpoise* (SS 172). Completed in 1935, she was lead ship of a class of submarine suitable for long-range, independent combat operations, yet with considerable growth potential inherent in her design.

When World War II erupted in the Pacific and our submarines were called upon to hold the line against Japan's powerful navy, we were ill-prepared. But once faced by the reality of disaster at Pearl Harbor, of war against a ruthless enemy, it did not take the United States long to renounce the London Submarine Agreement. Six hours after the attack on Pearl Harbor the order went out, "Execute unrestricted air and submarine warfare against Japan."

We had a total of 111 submarines in commission, 51 in the Pacific. Of these, 29 were on the Asiatic station, 22 at Pearl or San Diego. Of the 29 boats based on Manila, and thus earliest to get into action, 23 were modern, fleet-type, the other 6 being obsolescent, short-range S-boats whose living conditions had deservedly earned them their

5. Commander Submarine Force Seventh Endorsement serial SC26-38 dated July 27, 1938.

nickname "pig boats." All fleet boats were named for fish; the S-boats bore only a number.

We did not know how best to employ submarines in war. Our brief experience in World War I with a few primitive boats deployed in the vastly different Atlantic area gave little useful information. As to submarine operations in World War II in which the British had been engaged since 1939, we had only recently received action reports from our liaison officers assigned to their subs.

Swordfish, under quiet, meticulous Chester C. Smith, was first to sink a ship. On December 16, 1941, she sank *Atsutasan Maru*. A total of five marus was sunk that month, six more in January, 1942, and four in February. The number rose slowly but steadily, but time after time enraged, frustrated skippers would return to port with tales of torpedoes that exploded prematurely, failed to explode, or missed for unknown reasons.

The sinking of Japanese Navy ships also came slowly. The first torpedoing of an enemy warship came on January 27, 1942, when *Gudgeon*, under dynamic, aggressive Joe Grenfell, waylaid submarine *I-173* as she was returning to Japan on the surface from her shelling of our West Coast. In the first twelve months of war, fourteen Japanese warships were sunk, the major one being the 8,800-ton heavy cruiser *Kako*. She was sunk by the tired, old *S-44* under J. R. (Dinty) Moore, who camouflaged a sharp mind behind a soft, slow-spoken, Tennessee hillbilly drawl.

It was a lonely, frustrating period for the pioneer wartime skippers as they sailed on their solitary missions. There were no ships in company sailing against a common foe, a situation wherein, under a bold leader, the dynamics of visible support, of shared danger, of common action would sweep along even the faint-hearted. Plunged into the unforgiving realities of war, solely responsible for the actions and survival of eighty other men and their ship, they suffered the "first time syndrome." There was no background of combat experience from which to evaluate the enemy's capabilities or assess the worth of specific tactics. Deep within enemy-controlled waters, hundreds or even thousands of miles from the nearest friendly forces, the submarine C.O. had to devise his own tactics, weighing the chances of his ship against real or imagined enemy countermeasures. There was frequently a lack of aggressiveness and a tendency to credit the Japanese with better antisubmarine tactics and weapons than they had.

In the first year of the war about 30 percent of the skippers were relieved of command, some at their own request, others for ineffective performance. They went on to duty in surface ships, where many performed excellently, or to important submarine and Navy Department staff duties. Younger men who had commanded the smaller training boats, or who had been executive officers to their more senior skippers, were fleeted up rapidly. By 1943 the average age of a combat skipper was thirty-two, and among those who sailed on war patrol in 1945 some were only twenty-six. Under the same circumstances faced by our more senior predecessors, these younger skippers would, in all likelihood, have fared little better. We benefited from our own prior wartime experience, from the accumulated action reports of others, and from improved weapons and equipment.

It is hardly conclusive, but there is an interesting example in ten of us who served in *Argonaut* just before the war, and who each commanded his own boat later. The five youngest, Herm Kossler, Al Becker, Dick O'Kane, Jack Gerwick, and I, between us sank forty-four ships totaling 169,604 tons. Our five older friends, all fine submarine officers, accounted for twelve ships of 52,798 tons. On assuming their commands, the older group averaged thirty-seven years, the younger thirty-two, and the spread between oldest and youngest individuals was nine years.

Dick O'Kane's record was truly spectacular; he was the most effective of all U.S. sub skippers. In five war patrols in command of *Tang* he sank twenty-four ships with a tonnage of 92,824. Even in 1938, as my shipmate in *Argonaut*, it was apparent that Dick was an innovative nonconformist. He chafed under the constraints of outmoded custom and standard practice. He was the best man to leave to his own devices in the shipyard when something had to be done in a hurry and not all the niceties of paperwork and prior approval were in hand.

As to prewar training, our torpedo attack practices were relatively simple and conservative. This was in keeping with the fire control equipment available. There was no radar; sonar was very erratic; range was determined visually, very much by-guess-and-by-God; torpedo gyro angles were picked off of a primitive mechanical device called the "banjo" because of its shape. Overriding these material deficiencies was the fact that in the environment of peacetime a submarine skipper's record (and thus his chances for promotion) was enhanced more by his administrative skill, the material condition of his boat, and the cleanliness and smart appearance of his ship and crew than by proficiency and daring in torpedo attack. It seemed foolhardy indeed for a skipper to risk the loss of a periscope or more severe damage to his ship in demonstrating his aggressiveness or permitting his junior officers to do so.

The torpedo approach practices generally consisted of diving some eight or ten miles ahead of a destroyer or other small ship target, then proceeding to close to a firing position on the zigzagging, slow-speed target. The position sought was that which would result in a torpedo run of about 1,000 yards and that would intersect the target's track at an angle from 80° to 110° off its bow. In every case a torpedo gyro angle as close to zero as possible was sought. With the "fish" necessarily set to run under the target's keel, by projecting forward from the bubble track rising from the torpedo exhaust, the point where the fish actually crossed the target's track could be roughly determined.

I can't recall any night surface-attack training. That would wait for the innovation and daring of skippers in wartime. Nor were there any attempts at wolf pack tactics. In a few more advanced exercises the target would be escorted, or "screened," by another surface ship or by aircraft, and be free to take evasive action should the attacking sub be detected. There was also a requirement for at least one torpedo firing a year to be conducted using only information derived by sound. The inefficient sonars and crude fire control instruments rarely produced accurate data, but these practices did give valuable experience. They demonstrated that, though visually blind, a submarine need not surrender the initiative.

If the practices of the era did not promote aggressiveness, at least their frequent repetition did develop the ability to visualize the trigonometry of the torpedo attack problem and to evaluate almost instinctively the problems of relative motion. With his face pressed to the rubber eyepiece of the periscope, in the few seconds of periscope exposure above water, the submarine C.O. estimated through one eye the angle-on-the-bow the target presented, her range and speed, and remained aware of sea and weather conditions. Hardly had he ordered, "Down periscope!" when he directed changes in course, speed, or depth. Just as the pilot of a fighter plane becomes a part of his machine—the human sensing and reacting element—the expert submarine skipper is the guidance and control element of his maneuvering vehicle.

By the time I received my first submarine command, *R-11*, in 1942, I had served under seven different skippers. Each had his own style of leadership, emphasized particular facets of submarining, and left enduring impressions on his junior officers of traits to avoid or qualities to emulate. I learned the most about how to be an effective sub skipper from C. H. (Herb) Andrews in *S-24*. Herb was a Connecticut Yankee who worked hard and played hard. He was dynamic and unequivocal, good-humored and fair. He went on to become one of our top wartime skippers in *Gurnard*.

It was to *S-24* in the Atlantic that I went as exec and navigator in 1940. She was one of our obsolescent S-boats being used to provide target services to our antisubmarine forces, and to advance our own torpedo attack training. When *S-24* sailed from New London to Philadelphia in September, 1941, for overhaul in the Navy Yard, U.S. entry into the war seemed to be awaiting only some climactic event.

As we stripped our ship for the heavy-handed ministrations of shipyard workmen, we could see in an adjacent drydock the British cruiser *Liverpool*, a gaping hole in her underbody. Here was my first, direct view of the work of a torpedo warshot. From the one German torpedo hit she took in the Mediterranean, *Liverpool* would be out of action for twelve months.

As I looked at the torn and twisted metal and reflected on the fate of the sailors who had been within that hull, I saw for the first time the reality for which I was being trained. I felt no horror or revulsion. It was a professional, unemotional view, a clinical appraisal of what happened in combat between two ships. The fact that men lived and worked in those ships was beside the point. It was the ships that fought each other; they are what mattered.

3

Guarding the Canal

Sunday, December 7, was overcast and chilly but dry. Our overhaul was proceeding on schedule toward its completion date in January, and I would have the whole day free with my family. Our daughters, at the ages of one and three, were too young to understand the place of Valley Forge in our history, but a visit there would take us away from the grime of the city and give us our first look at that historic turning point in the war for independence. As we drove back home in the darkening afternoon, I reflected on history's irony. In 1777 Britain occupied Philadelphia; now her forces returned for vital support in her own crisis of survival.

Back in our Walnut Park Plaza apartment, I switched on the radio and romped on the floor with the children while Ginny prepared dinner. A local radio announcer was reporting what sounded like a war game, a simulated attack on Pearl Harbor like those I had taken part in. "Now we switch to Honolulu for a direct report from the scene."

The voice that came over the air waves from the speaker 5,000 miles away was fraught with excitement. I suddenly realized that this was Webley Edwards, describing events that were real. This was no drill! During our four years in Hawaii we had many times observed or listened to Edwards's popular radio program, "Hawaii Calls," originating at the Moana Hotel on Waikiki Beach. As his agitated voice described familiar places, now burning and billowing smoke, the reality of disaster became clear. Japanese planes had swept in from north of Oahu in complete surprise to bomb and torpedo our fleet moored placidly in Pearl Harbor.

Hurrying to the shipyard, I met with our new skipper, Lieut. John Corbus, the Californian who had relieved Herb Andrews. We strengthened our security watch and made plans to speed our completion and departure. Johnny Corbus was an intellectual, a most kindly and considerate man, who planned meticulously and left nothing to chance.

With the completion of our testing and loading, we provided for the security and support of our families as best we could, and on December 20 sailed for our secret destination. Only the skipper and I knew that we were ordered to Panama.

When we sailed out of Delaware Bay and took departure from Cape May, the track I laid down on my navigational chart headed us for Crooked Island Passage through the Bahamas. The chart desk was merely a hinged table over the gyro compass which stood in the starboard, after corner of the control room. It received the curious glance of everyone who ducked through the watertight door leading to the after battery compartment. When the lookouts saw the penciled track on my chart, they didn't need a reminder to keep a sharp watch; they knew that this focal point of shipping could quickly become a happy hunting ground for U-boats.

In this period of confusion and uncertainty that marked the opening weeks of our now formally declared war in the Atlantic, *S-24* made her way steadily southward. Our two Nelseco diesels could push us against the Gulf Stream at only ten knots as we plodded along on the surface in rough, wintry seas. We dived only briefly each day to adjust our trim and for the training we needed after our months in the shipyard. Christmas Day in the Caribbean was warm with bright sunlight on a calm, blue sea. It gave us a welcome chance to get down on deck to repair storm damage, and to clean and dry out our ship below.

At Coco Solo in the Canal Zone a couple of days later, we joined five other boats of our squadron who had preceded us, and the eight boats of Subron 3 that had already been based there before the war. *Barracuda, Bass,* and *Bonita,* unreliable as ever, were also ordered to this duty, demoted from more demanding operations in the Atlantic.

The job of our obsolescent ships was to form a defensive screen guarding the Pacific approaches to the canal. After the success of the Japanese attack on Pearl Harbor, a carrier strike against the vital canal was not ruled out. And, in spite of the vast distance from Japan, perhaps submarine or surface raiders would try to prey on the steady stream of shipping to and from the canal.[1]

1. We learned after the war that the Japanese had indeed planned an attack on the Panama Canal, but that the attempt was never made. Their submarine *I-401* had been designed for the specific purpose of destroying the canal. She had a displacement of over 5,000 tons and a deck hangar to carry three seaplanes whose mission it would be to bomb the canal's vital points.

Our submarine patrols were augmented by the air patrols of Army B-17 Flying Fortress bombers and Navy PBY Catalina patrol planes. We would learn that these planes and the recently mobilized, sketchily trained navy surface escorts were our chief source of danger, through mistaken identity or faulty ship handling. The hand-held Aldis lamp we had for signaling was not steady or powerful enough for daylight communications. We had to use our 12" searchlight and, on occasion, even semaphore flags to send slow, laborious identification signals to ominously circling planes. These time-coded, pronounceable three-letter groups of challenge and response came from code books which the British Admiralty gave our navy. We had so much to learn about fighting a war.

Each patrol, averaging about twenty days, required a round-trip transit of the canal. Under way before dawn in company with one or more sister ships, we'd pick up a canal pilot for the seven-hour transit through the "big ditch" and its locks. Safely through the canal, we'd be led through the army's controlled minefield which guarded the approach to Balboa harbor. Once clear of that, our surface escort, a small patrol craft or converted yacht, would lead us past San José Island in the Gulf of Panama to our point of departure for the open Pacific.

The first dive in the Pacific was always a test of diving officer Frank (Tiny) Lynch's computations in his diving book. Tiny was a superb naval officer. Six feet four inches tall, handsome and quick-thinking, he had been a powerful lineman on Navy's football team, and regimental commander of midshipmen in '38. When he said he had pumped overboard 8,000 pounds of ballast from our variable tanks to allow for the lesser salinity of seawater in the Pacific as compared to the Atlantic, I thought that was too much. Still, there was no harm in having our ship on the light side. Tiny was right; our 800-ton ship had to be lightened by four tons of ballast water to be in diving trim. As we steamed to our patrol station some 800 miles west of the canal, brief, daily dives kept our trim adjusted for rapid, safe submergence.

The season of the year brought many stormy days, with frequent torrential rains. Fortunately, so near the equator it was not cold, and the rains brought a chance for a freshwater bath. The foul-tasting water in our potable water tanks was too precious to use for baths. Sighting a heavy rain squall in our path, the O.O.D. would pass the word, and one man at a time would be allowed topside naked, carrying soap and towel, to scrub himself on the cigarette deck under the heaven-sent shower. And, in spite of the whistles and obscenities directed at freshly scrubbed shipmates, the removal of several days' sweat, grime, and stench from a lucky few was envied and appreciated by all.

But the rainy season brought problems to navigators. It was important, both for proper coverage on the patrol line and for safety from trigger-happy search planes, that we stay as close to our assigned stations as possible. In these unfamiliar waters, with currents not accurately known, a day without star sights or sun lines could result in being many miles out of position, 50 or 60 miles not being unusual. On one patrol, after seven straight days of heavy overcast, a boat ended up 105 miles out of position!

It was that week that I reached my zenith as navigator. The O.O.D. had standing orders to call me whenever it seemed there might be a break in the clouds. My assistant, Quartermaster Bob Windrem, would precompute the bearing and altitude of the sun or major stars so that I'd know at once where to look when I scrambled topside, cradling my sextant, at the call, "Navigator to the bridge!"

About noon one rough, cloudy day, patches of blue began appearing almost directly overhead, and, in succession, I was able to snap sights of the sun, the upper limb of the moon, and Venus. The clouds assisted in this rare combination by blocking out most of the glare that normally made a daytime sight of the planet Venus unlikely. Our low height of eye and the short, jagged horizon yielded no exact sextant angles, but at least we now had a chance for a three-line fix, rough though it might be. As the skipper paced nervously back and forth behind me in the control room, I leaned over the chart desk and made the special computations which these high altitude sights at 6° north latitude required. They produced a triangle some three miles on a side, showing that after a week's dead reckoning we were only fifteen miles out of position!

We returned from our first patrol on January 24, 1942. We had sighted no enemy, made no attacks; our only contacts had been with inquisitive but friendly patrol planes, one of which did, nevertheless, unload her bombs on a sister ship. We had, at least, carried out a wartime operation, kept our ship in fighting shape despite daily casualties requiring much hard work and improvisation.

Leaving San José Light to port we headed for Balboa in the gloom of a dark, overcast night. Outside the harbor we met *S-21*, *S-26*, *S-29*, and *S-44*, who had just transited the canal and were lying-to awaiting our brief rendezvous before proceeding to their patrol stations. Their escort was a converted yacht now bearing its navy number *PC-460*.

We went close alongside *S-26* to exchange information. Johnny Corbus talked with his fellow skipper, Earl C. (Droop) Hawk, while I chatted across the few feet of black water with my opposite number, Thomas V. Peters. Droop, from upstate New York, was noted in the Submarine Force for his talkative good humor and hilarious use of the language. In describing a snowfall in his hometown, he would say it was "ass-high to a tall Indian." Droop was well muscled but not tall, his short legs seeming out of proportion to his torso. Tommy, from the Midwest, was a quiet, modest, true gentleman. He was my classmate at both the Naval Academy and at sub school, where Ginny and I had become very fond of him and his pretty young bride Adeline.

Johnny and I were eager for news of the war, for what had transpired while we were at sea, and for what changes of duty were in the offing. In return we gave information which might be useful to our friends on their own patrol. In a few minutes, calling, "Good luck, Droop," "So long, Tommy," we proceeded on our opposite ways. *PC-460* led our friends seaward toward San José Light while we headed for the canal entrance and our nighttime transit.

When we reached Gatun Locks we heard, unbelievingly, a sketchy report that *S-26* was on the bottom, sunk with all hands. What could have gone wrong? Following the friendly exchange of just a few hours before, the news of disaster hit us like a blow to the solar plexus. Not till we moored at Coco Solo did we learn what had happened.

After *PC-460* sent a visual signal to her covey of S-boats that she was leaving formation to proceed on duty assigned, she turned to starboard in a circular sweep. Only *S-21* received the message. As *PC-460* continued her turn to the right in the pitch black night, *S-26*, on her original course, suddenly loomed up dead ahead. With no time for either ship to take avoiding action, *S-26* was rammed on the starboard side of her torpedo room and in just a few seconds sank in water over 300 feet deep. Of the four men who were on the bridge at the time, three survived: Captain Hawk, Lieut. Bob Ward, and one enlisted man. The dreaded "Event 1000," the signal signifying submarine sunk and the start of rescue operations, was initiated at once, but by the time divers landed on *S-26* many hours later there was no sign of life in the silent hulk.

Less than a month later submarine disaster came again off Panama, and once more at the hands of friends. The giant French submarine *Surcouf*, which had just been overhauled in the U.S. Navy Yard at Portsmouth, New Hampshire, was en route Tahiti via Panama when, on February 18, she radioed her position and reported that she would reach Colón the following day. She never arrived. A U.S. freighter, the *Thompson Lykes*, reported that on the dark night of the eighteenth she had struck a low-lying object some eighty miles northeast of the canal. The freighter's bow was damaged. In all probability the object she had struck was the blacked-out *Surcouf*, which had disappeared with all hands. The loss of two submarines in a few weeks due to faulty ship-routing procedures and negligent seamanship was tragic, not for the loss of two decrepit subs but for the waste of trained personnel. Forty-five men died in *S-26*, 129 in *Surcouf*.

With each patrol, monotonous though it was, we gained experience in maintaining tired, worn machinery, in fast diving and accurate depth-keeping, in keeping a sharp lookout, in living together in cramped, unhealthful conditions. As with all our squadron, it was a matter of pride to keep our twenty-two-year-old boat on the line, never missing a sailing date or aborting a patrol. We lacked only the experience of contact with the enemy, of actual attack with gun or torpedo.

When we returned to port after our fourth fruitless patrol, we were ordered to return to New London, there to receive a British submarine crew, train them in the operation of our boat, and then transfer *S-24* to the United Kingdom. All hands were elated. Not only did this mean a reunion with loved ones, it would bring for some of us a move from the minor leagues to the majors—assignment to a boat already fighting in the far Pacific, or to a new-construction boat soon to be deployed.

Much as every submarine officer wanted early command of his own boat, I felt greatly let down when, instead of being sent to the Pacific war zone, I was ordered to command of *R-11*. She was even older and more primitive than *S-24*. Built in 1919, the 680-ton boat was one of several based in Key West, Florida. Her mission was to provide target services for the underway training of the Fleet Sonar School students, while at the same time giving preliminary training before submarine school to young naval reserve ensigns who had volunteered for submarine duty.

Young wives also received training in navy ways. Answering an insistent ringing of the phone, they'd hear, "Honey, collect the children. Put up the shutters. There's a hurricane coming and I've got to take the ship to sea." They could well wonder, does he love his ship more than me?

Those of us assigned to Key West were not pleased. We were impatient, fearful that all the good targets would be sunk before we got to the Pacific and command of a fleet boat. Even in this place, remote from the main war zones, we saw evidence of the part submarines were playing in the war. Occasionally a burned-out tanker or crippled freighter was towed into port, a grim reminder of German U-boats operating close to our own shores.

But in six months the impatience and frustration were ended. I was ordered back to New London.

After the bus ride over the Keys to Miami, then the two-day, rattling, jerking train ride, two tired parents and two lively children settled in the only lodgings we could find, a cramped, uncomfortable room in the Crocker House Hotel on Main Street, New London.

4

Action in *Sculpin*

A new level of training had been instituted for commanding officers. Before a skipper without previous submarine combat experience could take his own ship on war patrol he must henceforth attend Prospective Commanding Officer (PCO) School at the Sub Base in New London. Following that, he would make a "PCO run"—that is, embark in a boat going on war patrol to acquire experience under a C.O. who had already been in combat.

The four-week course in tactics, weapons, and communications was taught by experienced commanding officers who had returned from the war zone for a welcome respite. It was their important duty to pass on to younger skippers their lessons learned, both in attack and in evasion of enemy counterattack. The course consisted of lectures, the study of war patrol reports sent back from the war zone, and intensive drill on the torpedo attack teacher. On this device, moving, scale-model ships viewed through a periscope permitted reasonable simulation of a real torpedo attack. There were also a few actual torpedo firings, day and night, under way in one of the school boats. For a long time no fleet boats could be spared for this duty, so the torpedo firing practices in Long Island Sound were done in the obsolescent R- or S-boats attached to the school.

I was the junior officer in our seven-man class, the others being George W. Kehl, Richard D. King, Charlton L. Murphy, Frank M. Parker, William B. Perkins, and Roderick S. Rooney. We were all lieutenant-commanders. Except for Rod Rooney, we all came through the war safely. Rod was lost in command of *Corvina* in November, 1943, when his ship was on the surface near the great Japanese naval base at Truk, and was torpedoed by an enemy submarine.

A preoccupation during our busy schooling was how to provide for the welfare of our families before we departed for the war zone. Some sent their families back to hometowns. Neither a small Midwestern town nor giant Manhattan appealed to Ginny or me, in our unspoken thoughts of what she and the children would do should I not come back. We chose to settle the family in New London, where Ginny would have the moral and practical support of the official navy and of the many other submarine wives in the area, enlisted and officer alike. Scraping together $5,000, we invested it in the first of our numerous houses, and I went off to war with a mind at ease. Most of my pay would go directly to my wife by navy allotment check each month.

My orders from the Chief of Naval Personnel read as follows:

1. When directed by the Commanding Officer, Submarine Base on or about April 10, 1943, you will regard yourself detached from temporary duty under instruction at the Submarine Base, New London, Conn., and from such other duty as may have been assigned you; will proceed to San Francisco, Calif. and report to the Commandant, Twelfth Naval District, for first available transportation, including air, to the port in which the Commander Submarine Force, Pacific Fleet may be, and upon arrival report to the Commander Submarine Force, Pacific Fleet, for assignment to duty as prospective submarine commanding officer, and on board a submarine of that force.

2. You are hereby authorized to delay for a period of sixteen days in reporting at San Francisco, Calif. in obedience to these orders. This delay will count as leave.

There was no emotional scene at parting. By this time we were a dedicated navy family; we took in stride the separations that were part of navy life. I had always come back. We spoke only in terms of "when" I came back, never "if."

We had enough rationed gasoline for Ginny and the girls to drive with me to the railroad station at the foot of Main Street overlooking the Thames River. Sunday, May 2, was warm and sunny. As we waited on the platform for the New York, New Haven, & Hartford train that would carry me to New York, I lifted the children so they could better see the clanging monster that would take their father away. They were too young to understand why the strange man in their lives would appear and disappear.

When the conductor called, "All aboard," I clung more tightly to Ginny for a last hug and kiss, then turned quickly away. Only when I was in my seat with Connecticut's familiar countryside rushing past did "if" invade my mind.

At Pearl Harbor on May 8, 1943, I reported to ComSubPac, Rear Admiral Charles A. Lockwood, Jr., and was soon ordered to join *Sculpin* for my PCO patrol.

By this time the early confusion in submarine force organization and command was pretty well shaken down. When the war started the submarines were still operating as an element of the Scouting Force, but were soon shifted to come directly under the Commander-in-Chief Pacific as a force of its own. Rear Admiral Robert H. English had taken over from Rear Admiral Thomas Withers, Jr., in May, 1942, as ComSubPac, but was killed in a plane crash less than a year later. This brought Rear Admiral Lockwood to Pearl in January, 1943, from Fremantle, Australia, where he was in command of the few boats operating from that remote base.

It was a happy choice for the submarine force. Lockwood was our most experienced submariner; he had served in the boats since 1914. He was still an ensign when he had his first command, the 123-ton *Adder*, which was the third submarine in our navy. Before the end of World War II he would be Vice Admiral in command of nearly 200 submarines.

In his numerous submarine commands afloat and in the top submarine billets ashore, Lockwood had constantly pushed for boats of improved design. He was truly the "Mr. Submarine" of his time. In the major submarine operational command, with war experience adding conviction and urgency to his demands, he continued his drive for improvement in all technical aspects of the fleet-type submarine. He had a quick, penetrating mind and a lively sense of humor. From his many years of submarine duty he carried an air of casual but effective command that put his juniors at ease and inspired their best efforts. His warm, genial personality was quickly felt in SubPac. He was a great example of "loyalty down," and received, in turn, the whole-hearted support and admiration of his skippers. To us he was "Uncle Charlie," the understanding, kindly critic and taskmaster of our lonely commands.

The boats based in Australia after their retreat from the Philippines formed Submarines Southwest Pacific (SubSoWesPac) and operated in two groups, some from Fremantle in West Australia, the others from Brisbane in the east. Their respective commanders, Rear Admiral James Fife, Jr., and Rear Admiral Ralph W. Christie, did not have Lockwood's personality or style of command. Jimmy Fife was noted for his intense, personal involvement in every detail, largely destroying his subordinates' initiative. His heavy-handed approach, trying to control operations from his headquarters ashore, reduced his boats' freedom of action and may have led to the excessive losses he suffered. On the other hand, fun-loving Ralph Christie, while a more likeable personality, would be remembered chiefly as the torpedo expert who for so long stubbornly refused to accept the fact that his pet Mark VI exploder and Mark XIV torpedo were defective.

At any rate, the three force commanders were slowly developing a coherent, consistent strategy for the use of their boats. The limited number of subs available had too long been spread thinly in *ad hoc* applications, reacting to special intelligence on enemy movements, responding to the frequent requests for special missions coming from General MacArthur or Admiral Nimitz, and trying to cover focal points of shipping.

For her forthcoming patrol *Sculpin* was given Area 3, the strip of ocean extending a couple of hundred miles up the east coast of Honshu from Inubo Saki, the cape just east of Tokyo. When assigned a specified geographical area, individual subs were free to attack any target in it, knowing that it could be only enemy.

Sculpin was one of our older fleet-type boats, without the newest radar and fire control equipment on which we had drilled at PCO School. Her torpedo data computer was the early table model, and was unhandily jammed into the already-overcrowded control room not accessible to the torpedo fire control party in the conning tower. Also, she had an operating depth of only 250 feet. Still, I counted myself fortunate in that her skipper, Comdr. Lucius H. Chappell, was a greatly respected, highly experienced submarine officer. He was a handsome, soft-spoken gentleman from Georgia with a ready smile showing dazzling white teeth. His officers and men were confident of his ability, and eagerly responsive to his cool, relaxed leadership.

In command of *Sculpin* on the Asiatic Station when the war started, Lu Chappell had already completed six war patrols when I joined in May, 1943, for what was to be my first combat experience. When war started—on December 8, 1941, by Philippine time—*Sculpin* was one of the first boats to leave Cavite Naval Base to take up a patrol station east of Luzon. Getting only repeated misses on his early patrols, Lu was one of the first to realize that something was drastically wrong with our torpedoes, and he angrily denounced them. Now, eighteen months into the war, armed with the same type of torpedo equipped with the same Mark VI magnetic exploder, *Sculpin's* next patrol would take her to the Japanese home island of Honshu.

Chappell's executive officer and navigator was Lieut. Comdr. Alfred M. Bontier, a Missourian. Al was slim and boyish, quick witted and talkative, with thinning, reddish hair that was exposing more and more cranium. A thoroughly experienced submariner with several war patrols under his belt, he could expect to go directly to his own command without the need to attend PCO School. Though two years senior to Al, as the embarked PCO I was not in the command line of the ship; his duties and responsibilities were unchanged. I know of no case during the war in which there was resentment toward or conflict with the PCO. The logic of the situation was understood, and the availability of an extra, experienced officer was used to advantage.

My duties in *Sculpin* were not confined to any particular task or watch station; my function was to learn all I could from my seasoned mentor, and to get firsthand experience of wartime operations. After familiarizing myself with the ship, I spent most of my waking time in the conning tower, since that was the C.O.'s battle station. Occasionally I'd take the watch on bridge or in the conning tower, and frequently I'd take over from Frank Alvis, communications officer, the chore of decoding the nightly message traffic radioed by ComSubPac.

Chats with the crew gave me a look at submarine war through enlisted men's eyes. The Chief-of-the-Boat, Chief Signalman Moore, held forth in the Control Room. He was called "Magic Eyes" for his uncanny vision, day or night, when on the bridge. On stops in the crew's mess for a cup of soup at any time of day or night, I'd overhear frank discussion of the girls they'd laid in Australia, or of the varied talents of the girls of many racial mixtures in the well-ordered whorehouses of Honolulu.

But they talked of more than sex. Most men lived in the small, steel world defined by their watch station, the messroom, and their bunk. Those who stood watch on the bridge, in the conning tower or control room, brought word of the broader world of the ship. There was always hunger to know where we were, what was going on, what the skipper said, or how he acted.

In the forward torpedo room, crowded with reload torpedoes and bunks, there was little room for an extra body. On days when the fish in the tubes were withdrawn for their careful, routine checks, it was well to keep clear of the sweating, swearing sailors. Their own brand of humor showed in the cartoon taped to a locker front: a man and a woman in profile seated facing each other in a bathtub. The caption read, " . . . and that's how the new torpedo works."

This patrol was my first experience with a procedure we had discussed at PCO School, but which was optional for each commanding officer—that of "reversing the clock." Nighttime was the most critical and dangerous period for a submarine in enemy waters. Since our boats were not equipped with snorkels, that was when we had to come to the surface and proceed at moderate speed while the diesel-powered generators recharged the storage batteries which the day's submerged operations had depleted. It was the time the sub shed its cloak of concealment and was itself susceptible to being surprised. On clear, calm, moonlit nights it was an especially naked feeling to be on the surface, subject to detection by sight, sound, radar, or even the smell of our diesel exhaust as we strained to recharge the "can" as fully as possible before having to dive again.

To ensure maximum vigilance and readiness during the period of darkness, some submarine skippers, Lu Chappell among them, turned night into day. Quite simply, instead of night being the time those not on watch were asleep, it became the active, alert "day" with all hands up and about. Meals were adjusted accordingly. Breakfast was served late in the day, about 1800—or six o'clock in the evening—if we were to surface at dark around 2000. Lunch would be some four hours later, and dinner would be shortly after submerging at dawn. I did not follow this procedure in my own command later. There were, of course, two periods of physiological and psychological adjustment required in such an inversion of the diurnal cycle, and I preferred to rely on the natural, intuitive, heightened sensitivity to danger of men on watch in the night.

Except for brief daily dives, the 1,200-mile run to Midway Island was made at fifteen knots on the surface. After topping off with diesel fuel and food we sailed for Japan. *Sculpin* still had 2,300 miles to go. If all went well, we would get there in eight days.

Steaming steadily westward, always on the alert for ships and planes, we remained on the surface except for brief periods. Tension mounted as we passed in the vicinity of Marcus Island. Via the nightly radio broadcast by ComSubPac, *Sculpin* was ordered to proceed to a point some 400 miles off her normal track.

The message was an Ultra. The code word designated that the information being transmitted had been derived by cryptanalysis— the breaking of Japanese naval codes by our Combat Intelligence Unit at Pearl Harbor. Utmost care had to be taken in the handling and use of the Top Secret data obtained. Even in the highest headquarters ashore, the dissemination of Ultra information was extremely limited, but to be of use at the action level, in the submarines at sea, it had to be transmitted to them.

The source of Ultra information was not even divulged to submarine C.O.'s, and we were directed never to reveal in any way that we had received such messages. Ideally, when it was seen that a message being decoded started with the word Ultra, only the communications officer, always that one officer, should continue with the decoding. However, that practice alone would draw the attention of others to the special nature of the message. Besides, the requirements of standing watch and the urgency of decoding made it impractical to adhere strictly to that procedure. Still, only the captain and exec would see the sheet on which were pasted the decoded strips, and never was oral or written reference made to it. The raw material was always burned. Insofar as our personnel knew, the information we plotted came from routine sources, our best guesses, or our fertile imaginations.

From Ultra information a hastily redeployed U.S. fleet had been able to surprise and defeat the Japanese fleet as it advanced on Midway. It was an Ultra that doomed Admiral Yamamoto, Japan's top naval commander, when our planes ambushed and shot him down. As for our submarines, Ultra contributed greatly to their success, allowing them to waylay important targets that might otherwise have slipped by.

Rushing to our newly designated position at our best speed of twenty knots in the smooth sea, we made contact with the target every submarine captain dreamed of. It was a sight I shall never forget, my first glimpse of the enemy, the focus in the remote Pacific of all the elements of my training as a naval officer in general and as a submariner in particular.

On this night, just at midnight, Lieut. George Estabrook Brown, Jr., an outstanding, aggressive, and very personable young reserve officer from New York City, had the deck when we sighted them— two large aircraft carriers and, soon after, a single escorting cruiser or large destroyer. In the clear, starlit night they were visible over 10,000 yards, and as the column seemed to slink noiselessly across our horizon it had an almost hypnotic fascination. What an awesome sight: three great warships jammed with planes and weapons, manned by thousands of our enemy, most of them now asleep, a few hundred alert, on watch, uneasily on the lookout for their enemy—us.

Every skipper longed for contact with a Japanese carrier; most went through the war without seeing one. Here, in my first sight of the enemy, were two, and only one escort to worry about!

I had wondered what my reaction would be on first sighting a real target, an enemy target, not just a friendly destroyer or tug poorly simulating the real thing in training exercises. Now I knew. The excitement of the moment descended to my kneecaps; they were jerking up and down in spasmodic motion. Since I was wearing khaki shorts that didn't even reach the knees, I was fearful that I would be shamed by someone's noticing. But I needed have no fear. In the blackness of the night, with everyone intently scanning his assigned sector or focused on the three ships, kneecaps went unnoticed.

The small bridge was crowded. George had the deck but Lu had come up to direct the attack. I was there as an extra number, and Al Bontier came and went from his station in the conning tower. The battle stations telephone talker, Yeoman 2c Delbert E. Schroeder, stood near the skipper relaying his orders. Our three lookouts, perched on their platforms a few feet above us, tried to confine their looks to their own sector as George directed. If we would have to dive in a hurry, we would lose precious seconds getting everyone down the hatch.

Over the phones, Lu asked quietly, "Mendy, what's the normal approach course?"

Burly, balding Lieut. Corwin G. Mendenhall was the TDC operator in the control room, sweating over his balky instrument. A Texan, Mendy had graduated high in his academy class of '39, and had been the five-striper, commander of the regiment of midshipmen.

"Two four two, captain."

"What speed are they making?"

"They plot at twenty-two knots, sir."

"Steer two four two. All ahead full," ordered Lu.

This course, placing the targets on our starboard beam, would give us the best chance to close the speeding warships that were moving so silently and steadily to the southward. We seemed to be running away from the familiar, deep, throaty roar of our four straining diesels. We were more conscious of a new sound, the hiss of water parted by our thrusting bow. Under the great dome of starry sky, the velvet smooth surface of the black sea seemed a stage on which a drama was unfolding. We spoke almost in whispers, seemingly fearful that the three chief players would be disturbed, yet knowing that was impossible at five miles range.

Try as we might to gain bearing and to close for a favorable torpedo track angle, it soon became clear that we could not manage it. We were too far abaft the beam of the targets, and could not match their speed. If we were to attack at all, it would have to be at long range, using low power (slow speed) setting on our torpedoes in order to get the long run required. This Chappell chose to do.

Sculpin had left Pearl with a full load of torpedoes; for ships of her class (four tubes forward, four aft) this meant twenty. These were our standard submarine torpedo, the Mark XIV, in which a miniature, alcohol-fueled, steam turbine noisily drove two counter-rotating propellers, leaving a prominent exhaust bubble wake. At their high speed of 46 knots they had a range of 4,500 yards. At their low-power speed of 31.5 knots, they could run a distance of 9,000 yards. Targets of such importance warranted any attack that had a chance of success.

When we got to the point of shortest torpedo run, the four bow tubes were fired. Being on the surface, the boat was shaken more than usual. As soon as one fish had run the few hundred yards it took to arm itself, it blew up dead ahead. Even at this mid-stage of the war, this serious flaw of premature detonation by the magnetic exploder remained uncorrected. Before we could fire more, the targets passed beyond torpedo range.

At this time, eighteen months after our entry into the war, with over 2,700 torpedoes already fired and hundreds of premature explosions, we were still required to use the magnetic feature of the exploder. Our primary weapon, the Mark XIV torpedo, was fitted with a very complex, very ingenious mechanism—the Mark VI exploder. This was designed to detonate the warhead of torpex through a chain of events initiated by magnetic induction when the torpedo passed through the magnetic field of the target's hull. A torpedo exploding beneath the hull of a ship would be more deadly than an equivalent explosion alongside, which would vent some of its force up into the atmosphere. Detonated under a ship, a warhead would open a greater hole in the ship's unarmored bottom, or break the ship's back. Indeed, in the case of major warships with heavy side armor, our small (in comparison to the Japanese) warheads were slightly more than irritants when they exploded against the armor belt. At the start of the war our fish carried a warhead of only 500 pounds; the Japanese submarine warhead was 900 pounds. The modest weight of our explosive added to the force commanders' reluctance to give up the magnetic exploder. And with fish set to run under a target, there was no chance for the impact exploder to function.

The Mark VI exploder had been developed by our Bureau of Ordnance and kept in such super-secrecy that most submarine personnel did not know of its existence until war was upon us. In 1940 in Pearl Harbor a carefully controlled few of us were introduced to this wondrous device. But it was only a passing acquaintance: a look at a sample, an explanation of its theory of operation, and quick replacement into its box. As a consequence, the Mark VI was inadequately tested, and there was almost no experience in its maintenance, installation, and use. It took the costly test of combat to prove to a stubborn bureaucracy that its brainchild was fatally defective.

Serious as this defect was, it was for a long time shielded by another. Skippers of the early war patrols reported that both the Mark X and the Mark XIV torpedoes ran deeper than they were set to do, passing so far beneath their targets that neither contact nor magnetic exploder could function! Getting no satisfaction from the Bureau of Ordnance, the submarine force commanders took matters into their own hands. In July, 1942, after tests which proved that the torpedo ran eleven feet deeper than set, they directed their boats to use correspondingly lesser depth settings.

There was still another defect in our torpedoes, one that hid beneath the others that had been so painfully isolated. This was the poor design and construction of the contact exploder's firing pin. Torpedoes that hit their targets squarely generally failed to detonate; only those that hit glancing blows on the hulls of their victims would explode! Again it was the forces afloat that isolated the fault and devised a "fix," but almost two years of war, of heartbreak and loss, went by before U.S. submarines went on combat patrol with a reliable torpedo. There is little doubt that many American lives would have been saved and the pace of the Pacific war accelerated had an effective torpedo been available from the start. How true this was, was confirmed by Japanese ASW expert Atsushi Oi writing after the war, "Luckily for the Japanese merchant vessels, however, some of the American torpedoes proved to be ineffective. Frequently ships' masters saw premature explosion of enemy torpedoes. Some merchant vessels entered port with unexploded American torpedoes thrust into their hulls."[1]

There were inklings from battle reports and intelligence that Germany's U-boats were also having torpedo problems, but it was not until after the war that the full story was disclosed. In his memoirs German Admiral Karl Doenitz treats the subject at some length.[2] A submariner with combat experience in World War I, Doenitz was the Officer Commanding U-boats from 1935 until Germany's surrender. In addition, he was appointed Commander-in-Chief of the German Navy in January, 1943, when the Fuehrer belatedly decided that U-boat warfare would thereafter receive primary emphasis.

Doenitz called the torpedo failures, so remarkably similar to ours, a "torpedo crisis," one with "grave and sinister consequences." The official inquiry conducted by the Naval High Command listed the failures as follows:

(a) Torpedoes running too deep
(b) Premature firing of the magnetic exploder
(c) Unreliable action of the contact exploder

Unlike in our case, the German Navy moved with utmost vigor (including the court-martial of four officials) but, as was true for us, the interrelationship between the three classes of defects confused and delayed their correction.

I learned these lessons well. Twenty years later, when I was in charge of our own weapons development and production, I stressed the need for simplicity and reliability, and sometimes drove home the point by reciting a British analysis of a weapon: "The extreme ingenuity of this instrument rather blinds one to its utter uselessness." Perhaps

---

1. From *The Japanese Navy in World War II*, second edition (Annapolis, Md.: Naval Institute Press, 1986) p. 396.
2. Doenitz, Karl. *Admiral Doenitz Memoirs* (London: Weidenfeld and Nicolson, Ltd., 1959) pp. 92–99.

that referred to the Mark VI exploder. Early in the war the British had examined and tested the magnetic exploder, detected its flaws, and turned it down. Unfortunately, we persisted in its use.

Dejected after our futile attempt to convert ComSubPac's excellent intelligence into a staggering blow against the Imperial Japanese Navy, we set course to return to our originally assigned area. Perhaps submarines to the south of us, alerted to the approach of the same targets, could get closer.

Whenever on the surface, every submarine religiously guarded the schedules broadcast and repeated regularly on the radio frequencies reserved for submarine traffic. These came at fixed hours and from more than one station, in order to circumvent enemy attempts to jam and to overcome the vagaries of radio transmission over the great distances and varying atmospheric conditions of the vast Pacific theater. The primary broadcast might be from Oahu, but San Francisco, Seattle, Balboa, even Brisbane, would retransmit on their own schedules. The copying submarines maintained radio silence, acknowledging or receipting for a particular message only when so directed in the text of messages of extreme importance.

When submerged we could still receive radio signals, but only on VLF, the very low frequency reserved for submarine communications from specially configured shore radio stations. These long wave signals at about 19 kcs. were not attenuated as readily as were higher frequency transmissions. They penetrated the sea to some extent, and could be picked up on our submerged antenna provided we were within about fifty feet of the surface. Our distance from the transmitting station, the time of day, and of course the power output of the station influenced the strength of the signal received.

In addition to key intelligence such as had sent us dashing hundreds of miles to intercept important targets, ComSubPac would inform patrolling subs of friendly forces they might encounter, changes in area assignments, new information on enemy ASW measures, results achieved in outstanding patrols, as well as "family grams"—personal messages from home—when time permitted.

At this time, mid-1943, the war in the Pacific was still primarily a holding action. Occasional raids and sharp battles were fought by our surface and air forces, but the brunt of offensive operations was necessarily borne by U.S. submarines and the few Netherlands and British boats available.

The strategy evolved by the Combined Chiefs of Staff under Roosevelt and Churchill called for the primary, major effort to be applied in the European-African theater. Dependent as actions in those areas were upon the seaborne supply lines from the United States, it was clear that the success of the Western Allies against the Hitler-Mussolini Axis hinged on winning the Battle of the Atlantic being fought by the Allied navies against Germany's aggressive and resolute submarine force. We eagerly awaited the day when our own augmented forces, both surface and submarine, would permit a truly massive, sustained offensive. To this end we avidly followed reports of the war's progress in Europe.

For boats on patrol, ComSubPac would include excerpts of important communiqués as his operational schedules permitted, but for lengthier reports the plain language news broadcasts on shortwave were constantly monitored, both in the wardrooms and the crews' messrooms, as we cruised on the surface at night. Quality of reception would determine which station, either on our West Coast or in Australia, would get our attention. Off the coast of Japan, reception of KGEI, San Francisco, was generally good, and as we ran on the surface the night of our unsuccessful attack, we sought news of action on other fronts. I thought a concise comparison of the state and tempo of war in the two widely separated theaters was given by two news items. The first said, "The night before it capitulated, Pantelleria Island in the Mediterranean was showered with 200 tons of bombs." Then, for the same day, it was reported, "General MacArthur's airmen again delivered a heavy blow at the enemy, blowing up ammunition dumps and warehouses, dropping 19 tons of bombs on Rabaul." In our state of frustration, it seemed that the most effective campaign in the Pacific was the many tons of MacArthur being dropped on our helpless, hero-hungry public.

Once in our assigned area, however, we had no time for bitterness in our ceaseless, stealthy search for targets. This was an area athwart the coastal traffic lanes from Hokkaido and northern Honshu to the major ports in southern Japan. It should be one rich in contacts, even though we fully expected ships to hug the rugged coastline as closely as they safely could. The importance of moving their shipping was so great that the Japanese left their major navigational beacons and lighthouses illuminated but at reduced power. The aid and safety they gave to their own shipping were more important than the minor assistance they were to the sporadic probing of our submarines. By running close inshore, Japanese shipping made it not only more difficult for our subs to see and hear them, it also permitted their antisubmarine forces to concentrate their search and screening efforts on the seaward side. There was also the possibility that an overeager sub might be tempted into shallow, poorly charted water, or into waters that might be mined, as she pressed to get within short torpedo range.

The waters of this region were extremely interesting. Here the counterpart of the Gulf Stream, the Kuroshio (the "black current") flowing northward from the Philippine Sea, met the Oyashio (the "cold current") coming down from the Bering Sea. In this season of the year, the mixture of strong, turbulent currents of different temperatures caused a virtual maelstrom of confused water. Though little effect was apparent on the surface, a slow-moving, submerged submarine would at times be bounced around like a cork. As we searched for targets through our periscope at a depth of sixty feet, we could hear a constant rush of water through the bridge and around the conning tower. At times we'd fear we had broached, inadvertently exposing our periscope shears or even the bridge. This was caused by the strong, often confused, current as well as by the extreme, rapid variations of water temperature. Our bathythermograph drew crazy patterns showing as much as 14° variation in ninety feet of depth change, and even 5° variation at constant depth.

Such sea conditions considerably complicated the diving officer's task, but we welcomed the acoustic shelter they provided. Enemy sonar, either active or passive, could not be efficient in searching for us through such extreme temperature and salinity gradients. Our own sonars were also affected, but we could at least vary our depth to find more favorable conditions, and, unlike ASW surface forces, sonar was not the primary means of target detection for submarines.

It was from such watery shelter that I had my first glimpse of Nippon on June 12 through a periscope extended above the surface some ten miles offshore. I had visualized this as a very tense and daring moment, fraught with excitement and danger as we evaded alert picketboats, watched anxiously for searching aircraft, and thwarted coast watchers by clever use of our periscope. The reality was far different. From a vacant, glassy sea I dispassionately viewed the land of our enemy, the land from whence sailed the forces which had treacherously attacked our own in Pearl Harbor. It was much like any other hilly, wooded coast at this latitude, and not an enemy ship or plane was in sight. I soon turned to the warmth of my bunk and a few hours' sleep. Though it was June, it was cold and damp within the boat on the day-long dives in water whose temperature was frequently only 45°. The diesels radiated heat for a long time after we dove, so the engine rooms and motor room were comfortable. In other parts of the ship we had to wear warm clothes and sweaters.

At this season, just as off our own northeast coast, there was much fog. Visibility could only be described as terrible, and largely accounted for our inability to make the number of contacts expected. When we were on the surface at night there was fog or haze, which transformed the surface into an eerie, silent, enveloping presence. This would add to the surprise of contact with the enemy the more mundane and equally deadly threat of collision as all ships moved through the night sans lights or fog signals. During the day the fog was not constant, but was a shifting, lifting one that varied our horizon from 100 to perhaps 6,000 yards. If it had been dense and steady we would have remained on the surface, but the skipper did not like the uncertainties of chance encounters in the drifting fog.

It was Lu Chappell's practice to close the coast at dawn to obtain a visual "fix" if possible, prior to submerging for the day's prowling along the coast. The most distinctive feature in the area was near its northern boundary, the small island of Kinkasan which, from seaward, gave the appearance of a very regular, conical mountain, a miniature Fujiyama. During the long days and nights of patrolling it became quite routine to close Kinkasan, either on the surface or submerged, to fix our position as exactly as possible by means of periscope bearings on prominent headlands, supplemented at times by fathometer soundings. Then, hour after hour, the watch officers would intermittently but carefully sweep the horizon looking for a target worthy of torpedoes, only to find, for the most part, fishing boats that had to be watched and avoided.

I was in the cold conning tower one morning when word came from sonar that the beat of a ship's screws was detected up ahead, apparently a considerable distance away. Since report of any contact was made immediately to the captain, Lu Chappell came quickly to the conning tower, and was given the salient information even as he was climbing the ten rungs on the ladder from the control room.

Raising the periscope on the bearing sonar reported, he searched long and carefully. No ship was in sight, but visibility low over the water was very poor in the patchy fog. It was not surprising that nothing could be seen on the bearing, from which came intermittent screw noises. Going to battle stations in anticipation of an early attack, we closed on what we hoped would be our first victim of the patrol. Sonar reported that the screws were becoming fainter, and soon our best sonarman, Grover W. Marcus, announced that he had lost the target.

Unable to sight a target through the scope, with sonar no longer holding contact, Lu sadly concluded that the target we thought we had heard was now far out of range or might have been only a fishing sampan along the coast. Meanwhile, Al Bontier was much concerned about our position along the rocky coast, so beset with strong currents. "Captain, we sure could use a fix. Could you give me a cut on Kinkasan or anything else? I think it will bear about three zero zero."

Kinkasan was about 1,400 feet high, and often only its peak could be seen jutting up from the belt of low-lying fog. Looking in its general direction, Lucius searched back and forth, initially with no result, then said, "Oh, yes; here it is. Stand by for a mark. Mark the bearing!" No sooner had he said this than he shouted, "It's a ship—trying to ram us—take her deep! All ahead full! Flood negative!"

We could feel *Sculpin's* deck tilt forward and sink beneath us as George Brown, the diving officer, impressed by the note of emergency in the skipper's voice, did his best to get deep quickly but without too large a down-angle. He knew that in the presumed ramming situation he should not tilt our very vulnerable stern closer to the surface.

As Lu pulled his head away from the periscope eyepiece, I snatched a quick look. Just before our scope went under, I saw the rust-stained side of a Jap freighter, Plimsoll mark and rivets seeming enormous as they passed swiftly across my line of sight, not ten feet away! As *Sculpin* was quickly forced deeper by the tons of seawater admitted suddenly into the negative tank, and by the fierce thrust of her propellers, the distinctive thrashing sound of a freighter's large, slow-speed screw passing overhead could be heard clearly through our hull.

What we had thought was the shape of Kinkasan looming through the fog was the bow of a freighter heading almost upon us!

Safely deep, *Sculpin* slowed and listened carefully all around to learn if there were other targets. The ship that had forced us deep was drawing steadily away, the "chunking" beat of her single screw fading rapidly.

The procedure for coming back to periscope depth after having gone below it was always painstaking, one that was carefully drilled into us at submarine school and in every training exercise. It had to be, especially so in waters such as these where such extreme sound transmission anomalies existed. Rising from the depths, visually blind, a submarine's safety is dependent upon the sensitivity and accuracy of its sonar. A careful sound search all around is essential to detect any ship approaching, or perhaps lying-to in the vicinity. Because active sonar might disclose to an enemy the presence of the submarine, it was rarely used in such search situations; even when attacking, it had to be used most discreetly.

An active sonar sends out a pulse of sound and locates targets by detecting the "echo" or sound beam which is reflected, much as a rotating searchlight beam reveals objects by reflecting light rays to the observer. Furthermore, since a two-way sound transmission is involved, the low-powered active sonars fitted in our boats in World War II could not detect targets at as great a range as could a well-operated passive sonar, which simply picks up and amplifies sounds passing through the water. While both types give the "bearing" or direction of their sound, only the active sonar gives the "range" or distance to the object in contact. In a search situation, range is not of primary importance; the stealth and greater range of passive sonar are of greater value.

"Listening carefully all around," in the jargon of submarining, a trained sonar operator could sort out from the background noises of the sea the telltale sounds of ships, the beat of their screws, even under certain conditions the noises of pumps and other machinery transmitted through the hulls into the sea. All captains carefully followed the running commentary of their experienced sonarmen as they translated the sounds of the sea: "slow single screw"; "small, high-speed propellers"; "distant depth charge or bomb"; "sounds like a school of fish"; and so on as the case might be.

At any rate, by the time *Sculpin* was back at periscope depth, visually confirming sonar's report of "all clear," the fog had lifted and our freighter was out of sight and sound. Close in to the coast as we were, it was not feasible to surface and give chase.

Later that day, with sunshine brightening the steep, green hills of Honshu, on one of his periscope sweeps Frank Alvis detects a freighter plodding northward. Verifying the contact, now seen to be escorted by two small patrol boats, Lu orders, "Battle stations, torpedo," and commences his approach. When we reach an excellent firing position less than 1,600 yards from the target, a spread of three torpedoes is fired from the bow tubes. Stopwatch in hand, Quartermaster Billie Cooper counts the seconds as the fish run toward their target. Suddenly a loud explosion and, at the periscope, Lu swears, "God damn it! Another premature!"

The two remaining fish seem to be running OK, but soon Cooper says, "They should have got there by now, captain."

Still watching the target, Lu can see no explosions, only the small escorts now turning toward us as they follow the bubble wakes of the torpedoes. Too small for us to spend torpedoes on, the patrol boats succeed in keeping us from making another attack on the freighter now belching smoke as she scurries up the coast.

A couple of days later, in a brief, smartly executed submerged attack, again close in to the coast, *Sculpin* thought she had sunk her first ship of the patrol. A spread of four fish was fired at a medium-size maru proceeding close along the shore. As soon as he observed a hit Lucius let me, as the novice along for experience, take a look at the result of a torpedo attack.

Just as I found the target in the field of the periscope, a second torpedo of our spread seemed to hit in her forward part, sending a great geyser of water skyward. But I noted a strange thing—even at the modest range of 1,500 yards and the detonation of over 500 pounds of torpex, we could hear no sound of explosion carried to us through the sea. Here was real evidence of the vagaries of sound transmission in these waters.

Going deep to evade the escort's counterattack, we could not verify the sinking. However, the timing and sighting of the explosions seemed conclusive, and there was rejoicing in the boat. But back in Pearl Harbor the code breakers soon knew that the freighter had escaped damage. What had seemed to be hits against her hull were actually premature explosions in the water. As the torpedoes neared their target, the overly sensitive magnetic exploders detonated the warheads!

Because of the unreliable performance of her torpedoes and the difficulty of finding targets along the rocky coast in the low visibility conditions even when her erratic radar was in commission, *Sculpin* had more inducement than usual to use her alternate armament, her deck guns. These were a 3″/50 caliber gun mounted forward of the conning tower, two 20 mm. rapid-fire guns, and two .50 caliber machine guns. These were all guns developed for surface ships or aircraft, but they had been adapted to the submarine for use against small targets not worth a torpedo, or for emergency, last-ditch action.

As they approached the coast of Japan our subs had to run a gauntlet of small craft, generally wooden-hulled sampans, ostensibly fishing, an occupation that in wartime was of even greater importance to Japan. However, many of them were equipped with radio transmitters to give the alert or call out ASW forces should they detect us. Armed with light automatic weapons, they formed an advance picket line guarding the approaches to the empire, sometimes as many as 600 miles offshore.

Since a submarine on the surface is very vulnerable to even small caliber ammunition, a surface gunfight had to be carefully planned and executed with utmost surprise and determination. Later in the war some submarines, specially armed, were designated to carry out coordinated gun attacks, chiefly as precautionary antipicket sweeps ahead of our advancing surface forces. For the most part, however, gun attacks were left to the discretion of the submarine commanding officers. Sound doctrine said it was best to reserve such risky operations to the withdrawal phase of a sub's patrol, when its presence had already been disclosed and most or all of her fish were expended.

The sinking of a sampan of perhaps 100 tons made only minuscule contribution to total tonnage sunk, but aside from the steady erosion of picket forces there was a very great psychological value in such use of guns. The nature of submarine warfare, relying on stealth both in attack and evasion, denies almost all her crew even a glimpse of their enemy. They must patiently and swiftly perform their individual tasks, making vicarious contact with the enemy only through the eyes of their skipper or through the dial of some instrument. What a welcome release of emotion, of pent-up hate, of frustration, of boredom—yes, even of fear—came with the order, "Battle surface!" And who could tell when the experience and confidence gained might one day be decisive in saving ship and crew, should she be forced to surface and fight it out there?

The first of two gunfights came as a result of a contact made in the moonlight as *Sculpin* moved well offshore to check her torpedoes in minute detail before making her next sweep along the coast. After tracking the target awhile on the surface, *Sculpin* dived, made a brief submerged approach, then made a "battle surface" at short range just before dawn. In the gloom at less than 1,000 yards range we could see no personnel, only the blurred outline of a steel-hulled sampan, perhaps 300 tons in size. Just sixty seconds from the time we were still at periscope depth, Lieutenant Joseph R. Defrees, Jr. (son of Rear Admiral Defrees), and his gun crew opened fire with their 3″ gun and soon began scoring hits. The lighter 20 mm. and .50 caliber machine guns poured streams of fire at the target; the barking of their rapid fire so close to us on the bridge seemed deafening. A few flashes of small caliber fire in return told us we were shelling not merely a ship but other human beings. The smell of gunpowder in the fresh morning air, penetrating even to those below decks, the trail of tracer bullets, the crash of 3″ shells exploding, were all part of the crescendo of violence, the upwelling of fierce, retributive emotion in men suddenly face-to-face with an enemy for the first time.

In a few minutes the sampan was a riddled hulk, roaring with flame, slowly sinking as we sped away to put her many miles astern before diving for the day.

Late the same day we came across another, smaller sampan, about a seventy-five-tonner. Once again *Sculpin* burst from the sea in a torrent of foam. Men swarmed on deck to cast loose their guns even as cascades of water streamed overside. This time the return fire came more quickly but no more effectively. Smothered by our gunfire, with sections of top hamper smashed overboard, the wooden sampan was soon dead in the water, her crew apparently all killed. Though her hull was holed and clearly lower in the water, the craft was not likely to sink. Like a drowning man clinging to wreckage, she clung to the surface, buoyed by her heavy oil- and fish-soaked timbers.

The unequal gun battle lasted only a few minutes. With the late afternoon sun intermittently obscured by fog patches, there was time to put a boarding party over to see whether items of intelligence, or perhaps a survivor, could be obtained. As we gingerly maneuvered our bow against the wallowing hulk, I could see two half-naked bodies in the waist of the ship, sprawled grotesquely near the light guns they had manned. How different, how personal was war when the target was flesh and blood instead of steel. The squat, strong Japanese bodies lay in the bilges, oily, blood-stained water sloshing over their firm flesh, tiny purple craters erupting where machine gun bullets had swiftly ended their involvement in a war not of their making. I recall thinking how firm and strong their bodies were, even though they ate mainly fish and rice.

There was no satisfaction such as comes from attacking and sinking a ship. Then, it is your ship against theirs, an impersonal contest, but one with the great satisfaction of being pitted against what is both symbol and reality of the Japs' power, their will and ability to sink you if you don't sink them.

Sculpin put her fiercely bearded, heavily armed boarding party on the sampan while all of us topside kept an uneasy lookout for Jap ships or planes. Leaping from our bow to the slippery, blood-splattered hulk, Joe Defrees and George Brown led three men on a quick search of the sampan.

As we impatiently awaited the return of our men, the two ships drifted apart, and the low-lying hulk disappeared in the patchy fog. Could we find the drifting sampan in the ghostly veil of low fog? Our always erratic radar was of little use at such short range, the wooden target giving no distinguishable return against the background of sea clutter. Cautiously inching our way lest we get too far from our quarry, we strained for sight or sound of our marooned shipmates. Suddenly, from abeam came a strong odor, sharp in the damp, fresh atmosphere. It was the smell of fish, an aroma which for years had permeated the timbers of our victim.

Soon we recovered our men. Of the Japanese crew of five, there was no survivor to take prisoner. There was only a motley collection of handguns, a wooden mock-up of a machine gun, and some charts and publications that might have intelligence value.

The gun attacks which had lifted the spirits of *Sculpin*'s crew and given them confidence in a new measure of their teamwork had eliminated two small ships, a few brave seamen, and silenced two radios that would no longer give warning of intruding submarines. There was exhilaration in the messrooms that night as *Sculpin* closed the coast once more, determined that her meticulously checked torpedoes would now account for bigger game.

In a few days two more freighters were attacked from favorable positions, but still the torpedoes failed to get hits. In five separate attacks nineteen fish had been expended, some from "can't miss" positions. We believed we had hit and sunk one maru. Angry and frustrated, reviewing each approach and attack, Chappell was convinced the fault lay with the torpedoes. On several of the spreads fired, at least one torpedo warhead had "prematured"—exploding soon after the fish started its run and long before reaching the target. Thus alerted, our targets had plenty of time to evade the other torpedoes that were approaching, or to counterattack. Other fish were seen to run straight to their targets, their bubble trails disappearing under their intended victims, but with no explosion. With so many torpedoes prematuring or failing to explode, the frustration and rage of torpedoman and skipper differed only in the choice of expletives.

As *Sculpin* plodded homeward on June 24, it did little to relieve the bitterness over excellent attacks frustrated and weeks of danger endured to receive Admiral Nimitz's order to discontinue use of the Mark VI.

On July 4 *Sculpin* moored alongside submarine tender *Sperry* in Midway lagoon. It was the second Independence Day of the year for us; the international date line was but a few miles west of Midway. And for a few hours we were all independent, immersed in the mail that had piled up for us during our weeks at sea—letters from loved ones, mothers, wives, children, the girls left behind.

Turning over the sea-stained ship to a relief crew, we moved ashore, officers to what had been the Pan American Airways Hotel, enlisted men to their own breezy barracks. The hotel was a simple, wooden, one-story building set in a grove of ironwood trees. Since 1935 it had served as a stopover resting place for passengers and crew of Pan Am clippers. Its individual bedrooms were austerely furnished, but they seemed large and luxurious after weeks in cramped, two-man bunkrooms. At one end of the central hallway was a lounge, the reading and recreation room with a shortwave radio receiver, a tired phonograph, and piles of old, dog-eared magazines. There we joined officers of *Sailfish* and *Whale*, boats which would soon leave for patrol.

A welcome visitor to Midway at this time was Comdr. A. C. C. (Tony) Miers, V.C., D.S.O., R.N. Tony was the Royal Navy submarine liaison officer sent to Admiral Lockwood's staff to tell of British submarine experience and tactics and to learn what he could of ours. He had won the Victoria Cross in 1942 when in command of the British submarine *Torbay*. After penetrating an enemy harbor in the Greek island of Corfu, he remained inside for seventeen hours, then in broad daylight torpedoed and sank two supply ships at anchor.

Tony was a burly, powerful man who played with the same turbulence with which he fought. "Yes, if there's no pink gin, a bourbon will do quite nicely, thank you." He was a very likeable, fun-loving companion who had not outgrown his junior officer days in the Royal Navy gun room or wardroom, where the games played were rough and boisterous. Here on Midway the long, after-dinner bull sessions with skippers, which Tony preferred to the more staid evenings on the *Sperry* with the squadron staff, sometimes ended in friendly wrestling matches to see who could put Tony down. He overpowered everyone but Lieut. Benjamin C. Jarvis, exec of the *Sailfish*. Ben was a big man with a magnificent physique who had been a great football player and wrestler at the Naval Academy. He upheld the honor of U.S. submariners in his friendly contests with Tony.

Our resting place had been nicknamed Gooneyville Lodge, after the handsome Layson albatross, or "gooney," who nested on Midway in great numbers. Our days were spent as we wished, sleeping, eating well, reading, playing tennis, swimming naked in the lagoon, or sunbathing on the magnificent white beaches we shared with tolerant gooneys. Nightfall would bring more poring over old magazines, poker, or bridge. Aside from unlimited quantities of beer, usually Primo brewed in Honolulu, the only liquor available was a poor grade of bourbon we called Schenley's Black Death. Liquor was a comfort to some, but there was little excess drinking. It seemed that the pattern set by each skipper was controlling.

In their own buildings our crew followed much the same routine. Most of our young men were unmarried; they would have preferred the temptations of civilization, the satisfaction of sexual appetites long suppressed, but there was not a woman within 1,200 miles. Officially the men had only beer to drink, but enlisted entrepreneurs on the tender or the navy's Seabees on the island could provide, for a price, a tolerable grade of alcohol with which to spike canned fruit juices.

Even so, the disappointingly wholesome life the men endured made them all the more eager to get to sea. Perhaps the next patrol would terminate in Australia, that Shangri-la for submariners.

From Midway Al Bontier left to become skipper of his own, new construction submarine *Razorback*. But the bad luck which had plagued our patrol seemed to follow Al. He was relieved of command along with his navigator when *Razorback* ran aground during her shakedown period. In time he was given command of *Seawolf*, old but famous for her exploits under Freddy Warder and Roy Gross. In September, 1944, while on the surface near the Philippines, she was bombed by a U.S. Navy plane that mistook her for a Japanese sub. *Seawolf* dived, only to be further attacked by our destroyer *Rowell* who sank her by depth charging. There were no survivors.

My own future was uncertain. Each day I eagerly scanned the radio messages, by which ComSubPac was ordering personnel changes. Several boats were due for change of command. Which one would be mine?

Lu Chappell would stay with *Sculpin* to make one more patrol in her, his eighth. When he returned from that successful patrol, in the East China Sea, he turned his ship over to Commander Fred Connaway and took up duties on ComSubPac's staff.

On her next patrol, on November 19, 1943, *Sculpin* was sunk in the Caroline Islands area. During an attack on a convoy she was detected by the escorting destroyer and heavily depth-charged. With his ship severely damaged, *Sculpin*'s new C.O. decided that her best chance lay in surfacing and fighting a gun action. In the unequal duel that ensued the destroyer's heavier firepower took quick effect, decimating those manning *Sculpin*'s guns and repeatedly holing the sub. Lieut. Joe Defrees was killed on deck forward as he directed the fire of the same 3″ gun I had watched him and his men use so effectively only four months before. Joe's mother had been sponsor of *Sculpin* when the ship was launched in Portsmouth, New Hampshire, in 1938.

Sculpin carried a total of eighty-four persons. Of them, thirty-eight men and three officers were picked up by the Japanese destroyer and taken to Truk. There they were divided into two groups, of twenty-one and twenty, and loaded on two aircraft carriers that were returning to Japan. Nearing Japan in a raging storm, the carrier *Chuyo*, with twenty-one of *Sculpin*'s survivors, was torpedoed and sunk by our submarine *Sailfish*. Only one *Sculpin* man survived.

It was *Sculpin* who stood by her stricken sister ship *Squalus* when that submarine sank off Portsmouth, New Hampshire, in 1939. It was *Squalus*—raised, refitted, renamed *Sailfish*—who intercepted and sank *Chuyo* with her cargo of helpless prisoners. After the war, twenty-one of *Sculpin's* crew were recovered from Japanese prison camps. The only officer among them was Lieut. Brown. He had succeeded to command of *Sculpin* when the ship's officers senior to him were killed in the gunfight. It was his bitter task to order all hands to scuttle and abandon ship.

5

Hunting off Honshu

My experience in *Sculpin* was ideal preparation for my first patrol in command. Two months after *Sculpin* left the cold, foggy coast of Honshu I was sent back in *Halibut*. I was familiar with the coastline and its sea. I had learned that the unpredictable sound conditions favored the submarine more than the antisubmarine forces looking for her. I was confident that a properly operated submarine, though 2,500 miles from its nearest support, could challenge the enemy at his doorstep and survive. I had seen Ultra at work. But most reassuring, I had seen the initiative, the courage, the teamwork of American sailors, officers and enlisted men alike, many of them reservists with no prior seagoing experience.

I took command of *Halibut* at Midway Island, on August 12, 1943. She was already a veteran submarine. She had been built in the U.S. Navy Yard at Portsmouth, New Hampshire, where she was placed in commission on April 10, 1942. Hurrying to the Pacific, she had compiled an excellent combat record in five war patrols under Comdr. Philip H. Ross in the arduous waters of the Aleutians, off Japan, and in the Carolines-Marianas islands area. She torpedoed and sank five enemy ships.

How proud and pleased I was to get her! Up to this time I had served only in older boats, all needing much hard work and ingenuity in maintenance and none equipped with up-to-date radar or fire control equipment. Now for my first combat command I would have a modern, deeper-diving, fleet-type, one with reliable, Fairbanks-Morse diesel engines, with all-welded hull, with longer, slimmer periscopes, and with the latest model radar and torpedo data computers. When I had inspected below, her living quarters, for both officers and enlisted men, seemed luxurious compared to what I had become used to. Only the outdated 4"/50 caliber, S-boat deck gun forward of the conning tower was disappointing. I preferred the rapid-fire, smothering effect of 40 mm. and 20 mm. guns. But never mind; after all the gun was only secondary armament.

Assembled on deck aft of *Halibut's* conning tower, in dazzling sunshine sparkling off the pale green water of the lagoon, seven officers and seventy-three enlisted men looked on as I read my orders and relieved Phil Ross. To almost all of them I was virtually unknown; only three men had served with me before. Chief Quartermaster Robert M. Robison had been with me in *S-24*; Albert A. Schwieso, motor machinist's mate 1c, and Richard E. Kelly, fireman 1c had been with me in *R-11*. In addition, I had obtained from *Sculpin* two men whom I had observed during my PCO run, firecontrolman 3c Silvio Gardella and seaman 2c Adolph Creighton. I knew none of the officers, and all that they knew of their new C.O. were a few sterile statistics: a thirty-two-year-old lieutenant-commander, ten years out of the Naval Academy, seven years in submarines, four years in *Argonaut*, two in *S-24*, one year C.O. of *R-11*, one war patrol in *Sculpin*.

Beneath their disciplined exteriors were concern and trepidation; was the new skipper foolhardy or wise, impetuous or patient, skillful or plodding, reckless or calculating? Their lives might depend on the answers. They knew only that from this time forward we were a team, *Halibut's* crew, shipmates with one purpose alone—to seek out and destroy Japanese shipping.

I was fortunate in that I could keep as my executive officer Lieutenant-Commander Ovid McMaster (Mack) Butler. The exec was a particularly important officer. As second in command he handled most administrative matters, but he was also navigator and, in combat, assistant approach officer. He exercised overall supervision of the torpedo fire control party in the conning tower and generally assisted the C.O. For example, I asked him to caution me should I expose the periscope too long, too high, or at too high a speed. He kept track of contacts that sonar reported, and was constantly alert to all that was going on in the boat.

I took a liking to Mack at once. He was three years junior to me, and had entered the Naval Academy from the District of Columbia, where his father was a forester with the government. Slim, reddish-haired, Mack was the quiet, intellectual namesake of a great-grandfather who had founded Butler University in Indiana. (It was a pleasant coincidence in Apra Harbor, Guam, once to see the Liberty ship *Ovid M. Butler* unloading war supplies.)

Mack had served two years in the new, large aircraft carrier *Lexington*, then went to the other extreme in an old four-stack destroyer for three years. Perhaps because of that look at two diverse segments of the navy, he did not resist when he was "drafted" for submarine school. In the summer of 1941 the navy was badly in need of officers for the submarine force buildup. Mack was one of those directed to take a physical exam and, if physically qualified, to report for submarine duty.

Under instruction at submarine school when Pearl Harbor was attacked, he later earned his submarine pin in a most unusual way. He was ordered to the S-27 and was soon on war patrol in the North Pacific off the Aleutian Islands, which the Japanese had invaded. S-27 was commanded by Lieut. Herbert L. Jukes. Herby had been an outstanding gymnast and captain of the team at Navy. He had a lively, engaging personality.

S-27 was on the surface charging batteries in a dense fog on the night of June 19, 1942, when strong currents carried her on to a reef 400 yards from Amchitka Island. All efforts to get off the rocks were futile. She sent six messages reporting her predicament, but only one, which did not give her position, was picked up. With the ship flooding and her batteries generating chlorine gas, she had to be abandoned. All hands got safely ashore via their rubber lifeboat. They made their way to a deserted village and took refuge in an abandoned church.

Herby was so pleased by Mack's performance during the ordeal that he said, "Well, Mack, if we ever get back to Dutch Harbor, you can write a letter recommending yourself for 'Qualified in Submarines'." Six days later a searching Catalina seaplane sighted the shipwrecked sailors, and air rescue followed. As did the letter qualifying Mack to wear his dolphins.

In *Halibut*'s wardroom I had four seasoned submarine officers, two young reservists who would be going to sea for the first time, and one mature ex-enlisted officer who would also be getting his first taste of undersea duty.

"Si" Lake was the oldest. He was a little older than I was, although his youthful appearance belied it. Slim and well-groomed, he was quiet, conscientious, and friendly, his ready grin disclosing the wide gap between his two upper front teeth. Edward W. Lake had enlisted in the navy at an early age. His family had a complex Polish name, but he preferred Lake. Early in his submarine career he was dubbed "Si" after Simon Lake, one of America's two chief developers of the submarine. An ex-Chief Radioman, Si's ability, reliability, and leadership brought him a commission. Now an ensign, he was our communications officer. Regardless of what time zone we were in, Si kept his watch set on New London time. That's where his wife and daughter waited.

Lieut. (jg) John J. (Jack) Hinchey was in the U.S. Naval Academy class of '42, which was hurriedly graduated in 1941, right after the Pearl Harbor attack. He was from Omaha, Nebraska, and had attended the University of Washington for a year before going to Annapolis. He had been a key member of the academy's swimming team. As our engineer and diving officer, his aquatic skills were being tested in a different way. He had graduated high in his class, and was a very mature, stable young man. I quickly recognized what a splendid diving and watch officer he was. He was a perfectionist and stickler for detail.

When a quartermaster of the watch was relieved he was required to report to the officer of the deck in a standard routine: "Quartermaster relieved, sir. Steering course two eight five. Going ahead standard on main engines three and four. Henderson has the watch."

Not satisfied with that simple, traditional pattern, Jack improved on it. Following the routine report he would always ask for some supplemental information: what's the seawater temperature; what time is sunset; what does the barometer show; what's the state of the battery charge? The boys quickly caught on to his special technique, and to help each other they logged all his questions in their quartermaster's notebook. At the end of one patrol there were listed 104 items on which Jack had queried them, and only 7 or 8 for other watch officers.

Ensign John Michael (Jack) Barrett had gone to the Academy from Chicago, where his Irish immigrant parents had settled. Their great contribution to American life included four successful offspring, among them not only Jack, who would ultimately rise to the rank of Rear Admiral, but Vincent, Catholic priest of a vibrant parish in California.

Jack's class of '43 was also speeded up to join the fleet a year early. His first love was aviation, but that required a preliminary year in the surface navy and he wanted no part of that. Eager for action, he chose submarines, but persisted in his desire to be a naval aviator. After the war he earned his wings at Pensacola and became one of the very few who wore both the dolphins of the submariner and the wings of the aviator. Jack's curly, dark hair, mischievous blue eyes, easy, natural charm, and ready Irish smile attracted pretty girls wherever he went.

Ensign Ray E. Stewart came to submarines by an unusual route. While still a senior at the University of Florida, he enlisted as apprentice seaman in the navy's V-7 program, wherein likely young college boys were quickly transformed into commissioned naval officers. Sent to Midshipman Training School at Northwestern University in Chicago, he was one of our so-called ninety-day wonders. These naval reserve officers were very important to the manning and fighting of our rapidly growing fleet. Most made splendid officers and fine shipmates; many attained their own commands; some transferred to the regular navy and reached high rank.

On being commissioned Ray had been sent to Pearl Harbor in March, 1943, bypassing New London and sub school. Assigned to *Halibut*, which had just returned from patrol and was in the navy yard undergoing overhaul, he became Jack Barrett's shadow and learned about submarines the hard way, crawling through bilges and ballast tanks, inspecting the ship from stem to stern. Replaced by a sub school graduate when *Halibut* sailed on her fifth patrol, he went to the sub tender *Sperry* at Midway Island. When I took command, I was happy to take Ray as one of my officers.

Also coming on board at Midway was tall, athletic Ensign Robert M. Gregerson. Greg was a brash, street-wise, cocky young man from New York. He had attended the College of William and Mary on a baseball scholarship, then went to sub school. He was a lively addition to our wardroom of young men getting old before their time.

Ensign Maxwell (Mike) Such was somewhat older. Like Si, he was a "mustang," an officer who had come up from the enlisted ranks. He had been a chief electrician's mate, but this was his first submarine. He was a short, stocky man with thinning hair, inclined to be introspective. His practical experience with electricity would be of great value when we struggled with electrical problems after depth charging.

As the new C.O., one of the first decisions I had to make was as to who would be Chief of the Boat. Chief Franklin (Doggie) Hearn had done an excellent job in that position up to now, but after five war patrols it was time for him to leave for a new-construction boat. With little knowledge of our men, I relied on Mack's judgment for Hearn's replacement.

The chief of the boat in a submarine is a key man. He is the exec's alter ego, the link between enlisted crewmen and the command in administrative matters. Like the top sergeant in an Army or Marine Corps unit, he wields much unofficial but effective authority, maintaining order and discipline, supervising operation of the watch, quarter, and station bill, disposing of minor infractions in his own way, and generally ensuring that life in the submarine runs smoothly, quietly, and efficiently. To that end he has to be an experienced, mature submariner, a man respected in his own right and not merely because he has the backing of the exec. His particular rating does not matter, but he is always one of the senior chief petty officers. In my previous boats, the chiefs of the boat had been chief torpedomen, chief gunner's mates, or chief quartermasters.

Mack recommended David Lee Roberson, chief motor machinist's mate. Dave was thirty-four, a ripe old age for a submariner, but he kept himself trim and fit. He was soft-spoken but determined, with an air of quiet, reassuring competence. He was an intelligent, good-looking, dark-haired married man who, we would find, could grow a beard as luxuriant as any on board. Jack Hinchey was reluctant to lose him from the engine rooms, but agreed on Dave's potential. I took Mack's advice, appointed Dave, and we never had cause to regret it.

In the few days of underway training we had off Midway, using the small, local escort vessels as targets, I quickly learned more of my officers and men as we shaped our battle station teams. Some of our new, young men, average age 18½, were going to sea for the first time. They would need more training, but we could do that on the long transit to Japan.

As for *Halibut*, she was all I had hoped for and more. She was of the *Gato* class, of which seventy-seven in all were built before the next class was introduced by *Balao*. The only significant, but important, change in that group was its 400-foot operating depth, as compared to 300 for *Gato* boats.

The *Gato* design was excellent, the culmination of many years of trial and error. *Halibut* displaced 1,526 tons, and had ten 21″ torpedo tubes, six forward and four aft. She dived smoothly and quickly to her operating depth. On the surface her 6,000 horsepower diesel-electric drive could give us twenty-one knots, and even more if we pushed her in an emergency. When submerged we could coax nine knots from our four main motors as they rapidly sucked amperes from the two 126-cell banks of Exide storage batteries. At that maximum submerged speed we would exhaust our batteries in about thirty minutes. Creep-

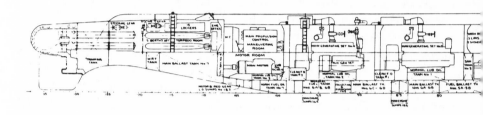

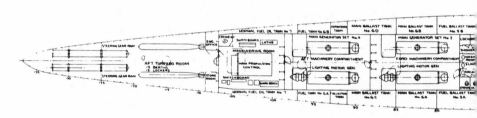

ing at two knots, however, we could stay submerged forty-eight hours. Battery capacity was the severe and ultimate limitation of every sub's submerged operations. In effect, when submerged, we were little more than somewhat mobile, intelligent minefields able to extend our lethal distance a few thousand yards through the torpedo.

We heard much of the snorkel used by Germany's U-boats in the battle of the Atlantic, but our navy did not adopt it until after the war. I had seen my first snorkel in 1938 in Pearl Harbor when a Dutch submarine of their O-class passed through en route to the Netherlands East Indies. They used it chiefly to draw fresh air into the boat when submerged. Taking the idea, the Germans improved on it. An enlarged

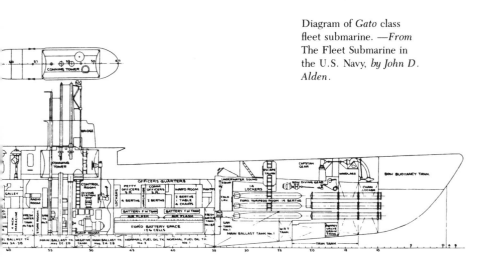

Diagram of *Gato* class
fleet submarine. —*From*
The Fleet Submarine in
the U.S. Navy, *by John D.
Alden.*

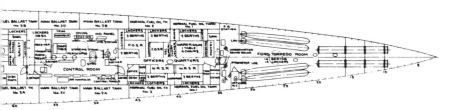

intake pipe and an appropriate underwater exhaust allowed them to
run their diesels while submerged.

Considering the inadequacies of Japanese antisubmarine measures,
we really did not need a snorkel. At any rate, unless attacking, our
speed submerged was kept to little more than steerage way, only two
or three knots.

Halibut had the Mark III, the latest model TDC. It was a compact,
upright design, fitted against the curvature of the conning tower. It
was a great asset to have it right at the skipper's elbow as he snatched
target information through the periscope.

The TDC was an electromechanical system of two main sections.

The position keeper section provided a continuous display of the relative positions of target and submarine. The angle solver section generated the corresponding, continuously updated torpedo gyro angle, and transmitted that data directly to whichever bank of torpedo tubes, forward or aft, was used. Up to the moment of firing a given torpedo, its gyro angle was kept properly set to hit.

It was the TDC which gave skippers such great latitude in approach maneuvers, surfaced or submerged, and permitted shifting fire rapidly and accurately to different targets. Of course the data generated was no better than that inserted, which was the data the C.O. or sonarman had to provide. Nevertheless, if asked which equipment was most important to them, most skippers would place the TDC at or near the top of the list.

Halibut also had the newly developed SJ, surface search radar, which brought a new dimension to submarine warfare. By giving our boats the means to detect targets at night or in poor visibility, and to get accurate ranges, it allowed them to keep the initiative as well on the surface as they traditionally did by stealth alone when submerged. Now that they were better able to pick the time and position for attack, the night surface approach became the preferred mode of attack, particularly in open ocean areas. And there was a priceless dividend. How satisfying it was, following the crash of torpedoes against an enemy hull, to evade counterattack by roaring off into the dark at full speed instead of settling into a deadly cat-and-mouse game trying to escape depth charging with a battery nearing exhaustion. Further, radar meant that an attack missed or thwarted need not be an opportunity irrevocably lost. It meant that it was possible to regain contact in the dark if time permitted, or, in daylight, to run around (end around) the target on the surface and dive in position ahead for another attack.

Thus, we were in fine shape on both counts, personnel and matériel, as we followed *Searaven* and *Pompano* out Midway's channel that August afternoon, and picked up our escort. A surface or air escort was provided for all submarines as they departed for patrol. This would protect us from the occasional misguided attacks by our own forces and, just as we liked to lurk off Japanese naval bases, it was prudent to guard against similar tactics by the enemy. There was nothing a sub skipper dreaded more than another submarine, an enemy submarine, submerged along his route. The antisubmarine escorts were by no means certain to detect an enemy lying off Pearl Harbor, Midway, Fremantle, or any other of the several submarine replenishment sites we ultimately obtained, but they would at least be a deterrent to overly aggressive tactics by the intruder. In addition, once clear of the channel, we would zigzag at high speed until nightfall.

Halibut was assigned the area off the east coast of Japan's two major islands, Honshu and Hokkaido. It included the approaches to Tsugaru Strait. This stretch of water, 100 miles long and 15 to 25 miles wide, separated Honshu and Hokkaido and led to the Sea of Japan. That sea, between Japan and the Asiatic mainland, had been a sanctuary through which Japanese ships moved unmolested until *Lapon, Permit,* and *Plunger* were sent there through La Perouse Strait in July.

Our area, Number Two on ComSubPac's master chart, was a welcome assignment; it should provide many targets. Furthermore, it was a region I was familiar with, for it was adjacent to and just north of the very area which *Sculpin* had patrolled when I was in her as PCO. The fifteen knots at which we proceeded to our station was a reasonable speed to hold, both for economy of fuel and for a ship with such low freeboard to sustain in the variable seas we would encounter. Only when we closed enemy shores would we trade our speed of transit for the stealth and security of running submerged. Each day we made brief dives for Jack Hinchey to adjust our "trim," or distribution of weight among the boat's variable ballast tanks. It was essential that we be able to dive quickly and safely at any moment.

Early in the morning hours of August 28 we entered our assigned area and headed cautiously for the coast. Hardly had we done so when our surface search radar made contact on two blacked-out sampans. Avoiding these and then three others, we continued toward Japan's coast and dived just before dawn. All day, submerged, we closed Honshu, trying to reach the shipping lanes, maneuvering to avoid other sampans.

In this area, so close to the enemy shore, it was necessary to patrol beneath the ocean surface during daylight, seeking targets by periscope and sonar. At this time of year at this latitude, about 40° north, there were only eight hours of darkness. The need to stay submerged sixteen hours meant that we had to use extreme care in expending battery power, hoarding enough to push home a submerged attack and then to get through the rest of the daylight period underwater until dark would allow surfacing to recharge.

Diving at first light each morning, our first order of business was the trim dive to compensate for changes or shifts in weight since our last dive. These came from fuel burned, water or stores consumed, torpedoes or ammunition expended, even changes in seawater temperature or salinity. Once we were satisfied with the trim at periscope depth, a brief excursion to our 300-foot test depth would give us a bathythermograph record of the temperature gradients we could expect on the day's operations. The BT operated in the ocean much as a barograph did in the atmosphere. On the smoked graph paper we placed on its revolving drum, a needle scratched the line showing variations in seawater temperature as we changed depth.

It was four hours after such a dive on August 29 that we reached a good position and sent a spread of three fish to destroy the *Shigure*-class escort that was guarding the Japanese freighter off the cape of Kuro Saki. I watched the torpedo wakes run right to their target, but there was no explosion.

As soon as she saw the tracks of our torpedoes, the destroyer turned sharply away to parallel them and dropped one depth charge. Simultaneously, we turned to starboard and headed for deeper water.

"Shouldn't we go deep, captain?" asked Mack, recalling counter-attack experiences on earlier *Halibut* patrols.

"No. No. Everything's OK. We can get this sucker." Only I could see the picture on the surface and feel confident that we had the upper hand. "Make ready the stern tubes."

Against our swift, maneuverable target we would have to be ready to fire from either bow or stern.

Halibut moved cautiously. In the glare of the bright, morning sun and with numerous whitecaps hiding our periscope "feather," we were intent on keeping the initiative, ready to fire at the first good opportunity. It was for all the world like my intercollegiate matches on the fencing team at the Naval Academy as, with épée poised, I'd watch for my opponent's guard to waver, giving an opening for a quick sword thrust.

At slow speed to prevent helping our enemy by emitting more noise or leaving a telltale wake, we headed seaward. I kept not only an eye on the searching, weaving destroyer but both ears, in the form of our topside and bottomside sonars. My frequent, brief looks at the *Shigure* showed he had not located us, and that we had a good chance to pick him off. As he searched he continued to drop single depth charges. Though it was clear to me these indiscriminate explosions were intended to deter us from being too aggressive, they had a much more evil sound to others in the boat. Each time I looked, the tension in the conning tower and throughout the ship mounted as Dempster passed word of what we were doing.

Once again Mack reminded me, "It's time to go deep."

Trying to give reassurance, not consciously trying to be funny, I said, "OK. Go deep, but don't go below sixty-four feet." That was the depth at which our periscope lens went under. Below that depth we would be blind, dependent solely on information from sonar.

Some twenty minutes after our first salvo the *Shigure*, still not certain where we were, crossed our stern, giving an almost ideal setup to a spread of three torpedoes fired with a zero gyro angle at a range of 1,000 yards. Not only did the zero angle setting of the gyros minimize their error or possible malfunction, but the geometry of the fire control problem was simplified to the point that an accurate range was not necessary. All that we needed was a good estimate of the target's angle-on-the-bow and a good determination of its speed. This was derived as twenty-one knots from my series of visual bearing and Paul Foss's "turn count" of the destroyer's r.p.m. Foss, radioman 2c, was our most experienced sonar operator. He was from Maine, a laconic Yankee who I sometimes had to prod into giving the steady stream of information, almost chatter, which is the mark of a good sonarman. The sounds he filtered through his earphones, and his own reaction to the acoustic jungle enveloping us, were valuable to me.

Certainly this time the destroyer was done for. In a few seconds the crashing roar of our exploding warheads would forever silence the sharp, metallic pinging, the frantic thrashing of her propellers. It was easy for me to ignore the probing pings of her active sonar as she searched for us. Not so for others in the boat. They were quiet but nervous and uneasy. They were at the mercy of my judgment and their own imaginations.

But no! I'm wrong! Once more the fish passed under their target or failed to detonate. And this time the hunter located us.

Turning hard to port, the nimble warship speeded up, headed straight for us, and "a dreadful sound" was truly in our ears as "the destroyer came upon us." Her sonar pinged strongly and rapidly on our hull, so loud that Foss had to turn down the gain on his receiver.

But worst of all, audible to everyone, was the rapidly closing beat of her pounding propellers. Would she ram us?

With my order "Take her deep, fast! All ahead full! Rig for depth charge!" Jack flooded negative tank, put a down angle on the boat, and headed us for the bottom. As our deck tilted forward sickeningly, all hands near a depth gauge watched the needle. Would it never stop pointing to 64? Was it stuck in that position? Would our hull be split by the sharp, speeding Japanese bow?

But soon the downward pull of eight tons of water suddenly admitted to negative tank at the ship's center of buoyancy, and the inclined thrust of two powerful propellers, force our ship down and down, under the protective cover of hundreds of feet of water and the blanket of a thermal layer we find at 210 feet. As we sink down I recall with satisfaction that British submariners have the right name for this tank; they call it the "down express" tank.

Mack remembers that we're in relatively shallow water and that the charted depths can't be trusted. "Captain, we'd better rig in the sound heads."

"Yes. Rig them in. We don't want to scrape them off."

Though operated from the stack in the conning tower, our supersonic transducers are mounted on two retractable vertical shafts extending below the keel of the forward torpedo room. Far forward like that, they're shielded from the worst of our machinery noises.

"Level off at two-fifty," I order.

"Two-fifty, aye, aye," says Jack.

Shortly before reaching there his calm, steady voice orders, "Blow negative to the mark."

Stocky, powerful Chief Motor Machinist Lawrence Perry at the blow and vent manifold twists the valve that admits high-pressure air into negative, forcing most of its water out its open, bottom sea valve. It's important not to blow the tank dry. That might let a bubble of air escape to tell our pursuer where we are.

"Blowing secured."

"Close negative sea valve."

Now we're at 250 feet, and Jack cautions his bow and stern planesmen to use their planes sparingly, just enough to keep us reasonably level at our depth.

Mack reports, "All compartments rigged for depth charge and silent running." Negative is almost dry, but it is also full of air at a pressure slightly more than outside sea pressure, now almost 120 pounds per square inch. We need to vent the tank into the boat as soon as we can, and certainly before rising to periscope depth where we may have to use it again. But we can't do it now, with the destroyer near. That volume of high-pressure air blasting into the boat could create a roar like Neptune's trumpet, audible for miles underwater.

In her first, mad rush at our estimated position, the *Shigure* dropped a pattern of four depth charges, close enough to shake us vigorously, put out all lights, shower us with fragments of cork insulation, spring a few small leaks, and, more serious, knock out the JP, our topside-mounted listening gear. With the bottom-mounted sonars rigged in, this left us for some time with no listening gear in operation, only the direct reception of sounds through our hull.

Brr-roomp. Brr-roomp. Brr-roomp. Brr-roomp. The four explosions slam against our hull, but all to starboard. They seem to be above us. Maybe the Japanese captain figures we can't go very deep here.

I'm sitting on the deck of the conning tower, my legs dangling into the trunk which connects it to the control room. That way I can talk directly with Jack and still quietly direct course and speed changes to Willard Ffrench, our steersman in the conning tower. Over 300 feet long, moving slowly, we're not very maneuverable underwater. We can't twist and turn easily, and we have no weapon with which to attack from this depth. We have to be patient and careful, using the background of roaring, rushing noises the explosions create to crawl silently away.

I console myself, and those who hear, by saying, "A depth charge sure is a dumb weapon. How can they expect a hit when they don't know what depth to set, and when to drop? Then the damn thing has to sink to the right depth all the while we're moving."

It's not very comforting, but it's the best I can do.

All unneeded lights have been turned off to save power, and the men not manning stations are encouraged to lie in their bunks in the semidarkness. The urge to "do something" gnaws at everyone, but this is the worst part of submarining: waiting, waiting and wondering, unable to do much.

Between the heavy blasts which try to split our steel shell but only blow luminous, green caverns in the ocean, it is quiet, save for the ominous drone of the destroyer's screws and the ping of her sonar.

When the roar of the frenzied water subsides, men lying motionless in their bunks hear the steady drip-drip-drip from a packing gland or sea valve. Why does that splash of water in the bilge sound so loud?

In the conning tower water is streaming down the shiny barrel of No. 1 periscope. Henderson quietly takes a wrench and takes up evenly on the packing gland.

There is no cursing or obscenity. This is no movie version of a submarine at war, of frantic men rushing forward or aft, grimacing, fright in their eyes. This is the real thing: men finger crucifixes; men pray silently; men rely on shipmates who guard each compartment and look for trouble. Only a few of us are directly involved in handling our ship's escape. The more serious the situation, the quieter we become.

"Twenty-three, twenty-four, twenty-five." Henderson is keeping a tally of the depth charges we receive.

With the boat rigged for silent running, all unnecessary noise-making machinery is shut down. This includes the air-conditioning plant and the ventilation blowers. The temperature in the boat rises steadily from the heat output of the batteries, from the many motors which must be kept running, from light bulbs in use, and from eighty-one bodies. Were it not for the cold northern seawater enveloping us, it would not take long to reach a temperature of 100° F, with corresponding humidity. In the hot, damp, stagnant atmosphere men sit in small groups, talking almost in whispers, or lie quietly in their bunks staring at the sag in the bunk above, just a foot from their face. Pipes and fittings that are exposed to seawater temperature sweat and drip their condensation on decks or floor plates that are now becoming slimy and slippery.

Occasionally the *Shigure* rumbles overhead, like an express train crossing a culvert. She drops depth charges when she thinks she has us. I use the time until she can turn and come back to make course changes, and gradually increase our speed.

The men in the after torpedo room feel a special strain. Locked in their narrow, small compartment, it seems to them they are moving in a separate capsule, cut off from their shipmates. They hear the constant, low rumble of our screws, the occasional shifting of our rudder, the louder screws of the Japanese destroyer, and the vicious crack of her depth charges. Undergoing his first depth charging, Fred Davis asks Racine, "Dusty, how long can this go on?"

"Shit, man, you might as well relax. This can go on all day," says Dusty, who likes to play the role of old salt to his young shipmates.

In the conning tower, which is now serving as the listening post for our evasive maneuvers, I know that we are slowly and quietly working our way to deeper water. We stay at or below our test depth, with our stern generally to our pursuers. A second hunter has joined our former target, and we keep track of her through the different tones of her pinging and her screws. We are gradually pulling away. The depth charging continues, but our pursuers are confused by their mutual interference and the bottom reverberations in the madly churned water. The explosions are farther away. The *brr-roomp* of each explosion is now preceded by a *click*, as the initial acoustic wave of each detonation reaches us.

Twice during the day we ease up through the thermal layer. If we can get to use our periscope, we can speed up our withdrawal. Each time we do this the hunters are drawn in our direction. Finally, at 1740 our third try is successful. *Halibut* is at periscope depth, and my quick sweep around in low power shows nothing in sight.

We vent negative, secure from depth charge and silent running. The ventilation blowers move hot, stale air throughout the boat. We have received forty-three depth charges, but there is no serious damage.

Mack has kept a dead reckoning track of our day's movements, and knows roughly where we are, out of sight of land. "Sunset's at 1932, captain."

When it's dark, at 2012, we come to the surface to recharge batteries and to complete repairs.

Time after time I reviewed the action of our two unsuccessful attacks, but could find no serious flaw in our tactics. In the patrols that followed in the months ahead, I would never again have the same poise, the same confidence, maneuver my ship so precisely into attack position with as little concern, as though it were an exercise on the attack teacher in New London. I had done my best for my men and my ship; all we gained was the bitter humiliation of crawling away in frustration to a future filled with nagging doubts of performance by man or weapon.

But my situation was no different from that faced by many other skippers on their first patrol. Behind the constant vigilance and instant readiness for battle we maintained, was the desire to justify the confidence placed in us, to show that the complex, integrated fighting machine of men and submarine had been placed in competent, aggressive hands. At the same time we felt a deep sense of responsibility and loyalty to the seven officers and seventy-three enlisted men who, denied even a glimpse of the enemy, placed their trust and hopes in their captain. In his lonely post at the periscope or when his boat was hiding deep below the surface, it was the skipper who made the decisions and gave the commands on which turned the ship's success and survival.

Failure of our attacks on the *Shigure* destroyer was a bitter disappointment. As I paced the cigarette deck on the night of August 29, fifteen feet aft and then fifteen feet forward, I reviewed our actions of the day. I could fault no one, not even myself. Had these attacks succeeded, as all data indicated they would, who can tell what would have transpired on future attacks, on future patrols? Would the sinking of an enemy ASW ship on my first attack, the very ship sent out to find and destroy us, have made me overconfident or rash to the point of pushing *Halibut* and crew into situations where less than perfect performance by man or matériel would be fatal? As it was, the bitter lesson of excellent training, perfect coordination, and bold action all being frustrated by faulty weapons and followed by merciless depth-charging would remain forever. Always, whenever I conned our ship into position to fire torpedoes, there lurked in my subconscious mind the dark memory of betrayal by imperfect weapons.

6

"Hot, Straight, and Normal"

Licking our wounds, determined to give retribution, we headed for the northern part of our area to try our luck in Iburi Wan, the large, open bay on the south coast of Hokkaido. At this high latitude, 42° north, the long daylight meant we had to dive at 0420, just as dawn was breaking. From our position eighteen miles east of Esan Saki, the southeasternmost point of Hokkaido, we headed toward the cape, which we believed would be rounded closely by all shipping moving between the island of Honshu and the important, steel-producing city of Muroran on Hokkaido.

Sure enough, as we closed the coast we sighted a column of three freighters making their way northward close inshore. After an hour and a half of trying to close their track, it was apparent that their initial range of 15,000 yards and large angle-on-the-bow made it impossible to intercept them. Reluctantly we abandoned the chase and turned once more for Esan Saki.

Four hours later we sighted smoke and made out the masts of a freighter heading north across Tsugaru Strait. Unlike the previous day, the sea was now a leaden, flat calm. If we were to reach this target, we could take only brief looks every thirty minutes, easing down to 100 feet in between and putting on bursts of speed. At a more shallow depth the chance of leaving a periscope feather or even the swirl of our speeded-up props was too great. Again we were thwarted as the freighter passed the cape close aboard and proceeded to hug the coast, safely out of our range. But we were certain now that Esan Saki would be a fruitful focal point.

Two hours later, now much closer to the beach, we sighted a freighter headed almost directly for us, escorted by a small patrol boat. A large turn away indicated that either he'd seen our periscope or else was zigzagging radically. As we worked gradually nearer, taking intermittent looks, another freighter came in view. This one would pass very near to us.

I shift targets, and give Jack Barrett a new setup. Taking a quick sweep all around, I see no other ships, nor any planes overhead. Being so close inshore, so close to Japanese air bases, I had wondered yesterday, and now again, why there were no planes guarding these vulnerable, important shipping lanes.

The new target is a medium-sized freighter, perhaps 6,000 tons. There is little need for *Halibut* to maneuver as she draws near. Compared to our deadly duel with the destroyer, this seems too easy.

As we approach, Mack orders tubes 4, 5, and 6 made ready. During the night torpedoman lc Emil Ade and his mates, Jim Soulis, Jack Perkins, and Ed Bertheau, had withdrawn the fish from their tubes, meticulously checked them, and reloaded. We wanted no more misses. The after torpedo room, where torpedoman lc A. J. (Dusty) Racine from Norwich, Connecticut, was in charge, had done the same. We had to be ready to fire from either end on every attack. Dusty's assistants were Grover S. (Sam) McLeod from Birmingham, Alabama, Tudor Fred Davis from Washington State, and Robert K. Warren. Sam McLeod, our garrulous, friendly "rebel," had come to us from *Finback*, but Davis and Warren had no previous submarine experience.

I take a look. On my "Mark!", Mack reads the bearing. It checks exactly with that generated on the TDC.

"Checking right on, cap'n. We can shoot any time."

"All right. I'll give you a final bearing, then shoot." It was standard procedure that, unless I said otherwise, on every attack we would fire three fish, spread to cover the length of the target.

Inserting the final bearing, Jack says, "Set."

"Fire 4!" orders Mack. The firing switch is in the conning tower, but the word also goes over the phones to the forward torpedo room where Ade stands between the two vertical rows of tubes, ready to fire by hand. It was 1432 in the afternoon.

Eight seconds go by. "Fire 5!" Eight more, and "Fire 6!"

We feel the slight shudder as the fish are blown clear, and I watch the exhaust trails streak toward the target. The spread of three torpedoes was fired at range 1,200 yards, track angle 104° starboard, gyro angles near zero.

Just before the fish reach their target, I see rapid tooting of the freighter's steam whistle. He has sighted the wakes of the fish and is desperately trying to turn inside them. Almost at once a torpedo hits just forward of his bridge, throwing a large cloud of water and debris three hundred feet into the air.

Throughout the boat, all hands hear the explosion. Dempster passes the word: "We got him. He's sinking." I can hear exulting shouts.

But now sonar alerts me to fast screws approaching on our port hand, and a last look at the freighter shows her settling rapidly on an even keel. The "fast screws" is the patrol boat, heading straight for us. Going deep, we head for the open sea. Hardly have all compartments reported "Rigged for depth charge," when the infuriated escort commences dropping. Being a small ship, lacking sophisticated fire control and launching mechanisms, he drops his charges one at a time, whenever he thinks he is close above us. In the relatively shallow water, not even 300 feet, he has little doubt as to our depth.

Between the exploding depth charges, over the sonar's loudspeaker, all hands in the conning tower hear the satisfying crackling, banging noises made by a ship breaking up. A second patrol boat joins the first, and for two hours they hold intermittent contact on us. Between them they drop twenty-four depth charges, probably all they are able to carry. None is very far away, but all seem smaller than those administered the day before by the destroyer.

As we maneuvered slowly eastward to deep water, diving officer Jack Hinchey and motor machinist's mate Bob Chalfant on the trim manifold had much to do. Whether because of the runoff of fresh water from the nearby mountainous island, temperature gradients, or other bathymetric phenomena, depth control was difficult. It took all their skill to keep *Halibut* from scraping the bottom or, conversely, from broaching. Either could be fatal. Their struggle for depth control was made more difficult by the need to minimize our noise output. Almost unbelievably, in only some 200 feet of vertical maneuvering, they had to pump out 15,000 pounds of water from our variable ballast tanks. Meanwhile, the patrol boats were making good use of their passive listening gear and keeping on our trail.

With the ship buttoned up tight against depth charging, free passage through her was prevented. Only the lower conning tower hatch remained open, so that I could speak directly to Jack. Reports on conditions throughout the boat were made by telephone to Control, where a talker relayed them to Chief of the Boat Dave Roberson. One report puzzled Dave, and he called up through the hatch, "Captain, men in the after battery report sounds like a chain scraping down the side."

"Oh, that's an old Jap trick—trying to hook us with a grappling iron." I wasn't at all sure, but I wanted to sound positive. There had been cases reported by our subs in which small Japanese ASW ships had attempted to hook on to them. Fortunately in this case, no one questioned why we did not at the same time hear the screws of a patrol boat passing overhead. As the seconds ticked by, and we moved 300 feet per minute toward the comforting deep of the open sea, tension subsided.

Not until after the war did I learn that what my men in the after battery compartment heard was probably the mooring cable or chain of a mine brushing along our side! Iburi Wan had been mined against inroads by our submarines. The six ships we had sighted in a few hours proved the importance of the shipping route we had found, and Japanese traffic passed between the defensive minefield and the shore. Because we were deep, hugging the bottom as we worked to seaward, we had not made contact with the mine itself, merely rubbed along the cable or chain which anchored it in position!

In this same area our submarine *Runner*, commanded by my Naval Academy classmate Joe Bourland, had disappeared without a trace in June. Postwar analysis charged *Runner*'s loss to a Japanese minefield. Was it the same one we had scraped through?

Before we surfaced that evening, the crew's messroom, so quiet when the chain scraped alongside, was full of noisy chatter and the loud good-fellowship of mealtime. The messroom and its galley were in the after battery compartment, on the platform deck just above the battery well. It was a very important place. The four stainless steel tables and their eight benches could accommodate thirty-two men at a time. Busy and crowded at each mealtime, the messroom was also the only place men could gather in numbers for recreation. It was never vacant. Even at night, men unable to sleep would hang out there. Once the tables were cleared of dishes, they became writing or reading tables, the place for card games, cribbage, or acey-deucey. (On a later patrol, when movie projectors became available, the messroom was our moviehouse if, due to torpedoes being worked on, the forward torpedo room was not available.)

The messroom was where our sailors compared notes, exchanged tales of what had gone on in their particular compartment during action, learned what had been said or done in conning tower or control room, or simply "shot the shit." The relaxation found there, the mutual support and fellowship, were critical to the attitude and performance of our crew.

In the crowded, brightly lighted room Albert A. Schwieso, brought up on an Iowa farm, takes a last swallow of hot coffee and heads for the watertight door en route to his throttle station in the after engine room. "Swede" had been with me in *R-11* at Key West. The big, easygoing, slow-talking, likeable man is always a steadying influence on his younger shipmates.

Jack Allison, from Titusville, Florida, is a hard-drinking, fun-loving sailor on the beach, but a tough, reliable motor mac under way. When he comes off watch he washes up in the cramped, steamy, wet washroom. It has three lavatories or "heads," and two shower bays. Of course, we can't spare fresh water for showers, so the bays are crammed with sacks of potatoes. Potatoes appear often on the menu. They spoil quickly in the hot, humid atmosphere, so it's better to eat our way through the pile.

Jack slides into his seat facing Dempster. "What's up, John? What's the old man gonna do next?"

"Oh, he just said we'd stick around and work this spot until it got too hot."

"Christ! Where's he been these last two days? My balls are fried like a coupla my Aunt Sadie's hush puppies!"

In the loud laugh that follows, men come and go. Some, a cigarette dangling from their lips, turn to toss a good-natured insult at a shipmate. Those just come off watch have time to linger, relaxing after hours of concentration, lazily enjoying the simple luxury of an extra cup of coffee and a slowly puffed cigarette as the mess cooks clear the tables and wash the dishes.

The release of tension gave words to the inarticulate. In the manner of men exposed to danger who lived from day to day, coarse good humor, a give and take of bawdy taunts, brought relaxation and comfort. The events of the past two days had fused all hands into an even closer bond. We had proven ourselves; we had sent a ship to the bottom in Japan's front yard.

In the wardroom, John McCrobey, our powerful steward's mate, serves our meal. We have a tiny serving pantry just forward of the wardroom to which he and Joe Cross bring food from the ship's galley, the same food that our men have. Joe is black, from North Carolina. He is a small, wiry man with a ready grin and the best night vision in the boat. When we attack on the surface at night, I keep him on the bridge.

Seated at the head of the table, I am wearing red goggles, as is Si Lake. We are shielding our eyes from the wardroom's bright, white light so that our night vision won't be impaired. As soon as we surface I will go to the bridge, and Si will take the deck.

Jack Hinchey has inspected his department since we secured from battle stations, and he tells me matter-of-factly that the battery is discharged more than usual, so we'll need a longer time to charge.

"OK, Jack. We'll loaf along in the vicinity, and let you jam her up. This is too good a spot to leave."

Mack's normal place, at the side, right next to me, is vacant. He is in the darkened, red-lighted control room fussing over the dead reckoning position report he will give me for 2000 hours. He has the constant concern of keeping our position along a strange coast, watching for unexpected currents, and guarding against rocks and shoals. The DRAI, the Dead Reckoning Analyzer Indicator, isn't perfect, but it's useful as it integrates speeds and courses we've steered.

Jack Barrett is bubbling over, exulting in the success of our attack. He and Mack had gotten brief peeks at our victim as she was sinking, but he was thinking of those that got away. "Too bad we couldn't reach the others."

Greg is quiet for the time being, soaking up the jargon of his seniors' shop talk.

Mack comes to the wardroom. "We can surface any time, captain. It's dark topside, and sound reports clear all around."

We surface into a pitch-black night. Three lookouts scramble onto their platforms and take up their uneasy search. Visibility is very poor because of a low-lying haze, and the heavy 7 × 50 binoculars are of little help. We are still close to shore, not far from major Japanese ports and the naval base at Ominato.

Lookouts are forbidden to talk to each other as they stand, not six feet apart, guarding their individual sectors. To relieve the strain and monotony of their task, every hour Dave Roberson sends topside a relief for each. These are men who have been sitting in the control room, waiting their turn, sipping coffee, exchanging stories of their hometowns or entry into the navy.

A favorite topic with the younger men is "Spritz's Navy." That's what they called their indoctrination into the submarine navy at New London. Charles Spritz was a chief torpedoman who had served many years in submarines, chiefly in China, some in Panama. He was a deep-sea diver as well. When he "retired on twenty" he stayed in the Fleet Reserve. Spritz was a burly, powerful man with arms and legs like limbs of an oak tree. His bushy, black eyebrows almost met over his disfigured, broken nose, smashed in a brawl with U.S. Marines in Tsingtao. His hard, dark eyes, his powerful jaw and bull neck, his harsh, loud voice, as compelling as a diving alarm, all struck fear in submarine recruits.

In 1940, when we called in the submarine reservists that we urgently needed to man the S-boats we were reactivating, Charlie Spritz was a security guard on the Moore-MacCormick Line piers in Brooklyn. When he was assigned to S-24, where I was exec, I thought he was just the man I needed as Chief of the Boat to meld our motley crew of recalled veterans and fresh-caught volunteers with our few experienced sailors and into a smooth-working team. He loved his return to the boats. With no family ties, he spent long days and nights in S-24.

Alas, I had misjudged Charlie's brand of leadership. He didn't lead, he ruled. He was as tough on our three respected CPOs as he was on our new seaman 2c. In a few weeks I had to report to our skipper, Lieut. Willard A. (Bill) Saunders from Maine, that we had to transfer Spritz. His heavy-handed approach was upsetting our whole crew.

Bill had seen this developing, and we soon had a plan. Spritz was just the man the sub base could use as Chief Master at Arms of the enlisted men's barracks. The raw, eager, young volunteers flooding into sub school needed a firm hand to keep peace in their ranks and to indoctrinate them with submarine discipline and obedience.

The C.O. of the base quickly concurred. Thus was born Spritz's Navy. The tyranny with which Spritz ruled his domain produced order and discipline, but also hatred. My personal experience with Spritz, unknown to my men, made me listen with special interest to the countless tales of Spritz's Navy. Sam McLeod was especially loud in his condemnation of Spritz—but Sam was the one who, years after the war, carried on correspondence with an aging Charlie Spritz, confined to the U.S. Naval Home in Philadelphia.

In the darkened control room of a submarine prowling off Hokkaido, half a world away from New London, I could sense that hate was giving way to grudging respect for the man who had left his mark on young sailors of the submarine navy.

As it became his turn to go topside, each relief lookout paused in the conning tower under the open hatch and asked, "Permission to come on the bridge, sir?"

"Permission granted," said Si, his eyes never ceasing their search of the blackness around us. He had to be constantly aware of everyone who was topside.

Si's quartermaster of the watch is Gene Jarzencska, from Chicago's huge Polish population. Gene comes under the conning tower hatch to relay word from Mack Butler. "Mr. Lake, the navigator says you should adjust course to zero-eight-zero, but stay at two engine speed."

"Zero-eight-zero, aye, aye," repeats Si, and so orders gunner's mate Leroy Fry, who has the wheel in the conning tower.

We need plenty of time to recharge batteries after their deeper than usual discharge. Going ahead on two engines while the other two generate power for the batteries, we head seaward at fifteen knots.

Once more Jarz calls to the bridge, "Mess cooks request permission to dump trash and garbage."

"Permission granted," says Si, and the nightly ritual proceeds. Tied in three gunnysacks is the day's accumulation of refuse, the sacks weighted with bricks we carry for this purpose as well as with smashed tins and bottles from the galley. Passed quickly up the hatch, the sacks are heaved over the side from the cigarette deck, their splash seeming louder than the rumbling of engine exhausts.

With our presence in the area known, we have been taking only intermittent sweeps with SJ radar; we don't want to provide too steady a beacon for searchers. At 2135 radar makes contact, bearing 170 relative (almost dead astern), range 13,000 yards and closing. I dash to the bridge thinking, any target is welcome, but why couldn't it be a little later, after the "can" is recharged?

We put three engines on propulsion while continuing the charge on one. This gives us a speed of eighteen knots, but the range keeps closing and radar now makes out two targets, about 600 yards apart. Giving up the battery charge, we put all four main engines on propulsion, and go ahead full power. If we can keep ahead of the targets while tracking and identifying them, we will pull off their track at the right moment and fire our stern tubes as they pass.

From the TDC Jack reports, "Target speed twenty-four knots." This is three knots more than we can make, and confirms my guess that these are destroyers.

As the range continues to close, and the bearing remains constant, dead astern, I conclude that a couple of radar-equipped destroyers have been sent out to search for us and are hot on our trail. Turning to get far enough off the track to fire torpedoes would be very chancy, exposing our length to the pursuers and inviting salvoes from their gun batteries long before we would be in a position to answer with torpedoes. A better tactic would be to dive while still dead ahead with a small silhouette, then turn out and fire torpedoes as the ships cross our stern.

Thirty minutes after first contact, with radar range 7,000 yards, we dive. I can't see the targets, try as I might through No. 1 periscope.

"Level off at five five feet!" That will give me plenty of scope out as I try to pick up our pursuers.

From control comes the word, "Bow planes won't rig out!"

We're hanging on the surface; our bow won't take its customary down-angle. We lack the downward thrust of bow planes on "hard dive." I've experienced this in other boats, and, in fact, all boats practice diving without bow planes. This is not serious for a boat in good trim, but this time there is urgency.

"Jack, we'll send twenty men forward."

Chief Roberson swiftly grabs all the men he needs from the crew's mess. "Get to the forward torpedo room on the double! Move fast!"

They dash through officers' country, banging against the aluminum bulkhead as they go, and jam up in the forward room. The extra weight helps, and we start under.

"Get the men back," says Jack. "I can hold her once we're under."

The trampling herd comes dashing amidships.

Lack of the bow planes vastly complicates Jack's job as I maneuver to bring our stern tubes to bear. But we can't check our descent in time and it continues until, at 250 feet, we suddenly bounce back to 220. A density layer acts almost like a trampoline as we descend on it. How we miss the bow planes! We're too deep and not far enough off the track to fire, but instead of the expected depth charge attack, the targets roar past, the sound of their screws gradually fading.

An hour's sweaty work in the crowded forward torpedo room finally gets the planes rigged out. With an almost discharged battery it's important that we get back on the surface. Sonar reports, "Nothing all around," but we pause at radar depth for a quick sweep around. Nothing shows on the scope, and we surface.

The latest contact, two high-speed men-of-war dead on our course, may have been a coincidence, but the persistent counterattacks of the past two days made it a fair assumption that they were sent out to find us. Do Japanese destroyers have radar? I wonder. If so, it was not efficient, for they did not detect our dive and failed to regain contact when we surfaced.

Now near midnight, all hands exhausted physically and mentally, we head for a far corner of our area for a day of rest submerged, and to make repairs.

As always following an hours-long attack or evasion, I nurse sore muscles. Since I do not raise the periscope fully for every look but expose as little of it as possible, I have to do a succession of deep knee bends. I grasp the scope's handles as soon as they come up clear of the well, press my eye to the rubber eyepiece, rise with the scope, and squat at the height desired when I call, "That's high!"

Next day the muscles in front of my thighs are stiff. The long-continued training of the periscope gives my arms and shoulders a good workout, and the constant twisting of the knurled handles to adjust line of sight or to change magnification, puts callouses on my hands.

Returning to action, we ranged along the coast by day, closed the beach on the surface by night, relishing the unfamiliar land scents, the aroma of wood fires, the smell of trees and grass and habitation as we prowled the blacked-out shore. Our many days at sea heightened our awareness of the crisp, northern land smells. To men who stood their watches below decks for weeks on end, denied the fresh air and skyward reach of those like Robison, Henderson, Jarzencska, or French who manned the bridge at night, it was a welcome change to be permitted topside. We allowed one or two at a time to come up to stretch their legs on the fifteen feet of cigarette deck.

Often, as their eyes adjusted to the blackness, the torpedoman's

1. Escape exercise, S-24, U.S.S. *Widgeon*, Lahaina Roads, Maui, Hawaii, 1939. Galantin is half-standing, left.
2. U.S.S. *Argonaut*, Hawaii, before war.—*Tai Sing Loo*
3. S-boats replenished their fresh water supply from this buoy off Cocos Island, Gulf of Panama. Ens. Howie Thompson, left, and Galantin.

4

5

4. Launching of the U.S.S. *Halibut*, 11:40 A.M., December 3, 1941, at the Portsmouth Navy Yard, Portsmouth, New Hampshire—*U.S. Navy*
5. Prospective Commanding Officers Class, Submarine School, New London, Connecticut, March, 1943. Standing, left to right: Comdr. B. E. Bacon, Jr., Comdr. G. W. Patterson, Jr., Comdr. T. C. Aylward. Seated, left to right: Student Lieut. Comdrs. Galantin, George Kehl, Frank Parker, W. B. (Si) Perkins, Rod Rooney, C. L. (Spud) Murphy, Bob King.—*U.S. Navy*
6. Aboard *Halibut*, at sea.
7. Jack Barrett.
8. Maintaining lookout at sea.

9

10

9. The coast of Japan, seen through *Halibut's* periscope. —*U.S. Navy*
10. *Halibut* officers and guests at party, Submarine Base, Pearl Harbor, September, 1943. From left, clockwise: Dora Trotter, Lem Stevens, Dixie Lindsey, Mack Butler, Kay Maurer, Jack Hinchey, Bob Gregerson, Si Lake, Mike Such, Jack Barrett, Mary Jane Tuttle, Galantin, Evanita Sumner, Phil Ross.
11. Dave Roberson, Bob Chalfant, Al Schwieso.
12. Bill Kidwell.
13. Clayton Rantz, at large in Honolulu.
14. Joe Cross and Jack Allison at Royal Hawaiian Hotel, Honolulu.

15. Silvio Gardella, John
O'Connell, Richard
Schoenlaub.
16. Ed Bertheau and
Gene Jarzencska.
17. John O'Brien and Alar
Braun.
18. Warren Easterling, Al
lan Braun, Dave Else,
standing; Art Grisanti,
Dick Kelly kneeling, dur-
ing recuperation period at
Royal Hawaiian Hotel.
19. Jim Conant.
20. James Soulis.
21. Jack Hinchey, left, and
Galantin in wardroom of
Halibut.

15

16

17

18

19

20

21

22-23. Photos made from observation plane showing test of *Halibut's* torpedo warheads, October 6, 1943, in Hawaii. At top: torpedo explodes successfully against base of cliff; at bottom: dud lies in water without having detonated.—*U.S. Navy*

22

23

mate, machinist's mate, or electrician's mate—men like Perkins, Kelly, Black, Gardella—would find me already pacing the short space abaft the periscope shears. Five thousand miles from our own shores, talking in hushed voices as though the enemy coast had ears, how rewarding were the frank, midnight conferences, as the gulf between captain and crewman disappeared in the night.

In the strange, unnatural life we led, in the tensions of submarine warfare deep within enemy waters, each man sought his private, personal assurance of safety and survival. What differing faith the voices in the night revealed. Some put their trust in matériel—in the fantastic equipment we had, or in the stoutness of our hull. As Ray Novakowski expressed it, "You know, when we were in the yard I saw how thick our hull is. It's almost an inch of solid steel. It sure is rugged."

Bob Black, from Brooklyn, was certain that our fine crew, our careful training, were more than equal to every challenge.

Still others sought assurance in the negative, in damning the enemy and denying his capabilities. Jack Allison, from Florida, ever ready for a frolic or a fray, swore, "Those slant-eye bastards can't take a fair fight. They can just stab you in the back."

Silvio Gardella, from White Plains, New York, he of the family of sixteen children, was convinced that I knew all the tricks of our trade and would certainly outwit any Jap C.O. "Skipper, a good Italian boy like me don't have to like it, but I can take it." He had been in *Sculpin* with me. Like me, he had gotten off in time.

In the darkness which hid men's self-consciousness when speaking of God and of love, some voiced prayers half-remembered from childhood, found comfort in the love expressed in letters from mothers, wives, or sweethearts. I could give confidence in our ship and in each other, but my own support came from the Ninety-first Psalm. Ginny had sent me a card on which it was printed. From frequent readings, I knew it by heart.

> I will say of Jehovah, He is my refuge and my fortress;
> My God, in whom I trust.
> For he will deliver thee from the snare of the fowler
> And from the deadly pestilence.
> He will cover thee with his pinions.
> And under his wings shalt thou take refuge:
> His truth is a shield and a buckler. . . .

The next few days brought several contacts, but always at such range that we could not get near enough to fire. Sometimes we would give chase on the surface after dark, but with no success. Perhaps the target slipped into one of the numerous bays or coves, or anchored behind a headland.

Then came a spell of foul weather, early fall storms bringing heavy seas and rain. Heavy gray swells were driven by the cold northeast wind blowing down from the Aleutians. Spray was whipped from the wave tops, and spume marked the dark swells. If we stayed on the surface in this sea and overcast, we could not count on sighting a plane first and getting down in time. The boat didn't dive as rapidly in heavy seas. Once submerged, depth control was difficult. The periscope watch officer would alert the diving officer before every look, but could never be sure whether his scope would be ten feet out of water or under a swell. Sonar was of little use. The topside JP, so close to the tormented surface, returned only the hissing, crackling noises of the sea; the bottomside QB, almost forty feet deeper, was only slightly more effective.

At night our surface patrolling was no more efficient. The SJ radar gave a confusing picture of sea return, and the lookouts, bundled in sweaters and sou'westers, lurched back and forth in their guardrails, unable to keep binoculars steady and dry.

Three stormy days of fruitless patrolling gave much time for poring over the chart, consulting tide and current tables, studying what limited intelligence we had on Japanese military bases in the vicinity. Ominato, the naval base on the north coast of Honshu, was the most ominous. Taking all this into account and reckoning our battery capacity, Mack and I decided that the tempting hunting ground of Tsugaru Strait was worth a probe.

When the seas abated we entered the strait in hopes of reaching its abundant traffic. Keeping to the deep water in mid-channel, taking infrequent periscope bearings but keeping a careful sonar watch, we headed cautiously to the west. Hour after hour our whirling propellers pushed against the eastward-flowing current, but we made little headway. We could hear the sound of distant screws, but in quick periscope looks only small craft were visible.

By three in the afternoon we had to turn back. We had to hoard enough amperes to get us out where we could surface at dark for recharging. Once safely in the open sea, the pitch-black night hid us while we charged batteries back to their full 1.210 specific gravity. We cruised through the night, silent but for the throaty, bass rumble of our diesels, our three lookouts intently alert. The SJ radar was used sparingly to avoid presenting a steady electronic beacon on which an enemy could home. We made no contact that night, nor all the next day as we patrolled submerged outside the strait.

Early the next morning, while we were still on the surface in a cold, clammy fog, probing the blacked-out coastline, radar made contact at 12,000 yards. From experience we knew this would be a ship of destroyer size or a medium-tonnage freighter, but as we closed in, radar revealed not one but three medium-sized ships and a small escort. Calling all hands to "battle stations, torpedo," we maneuvered for attack in the spotty fog. With Mack carefully minding our distance from the dangerous shore, we saw that we could slip between the escort and his convoy. When we passed him 3,000 yards abeam he flashed a light toward us, but we held on and soon vanished in the mist. Either he was challenging us or confused us with his flock.

As the predawn light improved we eased down to radar depth (a depth that submerged our hull and superstructure but kept the radar antenna exposed). Soon after, with daylight improving, we gave up use of the radar and went down to periscope depth. I could see nothing, but sound had good contact on one target who suddenly materialized out of the fog at a range of only 700 yards. A spread of three torpedoes fired at 650 yards "just couldn't miss." Sound tracked the whine of their propellers right to the target, but nothing happened.

As the freighter passed close ahead I saw that she was riding high, her single screw thrashing the water. Perhaps the set depth of ten feet on the fish was too great, or perhaps they simply had not had time to recover from their initial deep dive and settle at their proper running depth. Hurriedly resetting three fish to run at eight feet, we fired again at a range of 950 yards. Again, no hits. To miss on this attack seemed incredible. Through use of radar, sonar, and visual bearings, target course, speed, and range had been solved. Our postattack analysis showed we had enormous tolerance in target coverage.

So far we had fired fifteen of our twenty-four torpedoes against three different ships and sunk only one, a very poor score indeed. It was reasonable that I had made some mis-estimates of target angle-on-the-bow, and misjudged some masthead heights in taking ranges. Nevertheless, firing positions were all good to excellent. Deep running of torpedoes or exploder failure must account for some of the misses.

I felt enormously let down, as much for my men's sake as my own. In submarine warfare the ship, skipper, and crew interact to blend into a single organism. I could see each situation developing, was generally in control of it, and knew what was happening on each attack. My men needed to hear torpedo explosions to know that we were doing all right, and to reassure them that their blind imprisonment was nevertheless productive.

To redress so poor a performance I decided to return to the vicinity of our lone success. Close in to the coast of Hokkaido, between Erimo Saki and Muroran, just before dawn on September 6, we picked up a solitary target by radar. We had only four fish left forward while five remained aft. It was a bit more tricky to get into a good position for a stern tube shot, so we preferred to keep the bulk of our firepower forward. This seemed a fine chance to rectify the balance.

We maneuvered into position on the surface ahead of the slow, heavily loaded maru. When the range had closed to 5,000 yards we were sighted. Rather than reply to his blinker signals, we dived and proceeded to attack. Now no time could be spared, and this meant bow tubes once more. With such good target data a spread of two fish was enough. When I called "Final bearing, mark!", Mack read the target bearing from the scope's azimuth ring, Jack adjusted his TDC settings and sang out, "Set! Fire one!"

Chief Robison punched the switch which triggered the pneumatic firing valve on tube No. 1 and sent its deadly load on its way. I kept my line of sight on the target and saw that the actual bearings matched those being generated by the TDC. We fired No. 2. At the correct time of torpedo run I saw a very small splash, more of a mound of water alongside the target, and sound reported two light explosions. I could see no sign of damage. "I'll be damned! What the hell's gone wrong now?"

I answered myself. "Those lousy fish are duds! We hit that sucker! That splash must've been an air flask rupture."

Though puzzled and angry by the performance of our weapons, I was determined not to let a virtual sitting duck escape, and fired our last two forward torpedoes. At once I wanted them back. The rust-streaked maru was settling by the stern with a list to port, and sound reported his screws slowing to a halt. Our first two fish had hit after all! The last two passed ahead.

With no antisubmarine activity to bother us, there was time to give Mack, Jack, and the men whose battle stations were in the conning tower a quick periscope look at our victim. The freighter was tilting more and more to port, her deck cargo carrying away and sliding overside. Soon she rolled completely over, exposing about half of her almost flat, reddish bottom. Her stern was already completely underwater. Forty-five minutes after the splash I had seen, the maru slid under, while two boatloads of survivors drifted on the oily sea.

While my men enjoyed their rare and welcome experience, my mind was filled with questions. Why had we seen and heard no explosions? Unquestionably our fish had holed their target. Certainly a $10,000, 3,000-pound torpedo traveling at forty-five knots, hitting squarely, could punch a hole in a freighter's rusty side. We had just seen it done. But why didn't the warheads explode? Had we really missed on all those earlier attacks, or had we been victimized by our contact exploders? If *Halibut*'s experience on just one patrol in 1943 was typical, what a dreadful waste of ships and men to date. Upon our return to Pearl we would find the answers.

When we surfaced that night we had only five fish left, and all were aft. This made for an interesting and challenging attack situation. With our sting now only in our tail, I decided to concentrate on radar contacts where we could have a better chance to choose our position. There seemed to be no shortage of shipping along the coast of Honshu, and a night radar contact should not be long in developing.

Sure enough, not even an hour after surfacing on a pitch-black sea, radar made out a target at 9,500 yards, closing fast. Turning away to put the contact astern and to gain tracking time, we increased speed to eighteen knots. As the range continued to close it was apparent that once more we had a high-speed target on our tail, probably a destroyer. When the ship became visible at 5,600 yards, I shouted, "Clear the bridge! Dive! Dive! Hold her at radar depth!"

The hoarse "ah-oooo-gah, ah-oo-gah" of the diving alarm sounded throughout the boat. Even before the last lookout reached the conning tower hatch, the main ballast tank vents opened to release their trapped air like a gigantic whale blowing. It was the most exhilarating of submarine operations, a crash dive at full speed. It seemed as though *Halibut* herself was one of us, a being of mind and muscle, of sense and sinew, and not just an object of steel and copper, amperes and horsepower. Obeying the imperative alarm, she slid quickly beneath the waves. In thirty seconds we had virtually eliminated ourselves as a visual or radar target while we continued to track our quarry via our protruding radar antenna.

Soon after raising the night periscope, I could dimly make out the sharp bow of our contact at 3,000 yards, and classified her as a destroyer, type unknown. Easing down to periscope depth and turning right to a course which would give a 90° starboard track, our situation seemed too good to be true—exactly the attack situation suited to our torpedo status. Besides, with so sharp an angle-on-the-bow there could be little error in my estimates, and radar ranges and visual bearings were exact. We had an almost perfect solution of the target's course and speed, 112° and 21½ knots. This time I would be far enough off the track to let the torpedoes settle at their final depth of 6 feet, which should be shallow enough to avoid underrunning in the moderate seas we were in.

Fifteen minutes after making contact we fired, with results reported in our official patrol report as follows:

2125   Fired four stern shots at a range of 2,000 yards, 95° starboard track, depths set at 6 feet.

2126   At predicted time of hitting, the set-up was still checking perfectly on the TDC and both sound heads tracked torpedoes to the target. No explosions were heard in the conning tower, but men below reported a dull thud similar to the sound of this morning's hits and felt a slight tremor. Unfortunately this information did not reach the conning tower promptly and at

2129   When sound operators reported a whistling noise like a torpedo approaching, went deep. This was either one of our torpedoes running erratic, or one running "hot, straight, and normal" that was Made in Japan. While going deep sound reported screws somewhat slower, and bearing drawing in reverse direction. During venting of negative tank lost target for 30 seconds. Thereafter heard nothing specific except disturbance in the last known direction of the target. Decided to stay down until after moonset.

2131   Heard explosions of two of our torpedoes at the end of their run.

The end-of-run explosions were a normal event. Torpedoes which missed their target but otherwise functioned properly would continue their run until fuel was exhausted at about 4,500 yards at high speed. If they broached in a moderately rough sea, the erratic motion on the surface could cause the exploder to detonate the warhead, or, as they sank in deep water, they would reach a depth where sea pressure would crush the warhead and its encased exploder, probably actuating it.

We surfaced amid spectacular phosphorescence. It would surely disclose our presence to any searching aircraft, and even attract the attention of an alert surface patrol. Water thrown on our deck over our plunging bow made persistent puddles of light. Apparently the warm surface-water flowing northward from the Philippine Sea carried immense numbers of marine organisms that produced the eerie display of bioluminescence. In such waters, a submariner's instinctive dread of enemy torpedoes, combined with the rushing, luminous wake of a leaping tuna or dolphin, could make for a heart-stopping thrill.

There was no trace of our enemy destroyer. The postattack noises we had heard were not conclusive of a sinking; all we could claim was another dud hit, with damage to an enemy warship.

With only one fish remaining, we headed eastward to clear the coast, but did so reluctantly. We were now familiar with our area, and it was producing at least one contact a day. If only we had not had to expend so many torpedoes for so little return!

We were still quite close to Honshu and probably the object of a search by air and surface ASW units, so the following day had to be spent submerged, but when we surfaced and set course for Midway, it was a happy, light-hearted crew lustily and lewdly planning their next patrol on the beach. The long voyage home would be a lark compared to our eleven days in enemy waters.

But we were not yet fully clear. Running through the very dark night, lashed by intermittent heavy rain squalls, we found sampans patrolling and fishing at the eastern end of our area, just as when we had entered it. Occasionally one of these fishermen had the misfortune to hook a U.S. submarine.

With gun battle stations manned we closed cautiously on the unsuspecting target. Because of the poor visibility we had to get close for our gunners to see. It was important that we fire first. The sampan's guns could not be heavy enough to damage our ship seriously, but a volume of automatic, light caliber gunfire could greatly endanger our men on the guns and on the bridge.

All four main diesels were on the line, in case we should have to dash off at high speed, but we moved slowly, keeping a small silhouette, bow pointed toward the target. Would the throbbing of the engine exhausts or the smell of diesel fumes give us away? Suddenly a light flared up on the picket boat, and quartermaster Henderson said, "Captain, Radio reports strong transmissions on four-fifty." This was the radio frequency used by the pickets to report contacts.

Turning to put our target abeam to port, we opened fire at 800 yards range. The combined fire of our 4" deck gun, two 20 mm. and two .50 caliber machine guns quickly silenced both the frantic radio transmissions on 450 kcs. and the meager small arms fire we received. Leaving a battered and riddled hulk awash on the black, midnight sea, we made best speed for Midway.

Since leaving Midway we had logged 6,005 miles to Japan and back and in scouring our area for targets, but our stay would be brief. ComSubPac scheduled his boats so that after one refit at Midway they would have the next two at Pearl Harbor. After six hours alongside sub tender *Sperry* to receive fresh provisions, a few urgent repairs and fuel, we left the bright green water of the lagoon for the 1,374-mile run to Pearl.

Our brief stay at Midway brought a happy reunion. Clayton Rantz, from Mentor, Ohio, was a *Halibut* plankowner—one of the ship's original commissioning crew. He was of German descent, from a moderately well-off family, but had been a high school dropout. After enlisting in the navy, the big, homely, fun-loving extrovert volunteered for duty in submarines where he could fully indulge his passion for machinery. He loved the navy, his ship in particular, and the rough camaraderie of submarine shipmates. No matter how stormy the seas, his good humor persisted. His own watch station was the forward engine room, but he was always ready to take over from an incapacitated shipmate on the stern planes, in the pump room, and even on the wheel.

After he had made five patrols, in order to meet *Halibut*'s quota of ratings to be exchanged, it was necessary to include Rantz in the list of those being transferred. The lure of new construction and its few months of shoreside duty meant nothing to the steadfast sailor. He protested to Chief Roberson, who referred him to Jack Hinchey. Jack consulted with Mack and they agreed Rantz was an asset. A deal was struck with *Sperry*: if Rantz was available on our return from patrol, *Halibut* could have him back.

On the day we sailed the sorrowful motor mac helped haul our lines on board the tender, then walked to the rusty shell of a bombed-out aircraft hangar. Climbing as high as he could, he watched sadly as "his ship" cleared the channel, turned for Japan, and faded to a speck on the horizon. For the next four weeks Rantz haunted *Sperry*'s radio shack and implored the radiomen to alert him to any mention of *Halibut*. Sooner than expected they gave him word of our return. Early on the morning of the day we had reported for our arrival, he went as high as he was allowed topside and took up his eager search of the western horizon. By the time we moored alongside *Sperry* he was ready and waiting. He would make all subsequent patrols and stay with *Halibut* until her decommissioning.

On September 16 we entered Pearl Harbor. I knew that, whenever possible, Admiral Lockwood personally greeted each boat as it returned from patrol. The waterfront was visible from his office in the blockhouse on the base, and an aide would alert him when it was time to go down to the pier. As *Halibut* made her approach to Pier 4 the base band struck up "Happy Days Are Here Again," and I could see the admiral walking down to meet us. I wondered what he thought of our brief, hectic patrol with so many torpedoes fired for such meager return.

From the brief summary that boats radioed ahead after safely clear of their patrol areas, he knew generally what their results were, but he liked to meet his skippers and hear first hand the highlights of their action as well as any complaints.

I climbed down the ladder from the cigarette deck and waited just forward of the conning tower. As soon as the brow slid over from the pier, Uncle Charlie strode aboard, saluted the colors, and returned my salute. "Welcome back, skipper. Congratulations on a good job."

Seated in our wardroom, sipping iced coffee, I told him how pleased I was with the performance of my crew, but how bitter over the terrible performance of our torpedoes. Of the twenty-three fish fired, only one hit for a normal explosion, and three others hit as duds. Four torpedoes were positively tracked to enemy ships and went under them, while two others probably ran deep as well. Of the remaining thirteen torpedoes fired, the tracks were not observed because of visibility conditions. Some of them, too, might have run deep or been duds.

"I think we finally know what's wrong, Pete. By the time you go out again, we should have the fix."

For our efforts, our total return was two freighters sunk, one sampan sunk by gunfire, one destroyer damaged. The two freighters were *Taibun Maru* and *Shogen Maru*. In time, Naval Intelligence revealed that the supposed destroyer we had attacked with our final salvo was a light cruiser, which returned to port with one of our dud torpedoes sticking in her side! Only a ship sent to the bottom was out of the war for good.

The submarine tender *Griffin* would give *Halibut* her refit, using the work lists we had prepared. Turning our ship over to the relief crew, who started work at once to prepare her for her next patrol, we went off for our recuperation period.

A sad, grim postscript to our report of action in Area 2 came a month later when *Pompano*, who had left Midway the same day as *Halibut*, was declared "overdue and presumed lost." She had been assigned the area along Honshu's east coast just south of ours. After *Halibut* vacated her area,

> POMPANO was informed by dispatch that the area to the north of her own was open. Since that area was considered more productive of sinkings than the one she was in, it is quite possible that she moved into it. Both the one between Honshu and Hokkaido, and the one east of northern Honshu are known to have been mined by the enemy, with the greatest concentration of mines in the northern area. In view of the evidence given, it is considered probable that POMPANO met her end by an enemy mine.[1]

1. From Naval History Division, Office of the Chief of Naval Operations. *U.S. Submarine Losses, World War II*, fifth printing (Washington, D.C.: Government Printing Office, 1963) p. 54.

7

Bungo Suido

In the days of peace, prosperity, and tourism the Royal Hawaiian on Waikiki Beach was Honolulu's most posh hotel. It was owned by the Matson Steamship Co., but was now run by the navy as a recuperation center for submariners returned from war patrols. Being a skipper I was assigned a suite, the Kamehameha, a beautifully decorated, corner layout with large lanais, overlooking the beach and Diamond Head. The tariff posted on a door said this cost $105 per day. And this was in 1941 dollars! For all of it, meals included, an officer paid $2 per day.

Except for being separated from loved ones, it was two weeks of Hawaiian paradise for submariners whose boats were being readied at Pearl for another long trip westward. There was nothing to do but sleep, eat, swim, sunbathe, exercise, read and re-read the letters which had piled up for us. Our clothes and hair no longer had that submarine stench, that not-so-subtle essence of diesel oil, battery gas, body odors, and sweat. Everyone liked the clean, soft bunks that were motionless. You did not have to sleep flat on your back to keep from rolling out. And most of the time we didn't even get up for breakfast, preferring an extra, lazy hour in bed until the sun swung past Diamond Head and spilled into the rooms through the big windows, much like the whole Pacific did into the bridge when we dove. The food was good, with plenty of fresh stuff, and milk, too, that was a welcome change from seagoing chow even though submarine meals were the best in the navy. And something from the snack bar would tide us over for a swim and a loaf in the sun before lunch.

I had two huge bathtubs to choose from. One was quickly converted to a beer locker, filled with ice and bottled beer for the frequent visits from my officers and other friends. Best of all, I liked to stand under the shower and let the cold, fresh water splash on my head, trickle into my open mouth, and run down my body. It was what I longed for when we were being depth-charged, hiding as deep down as *Hal-*

ibut could go, steaming hot, the fans and air-conditioning secured hours before, and we were figuring ways to give the enemy the slip.

On another deck our enlisted men enjoyed the same sumptuous quarters at no cost, coming and going as they pleased. Women were not allowed in the hotel, and the men had little chance to meet local girls; they were pretty well preempted by the soldiers and sailors stationed on Oahu. Young men who wanted sex found it in the brothels of Iwilei which, since prewar days, were carefully monitored by the army for the good of their garrisons at Fort Shafter and Schofield Barracks.

The living was easy, better than for our families at home, who had to cope with shortages and rationing. Ginny's letters were cheery, full of news of the fast-growing girls, Joy and Vivien, now five and three. Though I could not tell her where my ship was, she could read between the lines of my letters. They held many memories of four happy years in prewar Honolulu: dances right here in the Royal, dinners at P. Y. Chong and Lau Yee Chai, parties at the Sub Base Officers' Club, "dancing under the stars" at Waialae, swimming at Kailua, and on and on. It was loneliest at night, when I woke to the rustle of palm trees and the sighing of surf, only to see the adjoining twin bed chaste and untouched.

But the sybaritic life was not for submariners eager to get on with the war, to use the new equipment now becoming available, to get enough patrols under one's belt to be sent back to command a new construction boat, and to a few months with the family. Long before our fourteen days of rest were up, Mack and I eased out to the sub base to see how work was progressing on our boat.

When we left *Halibut* for the Royal, sixteen of our men were designated to stay behind. They would work with the relief crew in repairing our ship, until the rest of us returned to the base. Following their own two-week rest at the Royal, they would be transferred to a new-construction sub or to duty in a relief crew, until needed again at sea. Among those due for a change, I had to give up Joe Cross,[1] Dempster, Chief Firecontrolman Claude Hitchcock, and Torpedoman

1. In 1978 Steward First Joe Cross was honored at the Sub Base, New London, with the dedication of an enlisted dining facility in his name. He had served in submarines since he enlisted in 1942 and was the only veteran of World War II in *Scorpion* when that nuclear powered sub was lost at sea with all hands on her way to Norfolk from the Mediterranean in 1968.

Pete Narowanski. Most replacements were new to submarines; only one or two were veterans of early patrols.

Our training task was a never-ending one. It started with the training aids and simulators on the sub base, proceeded to the intensive underway operations and exercise torpedo firings at sea south of Oahu, and continued with drills we could conduct on the long transits to patrol areas.

A strange but welcome sight at this time was a tall crane set up on the parade area in front of the enlisted barracks on the sub base. Like a pointing, accusing finger, it was evidence that Admiral Lockwood, loyal to his frustrated, irate skippers, was taking direct action. He would accept no more bureaucratic delay; if the Bureau of Ordnance couldn't solve the problem of torpedo duds, the forces afloat would. From the crane's ninety-foot height, dummy warheads fitted with actual exploders were dropped on to a steel plate, simulating the impact of a Mark XIV torpedo as it hit its target.

The tests showed that warheads which hit squarely, at right angles to the plate, resulted in duds. By slanting the plate to the line of impact, fewer duds were obtained. In other words, a perfectly directed attack, one which gave its torpedoes the benefit of maximum, broadside target length, was less likely to produce a sinking than an attack from a poor position!

The drop tests were set up after the firing of live torpedoes against a cliff on the deserted island of Kahoolawe in the Hawaiian chain had yielded a major clue to the problem. This practical test to get first-hand evidence was the brainchild of Captain C. B. (Swede) Momsen, whose innovative mind had previously produced the submarine escape "lung." The submarine *Muskallunge*, under my early skipper, Bill Saunders, had been sent to Kahoolawe to shoot live torpedoes against the cliff until a dud resulted.

The third shot was a dud. Divers recovered the warhead from the bottom, only some fifty feet deep at this point. The warhead was crushed, but when the exploder was extricated, it was found that its firing pin had been released by the impact, as it should have been, but had traveled only partway up its guideposts on its path to the fulminate of mercury firing caps. The guideposts had deformed on impact with the target (in this case the cliff), and restrained the firing pin from striking the detonator's firing caps.

With this major lead to go by, the dummy drop-tests quickly verified that the firing pin guideposts were too fragile to withstand the impact of solid hits on a target. They would deform and bind the firing pin before it could travel its short length en route to precise, sharp contact with the firing caps.

Perhaps because we had had such terrible luck with our torpedoes on our previous patrol, *Halibut* was given a load of ten war shots, all fitted with modified exploders, and sent to Kahoolawe to repeat the tests which *Muskallunge* had made with the official, Bureau of Ordnance exploders. Because of the danger of an erratic or circular running torpedo coming back to hit us, all fish would be fired from stern tubes, with *Halibut* on the surface. In this way we could keep our bow pointing to seaward and, with all four main engines on the line, be ready to maneuver at high speed if necessary.

I jockeyed *Halibut* carefully into position 1,000 yards from the island's sheer south wall. Each torpedo was set to run with a zero gyro angle for a hit as close to a 90° track on the underwater rock face as we could manage. With results being filmed by our own movie camera and by a navy photo plane circling overhead, we fired six consecutive shots, each giving a high order explosion. The seventh was a dud. We returned to Pearl knowing that progress had been made but that complete reliability still eluded us. Nevertheless, with the deployment that month of modified contact exploders, virtually all exploder problems vanished, and sinkings rose rapidly.

Our underway training was concluded in smashing style. Comdr. F. B. (Fearless Freddy) Warder was embarked as our training officer. Freddy, from Grafton, West Virginia, was of the Naval Academy class of '25, which had contributed more than its share of officers to submarines. Of short stature, Freddy was one of our tallest in courage and skill. He was a devout Catholic, extremely considerate of people. His officers and men adored him. Even today, at any reunion of submarine veterans, Freddy is the focus of admiring, respectful attention. He detested his nickname, which had been given to him for his aggressive, skillful attacks in command of *Seawolf* in the early, difficult days of the war. Late in the war he was Officer in Charge of the Submarine School at New London. Recounting some of Freddy's exploits, a Boston newspaper referred to him as a "bottle scarred" veteran. Quick to redress the inadvertent calumny, the next edition was corrected to read "battle scared" veteran.

On October 8, 1943, Division Commander Warder came on board to observe our day's exercises in the operating area south of Oahu. They would include a series of submerged attacks on which we would fire exercise torpedoes against a zigzagging target screened by a pair of destroyer escorts, one on each bow. Taking minimum periscope observations to prevent being sighted, I closed to firing position. A quick look all around showed that the starboard screen, the Destroyer Escort *Thomas*, should pass close down our port side, but that we would be in excellent position to fire at the larger target ship. Running the periscope up again after thirty-four seconds for the final observation before shooting, we felt the shock of something hitting the scope, rolled slightly with the impact, and heard the thunder of a ship passing overhead.

Responding to the collision alarm and my shouted order, "Take her deep! Go to two hundred feet!", Jack Hinchey proved again his expertise as diving officer. Using only a slight down-angle to avoid throwing our tender stern nearer the surface and possible collision, he quickly leveled us off far below the danger of surface interference.

A careful check throughout the ship revealed no damage. Meanwhile, sonar kept track of ships in the vicinity. When all was clear overhead we fired the appropriate smoke signal from our emergency signal ejector and came to periscope depth.

A rude shock awaited us. The attack periscope, No. 2, was damaged and not usable, and when I tried to use No. 1 I found that it too was out of commission. We had to surface blind, relying on sonar and trusting that the surface ships would keep clear. Scrambling to the bridge as soon as the conning tower hatch was flung open, I verified that not one but both periscopes were destroyed. No. 2, hit in its fully extended position when the escort's unexpected zig took her right over us, was bent grotesquely, while No. 1 had its upper four feet snapped off.

Proper procedure called for an unused periscope to be fully housed when under way, but our new quartermaster striker had lowered it only "to the taper," that is, with the thin, tapered neck protruding above the topmost steady bearing. This was the in-port position for periscopes. That way the periscope barrel would be fully seized by the bearing, and grit or dirt could not enter to scratch or bind its smoothly machined surface. Our new man had carefully conformed to this procedure in port and—to our sorrow—on his first watch at sea.

Loss of one periscope during realistic training operations was not unheard of, but to have both put out of action simultaneously was something of an event. (It had happened to *Seal* in combat the previous year when she had been run over by a Japanese destroyer.) With word of our mishap radioed ahead, we had the embarrassment of coming alongside a sub base pier jammed with grinning friends and onlookers, the evidence of our accident fully exposed.

This was exactly the kind of casualty which, in peacetime, would have resulted in a Board of Investigation, possible reprimand, or relief of command. My officers were very subdued as we returned to port, but in the agitation of the crowded messroom, ship's cook lc Thompson said, "The skipper'll catch hell for this. He might even be relieved." But in wartime skippers were not reprimanded for aggressiveness. Freddy's comments concerning the collision and *Halibut*'s reaction to it were generous, redoubling my admiration for that great submariner and warm-hearted gentleman. He considered our handling of *Halibut* after the collision a proper test of competence. To our squadron commander, Capt. Charles W. Styer, he recommended, "Give him new periscopes and let him go."

In a few hours both scopes were replaced, we were loaded out, and received orders to proceed to what was probably the choicest patrol area of all—the approaches to Bungo Suido.

Bungo Suido is the busy channel between the islands of Kyushu and Shikoku, one of the most important focal points of shipping in the Japanese archipelago. It can be compared in national importance to the Virginia Capes–Chesapeake Bay region in the United States, just as the Tokyo Bay–Yokohama complex compares to New York–New Jersey. It was to Bungo Suido that *Gudgeon*, commanded by Joe Grenfell, was deployed from Pearl Harbor on December 11, 1941, on the first U.S. Navy offensive submarine mission of the war.

I had high hopes for an outstanding patrol. On October 10, 1943, we set out, with my same officer team and with sixteen new men who were fitting smoothly into our organization.

We proceeded along the chain of remote reefs and islands which extend northwest from the main Hawaiian islands. On the morning of the fourth day we entered the familiar lagoon at Midway, and moored alongside sub tender *Sperry*. She replaced the 14,000 gallons of diesel we had burned coming from Pearl, and made our necessary voyage repairs. Chief among them was replacement of the motor-generator for the SJ radar. A new, high-power SJ had been installed in Pearl, but en route to Midway its generator voltage fluctuated so greatly that operation of the radar was impossible.

Late in the afternoon we were under way once more for the long run westward. For four days our passage was uneventful. Weather and visibility were excellent. After each morning's brief trim dive, we continued our surface transit at fifteen knots, keeping as sharp a look-out as possible. On the afternoon of October 19, 600 miles northeast of Marcus Island, a twin-engine Japanese bomber caused us to dive and remain submerged for two hours.

In general, in fair weather with not many clouds, enemy aircraft were not a major threat to our transitting subs. In daylight our topside lookouts could generally detect them long before we were in danger, and we would either dive until they passed out of sight from our periscope or would proceed warily on the surface, keeping a sharp eye on their movements. Even at night we could often sight aircraft long before they were a direct threat. More comforting, though, was the fact that our newly improved surface search radar, the SJ, though not designed for that purpose, frequently detected airplanes at 10,000 or more yards, giving us ample time to dive. The air search radar, the SD, fixed atop a retractable mast so that it could be extended above water before we came to the surface, was not very effective. It could not give the direction of its target, but could, in peak working condition, give an indication of an airplane up to thirty miles away. We used it only sparingly, for it was easy for an airborne detector to sense its pulses and turn the submarine's early warning device into the enemy aircraft's homing beacon.

As the war progressed, most submarine skippers preferred to keep radar silence in the vicinity of enemy aircraft, relying instead on the alertness and skill of their lookouts, and on constant readiness to dive before the plane could reach attack position. We had almost disdain for the threat which aircraft posed for submarines. This was more a mark of Japan's inferiority in ASW, of her poor airborne electronics in particular, than a tribute to our boldness or the efficiency of our lookouts.

By this time, in the Atlantic and Mediterranean, the Allies' ASW measures were taking a frightful toll of Axis U-boats. In the month of July alone the Germans lost thirty-seven subs! Among them was our own "opposite number," the German U-232, sunk by air attack in the Bay of Biscay. The escort carrier, the coordinated ASW attack groups, and the long-range ASW patrol aircraft combined to deny the surface to the U-boats and to hound them mercilessly to exhaustion. They were aided by HUFF/DUFF (high frequency radio direction finding) exploiting the excessive radio transmissions which Admiral Doenitz required of his boats, and by cryptanalysis such as Ultra.

Crucial to the success of these operations was the shortwave, 10 cm. radar installed in ships and planes, providing the capability to detect subs on the surface in all weather, day or night, while still miles distant. The Japanese had no equivalent, either of effective airborne radar or of coordinated ASW search and attack groups. Aided by our own radar, we were able to keep the surface and the initiative to a far greater degree than could the German U-boats.

However, there was peril in our confidence that we could detect and elude Japan's aircraft. A most remarkable incident occurred late in October. After a nighttime transit through the Nanpo Shoto island chain some 200 miles south of Tokyo, I decided to stay on the surface in hope of detecting a convoy along this busy route. Although the watch topside had been cautioned to be especially alert for aircraft at such short range from their bases, it was the sighting of an enemy plane from inside *Halibut* that saved us.

The helmsman on the forenoon watch this bright, sunny morning was Leroy Fry our gunner's mate. From his station at the wheel in the forward part of the conning tower, it was just a step to the open hatch that gave access to the bridge. Looking up through the hatch from below as he was, only a very small portion of the sky was visible as the gentle roll of the ship carved a recurring segment of the blue hemisphere and brought it to his vision. As Fry turned and lifted his head to make a routine report to the bridge he saw a plane high up in the patch of clear sky revealed to him. Disbelieving (was it a bird?), too surprised to sing out at once, he stared at the arc of blue. As the return roll disclosed the same patch of sky, he saw the plane was really there, high above us, positioning itself for attack.

"Plane overhead! Plane overhead!" yelled Fry.

"Clear the bridge! Dive! Dive!" shouted O.O.D. Si Lake.

Fry's hand, already on the diving alarm, pulled the handle twice and the unmistakable "aa-oo-gah, aa-oo-gah" of the raucous klaxon galvanized every man on board.

As the three lookouts leaped from their perches and jumped down the conning tower hatch, Si had just time to look up and verify the plane as he, in turn, scrambled for the hatch.

I was standing at the foot of the conning tower ladder when Si's feet hit the deck plates of the control room. "What is it, Si? Why did we dive?"

"A plane, cap'n, high above us."

With our ship already underwater, heading down at full speed, I ordered "Level off at 200 feet," and we awaited the explosion of a bomb or depth charge. But no explosion came. Was it only an unarmed search plane, or was his bomb a dud? I pondered in what strange ways were we safeguarded.

8

Impromptu Wolf Pack

The lonely nature of submarine operations gave infrequent opportunity to use friendly ships or aircraft as training targets. We were rarely in their company and had little chance to track them as visual, radar, or sonar targets. After a short indoctrination in a new piece of equipment or instrument, with perhaps a pass or two at a tame target during the brief, post-refit training period, we would sail and get our own "on the job" training. This was the case with the new, high-power SJ radar transmitter which replaced *Halibut*'s earlier model.

There was a great deal we did not know about phenomena associated with the interplay of high-power, high-frequency radio waves, atmospherics, and geography. Ray C. Welley, our radar technician 1c from Colorado who had done such a superb job maintaining our old, cranky SJ radar, was again central to our success. At age twenty he had enlisted at the navy recruiting station in Denver. Because of his prior experience in radio and electronics in general, he had entered as radioman 2c, but then spent a year in the navy's specialist schools at Treasure Island, San Francisco, at Texas A & M University, and at Submarine School, New London, learning about the radars that were so greatly transforming operations at sea. I was glad he had changed his rate to radar technician and had chosen submarine duty. He came on board *Halibut* when I did, and made all subsequent patrols with me.

Welley was serious and close-mouthed, a very conscientious workman. A worried frown was frequently on his face as he pored over his manuals and wiring diagrams. Hunched over his patient in the crowded conning tower, he diagnosed and dissected with the skill of a surgeon to make sure we would have peak performance when we surfaced. I often called him "Doctor" Welley.

It took several nights in the area to become familiar with the peculiarities of our new set. Pips on distant rain squalls and low clouds were especially confusing. When I quizzed Welley on this he replied, "Captain, I can't tell you what those gremlins are. I can only say the set is tuned right and puttin' out fine."

Once we tracked a pip for three hours, expecting it to materialize into a sizable ship, only to find it was caused by a low cloud. Small pips, at ranges of less than 4,000 yards, were continually appearing. Frequent, urgent calls, "Captain to the bridge!" gave me several sleepless nights. We finally learned that these "phantom" pips showed up only when we were within about fifty miles of land. With the mountains of Kyushu astride our horizon to the west, and the hills of Shikoku to our north, there was no shortage of land. The pseudotargets persisted for several minutes, changing in range and bearing. From the fact that they appeared only with a land background, we deduced that they were due to a secondary reflection of the high-powered beam from the land background.

At dawn on October 25, we dived twenty miles south of Okino Shima, and commenced patrolling the entrance to Bungo Suido. Bedevilled by unfamiliar radar performance at night, moving cautiously day and night to avoid the numerous fishing sampans, our first few days off Kyushu were not productive. As many as forty sampans could be in sight at a time in the rich fishing area, constraining our movements and observations. Exposing our periscope at even two knots left a prominent wake on the glassy sea. Fortunately the autumn days were growing short, and before 1900 each night we could be on the surface. Okino Shima Light was showing its normal characteristics as listed in the Coast Pilot, confirming the importance of this channel to Japanese shipping. When unable to get star sights, Mack had the reassurance of a radar fix on a lighthouse.

At 0320 on the morning of October 29 Jack Perkins, our slight, studious torpedoman, had the radar watch in the conning tower. "Target! Bearing zero six five." The range was 33,000 yards.

Hurrying to the bridge, I pause on my way to glance at the greenish pip dancing on the radar screen. This looks like a sure-enough target.

Even before Jack Barrett can reach the conning tower, Henderson has energized the TDC and is cranking in the target's range and bearing. As we track the contact, we find it is a single large ship accompanied by a small escort. She is zigzagging on base course 320° heading for the entrance to Bungo Suido. Her escort is about 2,500 yards on her starboard bow.

After checking the target's speed at 10½ knots, we gain a position on her port bow at range 10,000 yards. The target is just visible at this range as a dark, blurry shape, but the escort, at range 8,500 yards, is still not visible. It is a clear, starlit night with no moon and good visibility.

With the range closed to 9,500 yards, we dive to radar depth, and find the escort has moved over to our side of the target. He is displaying an amber light, such as we had seen on other ASW screening vessels. Perhaps it is a warning to his companion that he has detected a submarine.

At 0525 it is getting light and we can see both the freighter and her escort, a patrol craft of too shallow a draft for our torpedoes. We ease down to periscope depth. As we close in to attack the maru, the escort pings intermittently, not sure just where we are. When almost dead astern of *Halibut*, he drops two depth charges, not close but noisy. He hasn't yet found us, and we continue to approach the freighter.

When the escort drops two more depth charges, then two more, the freighter turns radically to the east and rapidly draws away.

With quick periscope looks I keep track of the depth charges as the PC boat searches for us in a 1,500-yard radius. To reassure all hands, I give a running account of what I see. They know that, loud as they might be, explosions I can see and report a few hundred yards away can't hurt us. But when the determined little craft closes to 200 yards on our port beam and drops two more, I decide it's time to go deep. As we head down, nine more charges explode, shaking the boat but doing no harm.

Two hours later we come back to periscope depth and find nothing in sight.

At 1610, shortly after he had relieved Jack Barrett at the periscope watch in the conning tower, Ray Stewart detected wisps of black smoke on the horizon. He changed course to head directly for them. If such gouts of smoke continued, in a few minutes their change in bearing would help determine in which direction their source is heading.

When I reach the conning tower, Ray describes what he has seen, and I decide to risk a higher periscope look. The sea is calm, with only a slight swell. Si Lake has the dive, and Dave Roberson is chief of the watch section.

"Si, how's your trim? Could you hold her at two knots if we slow down?"

"Yes, sir. She's real steady."

"OK. After we slow to two knots I'm gonna take a quick look with five more feet of scope. Then we'll go back down and speed up."

"Aye, aye, sir."

"All stop! Plane up five feet. Let me know when we're at two knots."

When the pitometer log indicator reads "2," Roberson calls out, "Making two knots."

"Up periscope!"

Willard Ffrench is quartermaster of the watch. Before the periscope breaks the surface he trains it dead ahead. With seven feet of scope out, I see the smoke and can tell it comes not from one ship but several, and they are outbound from Bungo.

"Down periscope! Go to one hundred feet. All ahead standard. Come left to one five zero."

The ships are still hull down. Only their telltale smoke has given them away. They're too far away for us to get in an attack before dark, so we close in as much as we can. It should be a busy night.

We pass the word that we have a convoy in sight, but can't get at it till after dark. That pleases most of the men. Like me, they like the freedom of maneuver which a good radar gives to running on the surface. Ray Welley comes to the conning tower without being called, and starts warming and tuning the SJ. He has his usual worried frown on his face, but I know that means he's reaching for perfection. We have only the basic A-scope on our radar. The PPI (Plan Position Indicator) scope, so enthusiastically received by boats who have it, is still in short supply. It gives the great benefit of continuous, 360° display, and was promised for our next refit.

Mack sends Dave Roberson to the galley to find out how soon we can have evening meal; no telling how busy we'll be once we surface. Our cooks, Tommy Thompson and Cooky Cookson, are well along in their daily routine.

"Cooks say they can be ready in twenty minutes."

"Fine. Pipe down chow as soon as it's ready."

By 1840 it is almost dark. Easing up to radar depth and taking a sweep around, we can count ten ships, about eleven miles away.

At 1845 we surface and commence tracking the convoy while we race to get ahead of it. We find that it is zigging on base course 120°, making good eight knots, and has at least three escorts.

We continue to draw ahead while we recharge our batteries, but about 2200 I'm startled when Welley says, "I keep getting radar interference dead ahead."

I take a look. Sure enough, the familiar, swirling pattern of an SJ radar trained in our direction is there. I know there are other boats assigned to the areas south of us. Can someone be playing the risky game of poaching in ours?

There's no need to go to battle stations yet. The tracking party is all we need until we get much closer and go in for attack. Not many men turn in. They gather in the crew's mess and torpedo rooms, awaiting the bong-bong-bong of the general alarm.

In the after room Sam McLeod is seated on a folding canvas stool. No longer the naive boy from Alabama who went to sub school and Spritz's Navy, he's a friendly, talkative sailor ready to describe his exploits on the beach or at sea to anyone who'll listen. He has made several patrols in *Finback*. Tonight our position off Kyushu reminds him that it was here in January that they almost lost the boat. Diving in a storm, *Finback*'s young quartermaster couldn't close the hatch in time, and the ocean poured in. It flooded the conning tower and roared through the lower hatch into the control and pump rooms. When they yanked the lower hatch shut, a man was left trapped in the conning tower. Sam might embroider his stories a bit, but I didn't mind him telling stories like that. They reminded everyone how alert and exact they had to be.

Up on the bridge it is quiet as we continue our end-around. It is a moonless but clear starlit night. A look through the periscope shows it's too dark to make a periscope attack, and the busy escorts are keeping us outside torpedo range. I decide our best course is to dive ahead of the convoy at dawn for a submerged attack.

The indications of another SJ radar in the vicinity persist. It's worrisome, but I finally conclude that the peak performance of our new radar is picking up another boat's transmissions at an unaccustomed great range.

At 0510 on the morning of November 1 we submerge to radar depth and turn toward the convoy. During the night we had solved their zig plan, but now we found that they were holding their right hand leg longer than usual. The smoke and tops of the ships were in sight, and when my looks showed no zig back to the left, I realized the convoy had made a dawn change of base course, leaving us considerably off the track. We had just worked up to six knots when the escorts commenced pinging.

My first good look at the convoy shows seven freighters in three roughly parallel columns. The largest ship, leading the center column, looks like the *Amagisan Maru*, which is shown in our recognition manual, ONI 208-J. The escorts are patrolling about 2,000 yards from the formation, two on each side. Since we can't get close enough for high speed shots, I decide to fire three low speed shots at the large ship. The several overlapping targets in the formation will give a good chance for a hit.

At 0652 we fire three torpedoes from our bow tubes at a range of 6,450 yards. When Robbie tells me, "The fish should be there," I can hear no explosions, but the ship leading the near column is sending puffs of steam from his whistle and turning slowly away. All the ships in the convoy now turn away, smoking heavily as they increase speed, and a large column of steam ascends from the freighter who had blown his whistle.

Four depth charges are dropped, and two of the escorts stand in our direction, pinging as they come. They are *Otori*-type torpedo boats. I stay at periscope depth, taking quick looks, and rig for depth charge just in case. When Dempster passes the word on what we're doing, fireman 1c Stedman (Rocky) Stone explodes. He's a profane, cocky, self-styled "tough guy" whose postwar plans call for joining the Mafia in Cleveland. "Jesus Christ! Why don't we go down? We didn't come all the way out here just so the Old Man can get a bang out of watchin' depth charges explode."

Chief Perry, his powerful, black-bearded boss in the engine room, glares at him. "Shut up, Rocky, or I'll give you a mouthful of knuckles."

I keep an eye on the torpedo boats, only one of them doing any pinging. They don't seem very professional, and never come closer than 3,000 yards. After a while, one turns to rejoin the convoy, but the other stays in our vicinity most of the day. At midmorning a single-engine land plane joins in the search as we head to the southward, planning to overtake the freighters during the night.

Surfacing as soon as it was dark, we broke radio silence to send ComSubPac a report of the convoy. Maybe headquarters could vector other boats to it. After thirty minutes of transmission we still hadn't gotten a receipt. Obviously we couldn't reach Midway or Pearl. To disguise our transmission, we changed the padding on the message, shifted operators, and tried again. It took almost an agonizing hour of transmission to get an acknowledgment of our message, and it came from Brisbane, Australia! But maybe some other of our boats in the vicinity had copied our broadcast and could get in position to make use of it.

All the while we were chasing after the convoy, the same puzzling, "friendly" radar interference we had noticed the night before could again be seen. As it turned out, on the night of November 1, *Seahorse* and *Trigger*, operating in areas to the south of us, each made contact independently. Unknowingly, our three boats had now become an impromptu wolf pack.

Seahorse, skippered by Slade Cutter, sank *Chihaya Maru* (7,089 tons) and *Ume Maru* (5,859 tons), while *Trigger*, commanded by Robert E. (Dusty) Dornin, sank *Yawata Maru* (1,852 tons) and *Delagoa Maru* (7,148 tons). Slade and Dusty were 1935 classmates at the Naval Academy, great athletes who brought victories to Navy in football, lacrosse, and boxing. Now, eight years later, they were bold and aggressive leaders in the deadly game at sea.

Just before dawn *Halibut* overtakes two ships of the disorganized convoy. They are without escort, but zigzagging radically, as they doggedly continue their southward transit. Submerged ahead of them, we fire three bow tubes at the larger ship, and maneuver for a setup on the next. I see and hear two hits, one under the mainmast, the other under the bridge.

Though mortally wounded, the freighter turns toward us and bravely tries to run over our periscope. She sinks before reaching us, but in evading her we lose our good position on the second target. The three other fish we fire from the bow tubes have to run 3,000 yards and they miss. The target draws steadily away.

"Mack, we're going to surface, close in, and give him another salvo. Pass the word, and tell the men what we're going to do." I can see no gun on the maru, but we need to work fast before surface or air cover can reach her. It would be nice to save our torpedoes and sink the laboring cargo ship, but the sea is too rough to use our gun effectively. Besides, it would be too risky to have men on our pitching, wave-swept deck.

Hardly have we popped to the surface and worked up to best speed in pursuit of the freighter when he shatters my scheme. A high explosive shell, probably about 4-inch, lands about 1,000 yards short, right "on" in deflection. Two more shots splash 500 to 1,000 yards away.

"Clear the bridge!" I yell, "Dive! Dive!"

Lookouts Marsh, Creighton, and Fojtik tumble down the hatch. I step on someone as I scramble down myself. Waiting with lanyard in hand, Edward J. French, quartermaster 2c, pulls the hatch down with a bang. (We have both a French and a Ffrench on board; both stand their watches in the conning tower. When we speak about them in the wardroom we sometimes have to specify: "Double Ff" or "Single F.")

We were lucky. The Japanese skipper should not have tipped his hand. He had nothing to fear from us until we got much closer. By then his gunfire could have been effective.

Safely underwater, we trailed our slowly disappearing target at the best speed our partly depleted battery permitted. Perhaps some engineering casualty would slow him down. Slowly he drew away. When only the tops of his masts showed, we surfaced and plodded along in the rough seas.

When we regain contact on the freighter, we can see the tops of two other small ships he has joined. Aware of his gun, we begin an end-around, using radar and high periscope looks. A twin-engine bomber forces us to dive for almost an hour, but after dark radar finds our target once more. It is a black, rainy night, ideal for surface attack, and a good time to use our stern tubes.

Not until we close to 2,500 yards can we make out the target, and then only as a dark blur. At 2259 hours we fire three stern tube shots. All miss. Apparently we have fired on and underrun the small escort, who now comes groping toward us, so close we can't get a radar range. It's so black and rainy neither of us can see the other.

"Reload the stern tubes," I order. "We'll try again."

In the after room, Racine, Davis, McLeod and their willing reload crew sweat and strain. In the lurching, heaving, crowded space, it is dangerous and difficult work.

Searching for the other two ships, we find one at a range of 1,800 yards. The sea is rough, and visibility poorer than ever. Closing to 1,300 yards, I can just make out the target through the binoculars of the Target Bearing Transmitter. When I tell him, French reaches around me with a wad of lens paper and wipes off the raindrops that are blurring my vision through the TBT. I keep the reticle of the TBT trained on the middle of the freighter, and send bearings to the TDC. At the same time Ray Welley is calling out almost continuous ranges. We are on the target's starboard bow. Our inputs are absolutely correct.

"Fire when you get a seventy-five-degree track," I say through the bridge microphone.

"Checking perfectly, captain. Stand by!" says Jack at the TDC.

There is the usual slight shudder when Robbie jams down the firing switch, and impulse air rams the fish out of its tube No. 8.

We are shooting with an eight-second interval, gyro angle 5°, depth set ten feet.

"Fire nine! . . . "Fire ten!"

One torpedo explodes after a run of three minutes, far past its target. The other two continue, and explode at the end of their runs. In the heavy swells the fish cannot hold a steady depth.

Seemingly long periods of idleness came between bursts of furious combat. After the exhilaration of a successful attack or the dejection of a failure had worn off, I could reflect on the curious nature of war at sea. It was an impersonal one. Naval warfare had evolved to the point that sailors no longer saw their enemy as people; they saw only the steel or aluminum vehicles in which their enemy sailed or flew, trying to bring their own weapons to bear. The ships or aircraft were the enemy of one's own ship; *they* were the enemy. In war at sea only rarely does one see the human flotsam marking the scene of battle: the oil-soaked survivor, the burned seaman, the scalded boiler tender, the drowned soldier.

Submarine war was even more detached, its special horror comparatively new to history, its action generally remote from human experience. Wrapped in tight security, our wet, silent war proceeded. Though our sinkings of enemy combat and cargo ships sent thousands of men to their deaths, this was but incidental to the real purpose— the strangling of an empire through cutting off its oil, its food, its raw materials. Part of the same grand strategy were our attacks on outbound shipping, those carrying fuel, food, munitions, spare parts for the Japanese army and navy deployed overseas.

Our area was a particularly busy one for both streams of traffic, and the residue of sinkings was a common sight. Letting the approaches to Bungo cool off for a while, we shifted our position to the southern end of our area. As we patrolled submerged just off the eastern outlet of Van Dieman Strait, which connects the East China Sea and the Philippine Sea, a mutely eloquent scene came into the field of our periscope—a seagull on a large, rope-bound trunk. The trunk floated past, the lugubrious bird perched on it.

What a tale that chest might tell; what imagination it inspired! Floating free from some ship torpedoed in the East China Sea, it was carried eastward by the Japan Stream, a gloomy symbol of futility, of defeat, and death. Did it belong to some officer coming home from duty in China, laden with spoils from Canton or Shanghai? Was some minor official outbound to a post in conquered territory? Or did it hold the finery of a geisha bound for foreign lands to entertain the Mikado's men?

All hands in the conning tower had a peek at the somber evidence of submarine attack. When it was his turn, Gene Jarzencska exclaimed, "We could haul that thing on board. Maybe it's got something valuable."

The impulse to find out, to retrieve the chest, was quickly suppressed. It would not pass through our hatch, and we could not linger on the surface.

9

Ultra Assignment

As we worked our way back to the north in mounting seas, there came from ComSubPac an urgent message that we be in a certain position at a given time. This was an Ultra. Messages so identified were sent only when headquarters judged we could exploit the vital tactical information they contained. They led to many contacts that would otherwise have been missed. But for normal errors in navigation by both sides, stress of weather, or engineering casualty, their contributions to the success of our submarines would have been even more remarkable.

Hurrying north at best speed, we rushed toward the entrance of Bungo Suido. The more than ordinary importance of the ships we had been alerted to seemed indicated by the night-flying plane which was patrolling the approaches to the strait. The night was clear with a quarter moon, and the sea was choppy. We slowed our speed to keep from cascading spray over our bow and leaving a highly visible wake. Tensely we watched the plane as it closed, but just then scattered cumulus clouds were drawn across the moon, effectively camouflaging the ocean surface with highlights and shadows.

The few cryptic words flashed 4,500 miles across the Pacific were sending us to a rendezvous with a Japanese task force, a hoped-for submerged ambush. But could we get there on time? Mack Butler checked and rechecked the computations of his evening star sights, plotted and replotted the course and speed changes we had made, even took moon sights against the fuzzy horizon. We were probably close enough to the enemy's track so that our new radar would pick him up, but we had to use radar intermittently and sparingly to prevent alerting warships, which could be expected to have the Japs' best in radar detection equipment. Furthermore, the high speed of the targets and the proximity to port meant there would be time for only one attack. We had to be right the first time, and as nearly dead ahead of him as we could get before dawn.

Only Mack and I knew what was really in the wind, but the special attention Mack paid to his precise navigation, the more than usual time he and I spent poring over the chart and visiting the bridge, revealed to our watchstanders that something unusual was afoot. Men who would normally be turned in following their watch were up, restless, loitering in the crew's mess or drifting casually into the gloom of the dimly lit control room to learn what the navigator's quartermaster knew or the chief of the watch might reveal. While the watch topside seemed normal, subdued in voice, restrained in motion as always, the restlessness below decks betrayed the expectancy and uncertainty of men scenting danger.

I had written my night orders carefully. I made no reference to Ultra, and stressed only the need to be very alert for targets in this fruitful area. The Night Order Book was read and initialled by each O.O.D. and chief of the watch before he relieved. Tonight Jack Hinchey and Chief Perry had initialled for the midwatch. During the night the five- by eight-inch notebook was kept on the navigator's chart table in the forward starboard corner of the control room, accessible to anyone. Its cryptic orders and information could easily be scanned by men passing through the room; they were eager for any tidbit of information concerning our patrol.

In the brightly lighted crew's mess some men made sandwiches from the platters of night rations always laid out. Those who would be going to the bridge for lookout watch were wearing night adaptation goggles with red lenses. If they played cards or cribbage to pass the time, they used the special decks on which the hearts and diamonds were boldly outlined in black so as to be visible under red light.

The midwatch passed uneventfully. Mack showed me on his chart that we would reach our desired position on the enemy's track at 0510. If we made no contact by then we would slow down, turn toward the task force on the reverse of its course, and await its approach.

There was no more I could do to improve the situation. Mack and our watchstanders were fully competent to react to sudden developments. They didn't need me around. To get what rest I could, I went to my stateroom, turned off its light, and lay on my bunk fully clothed. Normally I would kick off my shoes for my nighttime naps, but because tonight's events might unfold with unusual speed, I kept my shoes on. The slow roll of the ship, the swish-swish of the sea along the side so near my head, and the familiar drone of the ventilation blowers soon lulled me to sleep.

Hardly had the watch changed, the morning watch relieving the mid, when Tudor Davis, messenger of the watch awaiting his turn as topside lookout, rapped on the bulkhead of my room and spoke into its gloom, "Captain, radar reports contact at twenty-eight thousand yards."

Instantly alert, I swung my feet to the deck and dashed to the conning tower for a quick look at the radar scope before climbing to the bridge. The strength of the greenish pip dancing on the A-scope of our radar, from a target fourteen miles away, was confirmation that our contact was a large ship, almost surely a warship.

With more than two-thirds of the crew already alert, sounding of the general alarm for "battle stations, torpedo" was almost unnecessary. In seconds *Halibut* was fully ready. At this stage of our patrol we had only nine torpedoes remaining. Our six bow tubes were loaded, and a seventh fish was in reload position in its rack lined up with No. 4 tube. Only two fish remained in our nest of four stern tubes.

As he adjusted the gain on his receiver and tracked our contact by radar, Ray Welley quickly found that it was a formation of four or five ships. The shape and strength of the pips displayed on the scope were unlike anything we had ever seen before.

The targets were proceeding on course 300° at speed nineteen knots, but we were five miles off their track. This meant we would have to run very hard to get ahead of them, yet be wary of detection by radar or sight.

Going ahead at full speed of twenty knots, we strained to pull ahead of the enemy formation. Because the ships were zigzagging, we were slowly getting ahead of them on their base course, but the approaching dawn and closing range meant we would soon have to dive.

At 0512, when 14,000 yards ahead of the nearest ship, we submerged to radar depth, and turned toward the rapidly closing formation. Even though we presented a small silhouette, we dared not close in more on the surface. Experience with our own surface forces had shown us that their lofty radar antennas could usually pick us up at that range.

Six minutes later, when the range had closed to 10,000 yards and daylight was spreading, we eased down to periscope depth. The radar ranges we had taken, in combination with a few visual bearings, had given us ideal inputs to the torpedo data computer. When the formation zigged 20° to its right, it was clear that if it held that course it would pass very close to us.

By 0525 the picture was developing rapidly. The faint light revealed four large ships, the one closest to us being a *Tone*-class heavy cruiser. Slightly on her port quarter, about 4,000 yards farther, was every submariner's dream target—an aircraft carrier! Then, in an extension of the line of bearing, about 2,000 yards farther, on the carrier's port quarter were two even larger ships, their towering pagodalike masts identifying them as battleships. I could tell that the closer one was of the *Nagato*-class, but could not be sure of the other. I could see no destroyer or other escort, but our earlier radar sweeps had alerted me to the presence of a fifth ship. Nevertheless, with such important targets to attack, we would ignore any destroyer.

As my brief periscope exposures revealed the situation, I described the setup to the fire control party. "We'll fire six bow tubes at the carrier, then both stern tubes at the nearest battleship. Reload forward as quickly as you can."

Jack Barrett worked swiftly with the knobs and dials of the TDC. His assistant, Ray Stewart, manned the plotting table, backing him up should we have a TDC failure. Yeoman Glen Snell manned the phone to the torpedo rooms, relaying orders, verifying gyro angles and depth settings. Chief Robison at the firing panel stood ready to energize firing circuits.

With the rapidly decreasing range, sonar was almost overwhelmed by the beat of the ponderous screws of the massive ships. The steady drumbeat of the many powerful screws advancing on us was audible through the hull to all of us, but sonar operator Paul Foss concentrated on his own mental picture of the formation, ready to give sound bearings when I wanted them. As usual, Mack hovered over my shoulder, checking the periscope bearing and coolly coordinating the work of all in the fire control party.

Heading for the carrier, we passed 1,000 yards down the starboard side of the cruiser when the formation zigged to its right. This gave us a sharp, unfavorable track on our prime target. Still, the picture being generated on the TDC was checking so well with the angles-on-the-bow and bearings I was calling that hits at our short range seemed assured.

Ordering "Right full rudder! Port ahead full!" I turned hard to improve the firing setup. There was no need to pull down the periscope. So close in, even if our target sighted it in the dim morning light, it would be too late for her to avoid the spread of the six fish we were readying. We had only to wait a few seconds as our bow swung to the right before steadying on course 160°.

Suddenly the periscope went under. I could see nothing. "Hold me up! I've got to see! Ease the rudder!"

Jack Hinchey at his diving station, Red Creighton on the bow planes and Harry Metzger on the stern planes struggled with the unaccustomed forces of our sudden turn. In the sequence of going from the surface to radar depth to periscope depth, all in a few minutes, Jack had kept the boat trimmed heavy. This was a safeguard against broaching in the path of the task force, and useful if we had to go deep suddenly, but our fully extended periscope was now five feet below the surface.

The drumbeat of pounding propellers grew louder. Sonar could not sort those of the carrier from the general turmoil of sound. Should we fire blindly?

The seconds on the TDC clock clicked away. Each seemed a minute. At last the depth gauge needle steadied, hung at 70, then started up. It seemed an hour before the periscope broke the surface. Our loss of depth control for forty-five seconds would cost us dearly.

As soon as I could see through the scope, it was apparent that something was wrong with our data. The periscope bearing on which I saw the carrier had advanced 15° on the bearing generated by TDC, and I called the angle-on-the-bow 80° starboard, whereas 45° was generated from our previous inputs. The rate of change of bearing was so rapid that we knew our range was in error. The target was much closer than we thought. We'd have to fire at once.

Working frantically to crank in the new data, Jack pulled the range down 500 yards and set the final bearing I gave.

At 0539, at a range of 1,200 yards, we commenced firing our six bow tubes. The track angle was respectable, 115° starboard, but the fish had to have 30° right gyro angles. We used a divergent spread with 1° between fish which were fired at eight-second intervals. Taking no chances on underrunning this target, we set the torpedoes to run at a depth of ten feet.

Less than a minute later I saw, and all hands heard, one hit.

As soon as the last fish was on its way we turned hard to port to bring our two loaded stern tubes to bear. Gone was our plan to fire them at one of the battleships. Our first torpedo had hit the carrier far aft on her starboard side, but the other five all passed harmlessly astern of the big ship.

With her steering apparently disabled, the carrier was slowly turning to her right. Her flight deck was almost bare. I could see only three fighter planes lashed down amidships. No doubt these were damaged planes being brought home for repair.

At 0543 we fired our two stern torpedoes at her. Swinging the periscope swiftly to see what the other ships were doing, I could not see the hits, but the resulting explosions came at the right time for the distance the fish had to run.

My look around disclosed that the cruiser and battleships were fast disappearing, leaving the field free to a destroyer who had previously been obscured by the larger units. With the carrier turning slowly, listing to port and down by the stern, I carefully lined up our one remaining torpedo from a bow tube. This would be the coup de grace to the carrier now at a range of 1,500 yards.

At this close range I had a good look at our target. It had a silhouette like the *Shokaku* class as shown on page 25 of our warship recognition manual, ONI-14. I could see the many gun sponsons amidships and, in the growing light, the brown and green camouflage on the three planes.

Eighteen minutes after our first shot had crippled our victim, Robbie mashed down the firing switch for No. 4 tube. But we did not feel the shudder which normally signalled the impact of air under 300 pounds pressure forcing the torpedo out of its tube. Instead, the forward room reported, "Torpedo not ejected! Running hot in tube!"

As torpedo officer, Jack Barrett rushed forward to get precise information on our casualty. The torpedo tube's stop bolt had lifted, and the fish had moved forward enough to have its starting lever tripped. Its turbine was running, but it remained in the tube. With the pressure of our depth and motion through the water against its nose, it could not propel itself clear of the tube.

A "hot run" was literally that; without the cooling of seawater rushing by its afterbody and with its contrarotating propellers spinning madly in a void, the alcohol-fueled turbine would gain speed and heat until it could fly apart or melt, damaging the torpedo tube as well. To prevent this, an overspeed governor would in time cut off power.

But a big question remained: how far out of the tube did the warhead protrude? On the underside of the warhead was a recess containing the impeller that armed the exploder. Was it clear of the surrounding tube so that the impeller was free to turn? As a torpedo sped toward its target, the vanes of the impeller would be driven by the rushing seawater, arming the exploder after the torpedo had traveled a safe distance, some 400 yards, from the submarine. Were we pushing through the water a torpedo whose exploder mechanism was slowly turning, turning into an armed position where a sudden shock might actuate it?

I was angry. We had been given a once-in-a-lifetime opportunity, a chance to sink one of Japan's most important warships, and we had bungled it. What was wrong—our organization, our training, or me? I would have to find out. Possibilities raced through my mind, but this was no time for recriminations or self-doubt. It was not yet sunrise; we faced a whole day of Japanese search and attack; and we had no more torpedoes.

A look at the destroyer shows her swinging our way. I give orders loud and fast. "All ahead full! Take her deep! Go to 300 feet! Use negative! Rig for depth charge!" In the forward room torpedoman Emil Ade and his gang work desperately to get the fish, now idle, back into its tube.

As we pass eighty feet going down, a second destroyer, which I had not seen, rumbles directly over us. Perhaps he has seen our periscope or our wake and was trying to ram, for the expected depth charges do not come.

Once our tail is safely deep, Jack Hinchey noses *Halibut* down more steeply, and we look longingly at the BT for sign of a friendly thermal layer under which to hide. Not till we're near 300 feet do we find one. Going still deeper, we rig for silent running, shut down all unnecessary noise producers. Instinctively, without orders, we talk in subdued tones, step carefully and quietly when we move. The accidental clatter of a dropped wrench rings out like a village fire bell, bringing glares to the culprit from the eyes of startled shipmates. Some men not needed on watch lie quietly but sweatily in their bunks. They are not necessarily the ones who are most frightened. Most others prefer to sit wedged in some corner where they can have the reassurance of contact with shipmates.

Two depth charges are dropped by No. 1 destroyer. We can tell it is she because her screw noises are different, a higher-pitched *zum-*

zum, zum-zum, zum-zum. The explosions have a larger bang and shake us more than any we have previously endured. They are close. Their *whoomp-whoomps* slam into us without the telltale *click-click* which comes from charges exploding farther away.

Some locker doors fly open, spilling tools, spare parts, even clothing on the deck. Loose-fitting deck plates jump several inches high and fall in crazy patterns on their frames. Loosened dust and particles of dirt sift through the air, already hot and humid. In the maneuvering room Chief Braun and his electrician's mates, Grisanti and Mitchell, watch their meters grimly, listen for ominous arcing, sniff for the odor of burning insulation in the vital electrical control cubicle. A massive circuit breaker pops open. Grisanti shoves his control lever to neutral while Allan Braun braces himself clear of dangerous live leads. With gloved hands, he forces the circuit breaker shut. Sweat pours from his bowed head and spatters on the floor plate.

In the maze of the pump room's machinery and piping, Phil Carano struggles to control a leak on the discharge side of the trim pump. He curses when he slips on the wet, slimy floor plate and cuts his shin against a pipe flange.

I wondered what effect the explosions were having on our reluctant torpedo. Then I realized that as long as I could wonder, they were having none. Obviously the torpedo had not armed; it had not exploded even though exposed to full sea pressure at 360 feet and to the overpressure of depth charging.

There was no way to sight the torpedo or to tell just how far out of the tube it extended. If pressure from our forward motion had forced it back far enough, perhaps closing the muzzle door against it would push it back into the tube. Tudor Davis cranked the door's operating shaft until it would go no farther. He could feel the door coming up hard against the fish, but it would not budge. Apparently the tube's stop bolt had dropped into place behind the torpedo's guide stud, preventing any rearward motion. Somehow it had to be lifted.

Trying to be oblivious to the sounds of ships overhead and to depth charges, Ade and his men worked swiftly but carefully. The normally sacrosanct interlocks had to be disconnected. These were safety devices designed to prevent firing unless shutter and outer door were properly aligned, and to prevent muzzle and breech doors from being open at the same time.

The procedure was lengthy. The impulse stop valve was closed, and all air was bled off the firing valve. Working in the cramped space outboard of the tube, Jack Perkins and Ed Bertheau removed the No. 4 tube shutter bar interlock. Next the interlock disconnect flag was unlocked and disengaged. Now a stout line could be secured to the stop rod. Hauling back on it, the stop bolt was retracted.

In the forward room Jack Barrett took the phone and spoke to yeoman Snell in the conning tower. "Snell, tell the captain we've got the stop bolt up, and will try to force the fish back with the outer door. But we'd like an up-angle on the boat and maybe a little more speed would help."

"OK," I said. "Tell them to stand easy till we give them the word."

"Foss, search all around, and tell me what you've got."

The destroyers were in the vicinity, but unsure of our location. We could hear them echo-ranging for us. There were now three of them in the search. Sometimes one would slow his screws or lie-to so that he could listen with his passive sonar. They were coordinating their efforts well.

When all three were once more moving and echo-ranging, we made our move. Not knowing what the rest of the day would bring, it was best to boat our stubborn fish now.

"Jack, give us a three degree up-angle. Tell the maneuvering room to build up turns slowly to two-thirds."

As our bow lifted and our speed slowly increased, Davis and Bertheau cranked on the muzzle door. They could feel the resistance as it pressed on the nose of the warhead. "A little more angle would help."

"Control, give us a five degree up-bubble."

Cranked hard, the muzzle door slowly pushed the fish back into the tube and seated itself against the knife edge of the tube. With the torpedo safely on board, we slowed down and resumed our cautious evasion. Diagnosis of our casualty and examination of the fish would have to wait.

Sixty feet below our test depth of 300 feet, I kept a careful eye on how our ship reacted to the degrees of rudder and the slow speed we used. We were becoming progressively heavier from the compression of our hull and the accumulation of water from leaks around hull fittings. According to the submarine design experts in BuShips, we should lose 2,000 pounds of buoyancy for every 100-foot increase in depth.

The last time in port I had listened with envy to my "heavy hull" colleagues, skippers of the newest class of submarines, which had an operating depth of 400 feet. They dived to 400 or more feet with no concern, and had a correspondingly greater margin of safety than ours. However, I had little anxiety now about exceeding our peacetime test depth. Most of us had been forced far below that by Japanese counterattacks. We had great faith in the design and construction of our ships, but as the enemy's ASW improved, we yearned for the ability to pull a little thicker blanket of ocean over us.

As boats returning from action told of going by accident or intent to almost double their designed operating depth, there crept into the thinking of many submariners the belief that the collapse depth of their boats was much greater than the designers acknowledged. This attitude worried Admiral Lockwood as well as the navy's principal submarine designers, Captain A. I. (Andy) McKee at Portsmouth, and Comdr. Armand Morgan in Washington, D.C. It was pointless for ComSubPac to mandate a maximum operating depth; each skipper had to be free to act as he thought best in the situation he faced. However, it was the obligation of operational commanders and ship designers to lay out the facts as known. From these it was generally accepted that there was a 50 percent margin of safety, that is, a 300-foot boat should be able to go to 450 without collapse or serious component failure.

In our present predicament I did not want to use bursts of speed because of the hunters' good listening ability. I tried always to present them with a small sonar silhouette, so it was necessary at times to run right toward our pursuers or right with them. Several times they made good contact, shifted their echo-ranging to short-scale, rapid pinging, and started a run on us as we braced for a barrage of depth charges. Each time they lost us, their sound beams bouncing off the temperature gradient instead of our hull. Three times one of the destroyers passed directly overhead, close enough for all hands to hear the whine of turbines and the beat of screws.

Only thirteen depth charges were dropped, one or two at a time. They were close, but always above us. Normally, there seemed no limit to the number of charges the Japanese were willing to expend. Why were there so few now? Were they using a new antisubmarine weapon, something like the "hedgehog" which our own and British ASW ships were now using? These fired salvos of small, fast-sinking charges that detonated only on contact, any one being sufficient to hole a sub. But no use brooding about that. It was better for all hands to believe we were fully in control of the situation, deftly maneuvering to outwit the Japanese skippers, cleverly avoiding their depth charges. After all, maybe these homeward-bound ships really were low on depth charges. Perhaps this group had already been under submarine attack, real or imagined, and had expended most of their store.

Though few in number, the depth charges seemed bigger than those we'd gotten used to on other attacks. Our superstructure rattled and banged more; our ship shook and bounced more; our hull seemed to groan more. The ASW search was the most persistent and professional we had endured to date. No doubt a submarine attack at the very entrance to one of the homeland's major channels provoked the enemy's best antisubmarine efforts. Deep beneath the surface, we had no way of knowing, but because we were so close to Japanese naval bases it was almost certain that aircraft were also on the scene hunting us.

I did not consider the day's events particularly harrowing, but the cumulative impact of the past few days—surface running in daytime, gunfire, depth charging, penetration of a Japanese naval task force, now this prolonged evasion—unnerved some men. One young seaman had hysteria, and, with Mack's permission, Pharmacist's Mate "Doc" McClain gave him a sedative. Even one of our officers, hard-working, intense Mike Such, had been on the verge of active hysteria since the first depth charging on this patrol—the minor one shortly after our first contact in the area. We knew he was concerned about his wife, soon to deliver a baby, and that he was fearful of complications. His mind was not at ease when we sailed, and he lived each day half-dreading the "family gram" that might come for him on one of ComSubPac's nightly broadcasts. My reassurance that no news was good news was of slight comfort, and Mike was embarrassedly confined to his bunk for a few days with a pronounced swelling of the joints and a skin rash.

Fortunately, action on this patrol was about over. We would soon be bound for home, and in a few days could transfer our patients to the submarine tender at Midway.

As the day wore on we gradually worked our way off our pursuers' track and crawled slowly, silently away. We were being carried along by the deep, cold current flowing eastward south of Shikoku at a speed of about three knots. As the hours dragged on and hunger replaced tension and fear, our cooks passed platters of sandwiches and cold drinks. No electricity could be spared for cooking. The sandwiches were thick slices of bologna sausage (reviled as "horsecock" by sailors and marines) on bread plastered with artificial butter.

On some evasions, when our attackers held good contact on us and made repeated runs over us, and their depth charges were close enough to shower us with leaks from hydraulic oil or water lines, or knocked chunks of cork insulation from our hull, I would abandon the conning tower, ordering all personnel down into the control room. By securing the hatch between the two compartments we gained some measure of structural integrity. However, I did not like to do this. To some men it would mean we were in serious trouble, if not in extremis. Besides, I would have to give up the ready, instant access to the operator of the conning tower sonar console. The same sonar could be operated from the forward torpedo room, but then I would have to rely on data passed via telephone. At deep submergence I needed the mental picture which sonar painted. It was chiefly on the steady stream of bearings and the comments of sonar operators Paul Foss, Don Bice, and Joe Janus that I based our evasive tactics.

In this case I did not consider our situation precarious. I remained sitting on the deck of the cold, clammy conning tower, my feet dangling into the trunk leading up from control. This way I could absorb information directly from sonar as well as that which my unaided ears could detect. At the same time I was in direct voice contact with the diving station.

Mack and I shared a liking for chess and cribbage. After he'd completed his evening star sights, if time and circumstances permitted, we'd match wits over a chess board across the wardroom table. If less time was available, cribbage was our game. Ever since leaving Midway we'd been conducting the Great Transpacific Cribbage Tournament, and Mack was several games up on me. Here in the quiet, cool conning tower, with only the sound of distant pinging to distract us, was a good time to correct the imbalance.

Sitting on the deck, our legs dangling through the access hatch, we slapped our cards successively on the green linoleum surface, and "pegged" happily on, the progress of captain and exec duly reported throughout the boat. I won two games of three.

Six hours after our attack, our trackers lost contact with us. A final flurry of six depth charges, telegraphed by *click, click, click, click, click, click,* was so distant it must have been on a false contact. By midafternoon we were at periscope depth, clear of all pursuers.

It was comforting to hear our ship come to life. It seemed that she, too, had been holding her breath, suspended in limbo between the sunlit surface churned by avenging furies and the deep, dark bottom of eternal calm. Electric motors and hydraulic pumps started; ventilation fans whirled; lights came on, as electric and liquid currents flowed once more through copper veins and tubes. Men went loudly about their tasks, cleaning up the debris of depth charging, repairing the modest damage we had received, pumping overboard the excess water accumulated in the bilges. From the galley came the rattle of pots and pans as Tommy Thompson, Cooky Cookson, and Norm Thomas went ahead with preparations for a hot meal.

Surfacing at dark, we set course for Midway, 2,800 miles away. In the locker behind my bunk, I still had the six bottles of "medicinal" liquor issued to each skipper at the start of each patrol. They could be dispensed as he saw fit. I always distributed mine share and share alike, but I knew one skipper who reasoned that the limited quantity would be of greatest benefit to the war effort if judiciously rationed to himself alone. My crew and I had shared a trying day; it was time to break out the grog.

This time I had three bottles of a poor Maryland bourbon and three of an equally raw California brandy. They would provide only two small jiggers per man for an entire patrol, but after being without alcohol for four to eight weeks, what wonders of relaxation even one ounce of booze could perform.

Their doses carefully doled out by Dave Roberson, some men took their share in coffee, some in water, and some would sip it straight just before climbing into their bunks. I was sure there was some bargaining between old salts and the few youngsters who didn't like hard liquor. Those on duty collected their ration when they came off watch, and for the first time in many days men slept soundly as we sped away from Japan.

The long voyage home seemed like a health cruise. By this time we had eaten our way through the food stored in the shower stalls, and fresh water could be spared for showers. In a few days the sweat, grime, and stench of unwashed bodies had almost disappeared. Only our clothing and bedding retained the characteristic submarine essence of diesel oil, battery gas, stale air, and cooking odors.

As we steamed eastward, we let men who hadn't seen the sun in weeks come topside. While they soaked up sunshine and inhaled pure salt air, they served as additional lookouts. I had not seen some of the engine room gang since we left Midway and buttoned our boat up tight for sea. They had lived in a small world of their own, moving between the oil-fogged engine rooms, the noisy crew's mess, and their sour-smelling bunks in the crew's quarters. All were pale and spent, weak from lack of exercise and fresh air. The climb up the ladders from control room and conning tower left them breathing hard, legs weak and wobbly. Only their bushy beards looked strong; like mushrooms, they had thrived in dim, dark caverns. On warm days, when the wind was abaft the beam, shirts would come off for a cautious sunbath. In contrast to pale skin, the blue-green tattoos on chest or shoulder seemed livid bruises.

The seven-day run to Midway gave us plenty of time for a postmortem: why had five of our salvo of six torpedoes missed, and why had one misfired?

When about 100 miles from Japan we had broken radio silence and sent ComSubPac a brief summary of our patrol results. Most important was the attack on the carrier, but we did not know her name or her fate. We could certify only one torpedo hit in her, with two other probables. When we last saw her she was down by the stern, circling slowly. But the code breakers in Pearl knew. She was *Junyo*, a light carrier of 24,100 tons. Our warhead with 668 pounds of torpex had hit far aft on her starboard side, disabling steering and propulsion. While *Halibut* was being harried by destroyers, *Junyo* was taken under tow and safely brought through nearby Bungo Suido to her dockyard.

Repaired and returned to combat, unlike nineteen other Japanese aircraft carriers, *Junyo* would survive the war. In June, 1944, she took part in the Battle of the Philippine Sea and was severely damaged by a bomb hit from a U.S. Navy aircraft. Repaired again, in October she had to remain in the Inland Sea while Japan fought her last desperate naval battles off the Philippines. There were no planes available by then for battle-scarred *Junyo*. On December 9, 1944, while under way off Nagasaki, she was torpedoed by our submarines *Seadevil* and *Redfish*, suffering damage that kept her out of the war for good.

*   *   *

Trying to account for our failure, we played back all our fire control data from the time of first contact. It became clear that unfamiliarity with our new radar's performance, ineptness in its use, was the chief culprit. The battleships in the task force formation towered high above the carrier's low platform, and the one on almost her same bearing returned the dominant "pip." While we thought our fire control data was solving the problem to hit the carrier, we were, in fact, tracking the battleship just beyond her. We were using for the carrier a range some 2,400 yards too great. The loss of depth control at a critical time had denied us a look for forty-five seconds. During that time the convergence of our own motion and the carrier's at close range produced the large discrepancy in bearing when I next could see. There was time only for an arbitrary down "spot." The 500 yards applied was not enough, and only the first fish could hit.

As for the hot run, disassembly of the torpedo tube firing valve showed rust flakes fouling its smoothly machined inner surface. They could have come only from the impulse air volume tank, perhaps dislodged by depth charging.

With those bitter experiences behind us, Mack Butler assembled the data we had been compiling for weeks past, culled quartermaster's logs and records, and put our patrol report into final form for yeoman Glen Snell to type. Immediately on return to port each boat had to turn in a smoothly typed set of stencils, ready to be run off on the waiting mimeograph machine, as well as a track chart of all our movements in the area. As the report moved up the command chain, it would be critically reviewed and endorsed by our division commander and our squadron commander before final review by ComSubPac.

One part of the report called for a tabulation of miles steamed and fuel used. Our data told the story of superb reliability and long-range performance built into our fleet boats just in time to cope with war in the Pacific's vast expanse. Our round-trip from Pearl Harbor required 8,327 miles of steaming to make possible only 1,957 miles of action in our patrol area.

Our stop at Midway was brief. In seven hours *Sperry* refueled us, gave us fresh provisions and ice cream, and returned, still warm from the dryer, the huge bags of clothing and bedding we had rushed to her laundry. Under way by midafternoon, we headed for Pearl. Thirty-eight days after we had left, we moored again to Pier 4 at the sub base, and were warmly welcomed by old friends.

Admiral Lockwood could not be present. He was attending a conference at Admiral Nimitz's headquarters up on Makalapa Hill, but had sent word that I was invited to lunch in his quarters nearby on Makalapa Drive just across the highway from the base. The stack of mail which had piled up for me would have to wait a little longer.

At ComSubPac's quarters I joined Chief of Staff Captain S. S. (Sunshine) Murray and Captain John H. (Babe) Brown, ComSubRon 4. While we waited for Uncle Charlie we sipped beer and threw darts at the target hanging on the wall of the cool lanai. Soon we heard a car door slam, and the admiral came in with his usual vigorous stride and pleasant smile.

Over the light but tasty lunch prepared by the admiral's Filipino cook, I described our attack on the carrier and our analysis of why we had failed to sink her. Admiral Lockwood was not critical; he was more interested in the Japanese antisubmarine measures. He was constantly pressing scientists and the Bureau of Ordnance to develop equipments and weapons that would permit his boats to fight back under attack, and not just be passive targets.

In his official endorsement to our patrol report, ComSubPac credited us with sinking one freighter (*Eihuku Maru* class)—3,520 tons, and damaging one carrier (*Shokaku* class)—15,000 tons. Nowhere was there written reference to Ultra, its part in making the contact or its intelligence after the attack. Even reference to *Shokaku* and its incorrect tonnage was designed to avoid any hint that decrypted intelligence had been involved.

10

New Tactics

The recuperation period following our return from Bungo Suido was exceptional. Refreshing as was a stay at the Royal Hawaiian, it could not compare with what George P. Cooke and Sophie Judd Cooke shared with us at their ranch on the island of Molokai. Each was a descendant of the earliest Caucasian families in the Hawaiian Islands, and their own contributions to the cultural, social, and commercial life of Hawaii were great. Their own sons and sons-in-law were directly committed to the war effort, and they too sought a personal involvement by opening their home to submarine officers for rest periods following war patrols.

I was one of five invited to spend five days at Kauluwai, their home on the 72,000-acre cattle and pineapple ranch on Molokai, in the hills above Kaunakakai. This was the village made famous by the popular hula, "The Cockeyed Mayor of Kaunakakai." On the short flight eastward from Oahu to its neighboring island, my companions were Mack Butler and Jack Hinchey from *Halibut*, and Roy Davenport and Curtis Bunting from our sister ship *Haddock*. Roy was my Academy classmate. He had just completed four successful patrols in command and was on his way to the States for command of newly built *Trepang*. He was a most sincere and devoted Christian Scientist, known in the submarine service as the "Praying Skipper."

The youngest Cooke daughter, Phoebe, was our daily guide. Caring for their two young children while husband J. D. (Twink) Fitzgerald was on Army Air Force duty in the southwest Pacific, Phee somehow found time to lead us each day on new adventures: deer hunting, crabbing, fishing, surfing, horseback riding, sightseeing, and a *luau* with natives of Kaunakakai. Only Mack could bring down a deer, a descendant of the few imported from Japan many years before, but only Phee was able to skin and dress the prize while five submarine samurai stood by helplessly.

Barely fifty miles distant from Pearl Harbor and its grim evidence of war, the serenity of Molokai's green hills overlooking Kalohi Channel made the war remote for a few days, and depth charges only a bad dream. To many submariners the warm and gracious hospitality of George and Sophie Cooke was a fond wartime memory; to a few it was a last nostalgic glimpse of family life before sailing into oblivion.

Our visit included Thanksgiving Day. As George pronounced grace before the traditional feast, my thoughts were of Ginny and our girls in faraway New England, where Thanksgiving was born. It was seven months since I had left them. Joy, our oldest was a *kamaaina*; she had been born here in Hawaii. Vivien came to us in New London. Ginny's letters told of their antics: Joy adjusting to her expanding world in kindergarten, Vivien trying to emulate her big sister. The letters carried no complaints. Car pools coped with gasoline rationing; food shortages were tolerable; neighbors, navy or civilian, were always ready to help. I was kept current on new teeth. Often a childish crayon scrawl—a letter to Daddy—was included with Ginny's always optimistic, encouraging words.

Upon our return from "The Friendly Island" we were plunged into training for what was for us a new form of submarine warfare—coordinated attack, or "wolf pack" tactics. Up to this time our navy had not employed submarines in attack groups. There had been some effort in peacetime to develop a doctrine for coordinated submarine attack, day and night, but it had not been pursued with vigor. The basic difficulty had been the unreliable, inadequate communications of those days, shore-to-shore, sub-to-shore, and, more importantly, sub-to-sub. Unable as we were to exchange information securely and reliably with other boats close by, there was considerable danger of collision and of mistaken identity. Furthermore, no submarine skipper relished sacrificing his freedom of movement and independence of action to a commander remote from the scene and unfamiliar with a rapidly changing situation. Thus, we entered World War II with no doctrine for coordinated submarine tactics, and, in fact, with a predilection against them. It should also be said that far too few boats were available in December of 1941 to mount any effective campaign of wolf-packing. There were in the Pacific then only thirty-nine modern fleet-type submarines, and many of these were diverted from attack missions to perform special missions evacuating high-level personnel, supporting coast-watchers, transporting gold from the Philippines, landing raiders, and making reconnaissance in advance of amphibious assaults.

The first use of a rudimentary form of wolf pack came in the spring of 1943 when Rear Admiral Jimmy Fife, headquartered in Brisbane, Australia, deployed pairs of his boats along the most probable path of enemy traffic, in order to increase the likelihood of contact. Any reports they made of contacts would be rebroadcast by headquarters. However, they operated independently, responding to strategic direction from Fife but in no way coordinating their tactical operations. It was at this time that the Commander-in-Chief U.S. Fleet (CominCh), Admiral Ernest J. King, probably influenced by the great successes Admiral Doenitz had achieved with his U-boats, directed that wolf pack tactics be developed for U.S. submarines.

Unlike the U.S. submarine service, Germany's had methodically prepared in peacetime for the application of what they initially called "group tactics." From October 1935 onward they had conducted intensive training in and refinement of a doctrine for submarine coordinated attacks. Then-Captain Karl Doenitz was put in charge of the German Navy's nine small (250-ton) U-boats and directed to build up an effective submarine force. During World War I Doenitz had commanded the submarine *UB-38*, which was sunk under him following an attack on a convoy in the Mediterranean. Rescued and imprisoned, he had time to reflect on the lessons of Germany's unsuccessful war at sea. While the U-boats had initially achieved considerable success with their lone attacks, the introduction of the convoy system in 1917 thwarted them. Although not new in the long history of war at sea, the use of convoys was particularly effective in defending against submarines.

The convoy system meant that a solitary submarine on patrol would find for long periods nothing but vacant sea and fruitless search, followed by sudden, overwhelming contact with large numbers of lumbering, heavily loaded freighters and tankers, strongly escorted by warships. When the submarine was fortunate enough to make contact with so rare and so juicy a target, she would probably sink a ship or two, but her limitations in human and torpedo resources would not permit her to sustain the level of attack so rich a prize warranted. From this experience, and his conviction that the submarine was ideal for close range torpedo attack on the surface at night, Doenitz evolved his concept of group tactics, applying in submarine warfare the age-old principle of concentration of force.

The fundamentals on which he based his strategy, as stated by Doenitz, were:

a. It is essential in an attack on any given objective, to be able to deliver the attack in as great strength as possible—in other words, by means of tactical cooperation and tactical leadership, to bring a number of U-boats to attack simultaneously the given objective. This applies to any attack on a really valuable, individual objective but it becomes particularly desirable in the case of an attack on an accumulation of targets, such as a formation of warships or a convoy. A massed target, then, should be engaged by massed U-boats.

b. The U-boat has but a very restricted radius of vision and is slow, even on the surface. In terms of time and space it can cover only a comparatively small area and is therefore not suitable for reconnaissance purposes. Tactically, then, it must act in co-operation with a branch of the armed forces more suited to reconnaissance duties. And for these the best instrument is the aeroplane.[1]

The object of the wolf pack tactics developed from these principles was to locate the enemy, to report his position, and to attack him with the greatest possible number of U-boats.

In the search phase one or more boats were deployed across the most probable convoy route, and they remained on the surface as much as possible. The boat which first made contact would report that fact, giving its position, before moving in to attack. It might even be held back, directed to shadow and report on its contact. The command authority receiving the report would then order other boats within striking distance to move into geographically designated positions for night surface attacks.

Early in the war the U-boats had great success with these tactics. The Western Allies had concentrated their prewar ASW efforts on countering classic underwater tactics, wherein single boats attacked by daylight. As the number of boats available to Admiral Doenitz

---

1. Doenitz, Karl. *Admiral Doenitz Memoirs* (London: Weidenfeld and Nicolson, Ltd., 1959) pp. 14–15.

increased, the toll taken by his aggressive night raiders became devastating. The chief weakness of his system was the excessive use of radio communications required. This frequently disclosed the position of his boats. In time the Allies developed the technical and tactical means to deny the surface to the U-boats.

Thus the start of World War II found the German Navy ready with a submarine attack doctrine which was sound for the time in which it was introduced, considering the state of the art of ASW then existing. It needed only adequate numbers of U-boats to produce sinkings on a scale that might well have been decisive in winning the Battle of the Atlantic. Fortunately for the Western Allies, Germany's land-oriented high command started the war with only 57 U-boats, not the 300 that Doenitz estimated could be decisive against the convoy system.

Our problem in the Pacific was quite different. Early in the war Japan did not resort to large convoys. She knew our submarine resources were limited. The available boats would have to be spread very thin and traverse enormous reaches of the Pacific in order to cover the focal points of Japan's rapidly expanding area of conquest. In addition, unlike Germany, Japan had started war against us with a well-developed fleet, one strong in surface ships and aircraft carriers. That had been the means by which she tried to neutralize our power in the Pacific in the boldly conceived, ably executed attack on Pearl Harbor. Thus topmost priority on our submarine target list had to be given to carriers and heavy warships, not merchantmen. Until our shattered surface fleet could be restored and expanded, our small number of submarines, augmented by nine Dutch and three British boats, operated singly in widely separated areas. Not until 1943 did we apply wolf pack tactics, and then in a form and in numbers very different from the German pattern.

In response to CominCh's directive, ComSubPac designated Captain Babe Brown to set up and conduct a training program. As the Submarine Force grew, he would be promoted to Rear Admiral and head up the Submarine Force Training Command. One of the Naval Academy's all-time football greats, from the class of 1914, the towering but soft-spoken and genial Babe had excellent rapport with all of the skippers, by now almost twenty years his juniors. His program for wolf pack training was dubbed "Convoy College," and its campus was the open-air dance floor of the Submarine Officers' Mess at Pearl

Harbor. The large, square dance floor was covered with a checker-board pattern of highly polished, foot-square, black and white tiles. Most of us, during prewar assignments in Pearl, had spent happy evenings there with our wives, dancing under the stars among the graceful palm trees encircling the floor. Now the same floor was the gameboard of a grim curriculum, learning the new procedures and vocabulary for pack tactics.

It had been decided that our wolf packs would generally be formed of groups of three submarines, and that the group commander would be a senior officer at the squadron commander or division commander level, embarked in one of the boats. By this time our radio communications between ships was considered reliable enough for coordinated operations, and a technique had been developed for intership communication by means of our surface search radar. Nevertheless, there was a general antipathy among skippers to the emission of signals in any detectable form. We knew of the great success the United States and Britain were having in direction-finding German submarine transmissions. However, group tactics could succeed only with radio communications between boats; it was up to us to accept that, using practices that minimized the risk of detection. To this end special, two-letter codes were devised for passing intelligence between boats and for transmitting the group commander's instructions. The intent was not for him to exercise combat direction but to bring all boats into contact with worthwhile targets, so that successive attacks could be made by the different skippers using their own tactics.

Rather than attempting to attack simultaneously, our doctrine called for successive attacks. At any one time there would be one "attacker" and two "flankers," the attacker becoming in turn a "trailer" to reload and pick off stragglers. This was a much less formalized and less rigid procedure than the German tactics, and did not depend upon the submarines transmitting information to the force commander and his remote control. In fact, the only function of our submarine headquarters was to keep the pack informed, by one-way transmissions, of intelligence pertinent to its position and operations.

To train in these procedures, each of the three boats comprising a wolf pack would be assigned a corner of the game board. Each C.O., with his torpedo fire control party and communications officer, would take station behind a screen and simulate maneuvering his ship solely on the basis of signals sent between boats. Meanwhile, from the fourth corner of the board, the target convoy was maneuvered by the Convoy College "faculty." At appropriate times, after contact had been established, brief looks at the convoy were permitted, as would be the case in action.

After a practicable doctrine had been worked out by the "College," Commander-in-Chief Pacific permitted realistic at-sea exercises in which subs formed into attack groups could practice locating and attacking U.S. convoys that were approaching the Hawaiian Islands from our West Coast. This concentrated period, usually involving a succession of attacks for one night and the following day, was an excellent test for both men and material.

The first U.S. wolf pack to sail left Midway on October 1, 1943. It went to the East China Sea and was formed with *Cero*, *Shad*, and *Grayback* under command of the resourceful Swede Momsen, ComSubRon Two, embarked in *Cero*. The results reported by the boats on their return indicated the pack had accounted for five ships (38,000 tons) sunk, and eight ships (63,000 tons) damaged. However, postwar analysis confirmed only three ships (23,000 tons) sunk, hardly a testimonial to wolf pack efficiency.

The second group to sail left Midway on November 3 and was composed of *Harder*, *Snook*, and *Pargo*, commanded respectively by veteran fighting skippers Dealey, Triebel, and Eddy. Freddy Warder of *Seawolf* fame, at this time a division commander, was embarked as Officer in Tactical Command (OTC) in *Pargo*. Their assigned area was the Marianas, where it was expected that our invasion of Tarawa would result in considerable enemy traffic. Between them the boats sank seven ships totaling 31,500 tons, but their operations were hampered by poor communications, and none of the skippers was enthusiastic about wolf-packing. In addition, Freddy Warder saw that a separate commander embarked in one of the boats was superfluous, even a handicap, under our concept. True to his forthright character, he recommended that future groups be left to the command of the senior skipper.

The third wolf pack to be sent out would test Freddy Warder's idea. Charles F. (Brindy) Brindupke, skipper of *Tullibee*, would be OTC of our group, which included *Haddock*, captained by John P. (Beetle) Roach, and *Halibut* under my command.

Brindy, from San Francisco, and Beetle, from Paris, Texas, were 1932 Academy classmates, but Brindy had graduated fifty numbers higher than Beetle. In addition, he had already taken *Tullibee* on war patrol. For Beetle, who had just relieved Roy Davenport, this would be his first patrol in command. Both my packmates were very likeable, outgoing, fun-loving characters with a great circle of friendships in the submarine force. Beetle never left anyone in doubt that he was from Texas, but he was always a southern gentleman. He once apologized to my wife for having called her a Yankee.

We three skippers were warm personal friends. We had trained together in Convoy College as well as under way in a two-day convoy attack exercise. We anticipated no difficulty with the command arrangement. We were eager to make it work and to bring back a bag heavier than those of our predecessors.

Just at this time my Naval Academy roommate, James Bizzell Grady, of Clinton, North Carolina, arrived in the Pacific from command of the training submarine *R-6* in the Atlantic. Jim had already experienced air attack; an Army Air Force plane had bombed his ship when it was proceeding on the surface in Block Island Sound. Nevertheless, he would have to make a PCO patrol, just as I had.

Jim, called "Iron Man" at the Academy, was immensely strong, and had been a member of Navy's wrestling team. He had fought a successful delaying action with the fair sex for ten years, but when he was hospitalized in New London in 1943 he quickly capitulated to his pretty navy nurse, Lieut. (jg) Betty Plum of Moorestown, New Jersey. Now, a few months after their wedding, he was in Pearl Harbor awaiting assignment.

I was delighted when Jim said he'd like to go out with me in *Halibut*. Ten years after leaving Bancroft Hall, we were roommates once more, sharing the tiny skipper's cabin of a submarine where Jim took the spare upper bunk.

Jim's arrival was most timely, for our officer team was changing considerably. Jack Hinchey was due for a rest and assignment to a new-construction boat. Rather than give him up permanently, I agreed to send him on leave for thirty days, after which he would have temporary duty in a relief crew awaiting *Halibut*'s return. Mike Such had to leave submarine duty. As replacements, I received Lieut. (jg) Joseph G. Galligan and Ensign James R. Conant, both freshly arrived from sub school. Both young men were from Massachusetts, Jim from Cambridge where his famous father, James Bryant Conant, was president of Harvard University and head of the National Defense Research

Committee which guided the nation's scientific and technical programs. Joe was from nearby Canton. He described their introduction to submarine duty as follows:

"Shortly after our arrival in Midway we were summoned to visit the Division Commander, Captain Karl G. Hensel. We wandered past the gooney birds to Captain Hensel's office and reported in. I was senior, so I nudged Jim ahead. The captain asked Jim where he had gone to school. Jim replied, 'University of Michigan.'

"The next question was, 'What did you major in?' Answer, philosophy.

"The captain's eyebrows arched. I could see that was not considered a good answer. When it was my turn I had the same questions. My answers, 'Holy Cross' and 'Economics,' did not impress him.

"He said, 'I don't know what's happening back there. Last week they sent me a gravedigger.' But he added, 'Good luck, anyway.' "

Nevertheless, it was the contribution of bright, eager, young reserve officers like these, and of hundreds of even younger enlisted reservists that made possible the growing effectiveness of our submarine force.

Jim Conant was a highly intelligent man. He had attended Philips Andover Academy, then went on to the University of Michigan, where he graduated at the age of nineteen. Knowing that it would not be long before I would have to give up Jack Barrett, I assigned Jim to be his assistant and understudy on the TDC, that position so important to our success.

Jim was a gangling six-footer, who never gained weight even though he was a prodigious eater. Whether seated or afoot, he had an atrocious posture. He seemed to be all elbows and knees, about to fly apart at any moment. If I was in the cramped space of the bridge when Jim had the deck, I took care to avoid being bumped off the upper level as he shuffled restlessly about. And when he yelled, "Clear the bridge! Dive! Dive!" it was every man for himself. Whoever was ahead of him as his rawboned frame came hurtling down the hatch quickly learned to get out of the way.

It was clear that sports had not been much of a factor in Jim's young life. There was no smooth coordination of muscle to match the elegance of his mind. Still, by the time we reached our patrol area, I knew I had another alert, competent, trustworthy officer of the deck.

Our other Bay State native, Joe Galligan, came to us with much more seagoing experience than the average young submarine reservist.

He had served the first two years of the war in the old destroyer *Tattnall*, operating on convoy duty out of Panama. There he had become friendly with submarine skippers Karl Wheland and W. B. (Si) Perkins, and had gone out in their boats. For my money, anyone who was inspired to go to sub school by riding S-boats was the kind of man we wanted.

Joe was a good-looking young bachelor. He was of medium build, well coordinated in mind and body. He was articulate but not loquacious. His thought processes and actions were deliberate and precise, qualities which helped bring him success in his postwar law career. Perhaps it was his Irish heritage that gave him the tolerant understanding of Democratic politics, Boston-style, that enlivened wardroom bull sessions when they turned to the subject of President Roosevelt's unprecedented quest for a fourth term.

Creating and keeping an efficient ship was not a simple matter. Compared to our prewar submarine complements, the youth and limited experience of officers and men alike were amazing. This was partly due to losses, but mainly due to the great expansion of the force. In the twenty months of war to this time we had lost only sixteen boats. The number would grow rapidly as more boats were deployed, and as Japan's shrinking defense perimeter required our subs to penetrate more dangerous waters. In the same twenty-month period, seventy-six new boats were placed in commission.

On each patrol we sailed with 25 percent of our crew made up of new men. Many were youngsters who had never before gone to sea in any kind of ship, let alone a submarine. They were all volunteers, carefully screened mentally, physically, psychologically; but the knack of living and working together in a crowded submarine, and learning the seaman's need for alertness, reliability, and forehandedness take months of training under older hands.

War conditions were not conducive to thorough training; shortcuts and simulations were essential to provide on time the numbers of officers and men needed. During our refit and training periods in port we made maximum use of the attack teacher and other training aids, and each refit was followed by a few days concentrated underway training. Unlike surface ships, which almost always operated in company, once deployed we were alone. Even in a wolf pack we rarely saw the other subs. The very fact that under way we were constantly "rigged for dive," with torpedo tubes loaded, and had to spend long days submerged, silently on the prowl, denied many opportunities for comprehensive training.

The transfers of personnel required after each patrol were a painful loss of valued shipmates as well as a blow to the greater effectiveness we could have achieved with more stability. In my latest patrol report I had protested:

> When several short patrols occur in succession, rate of personnel turnover becomes excessive as long as one-fourth of the crew is transferred after each patrol. If this vessel is required to transfer the usual sixteen men during this refit, a seventy-five percent turnover in the last 120 days will result. While the need for personnel for new construction is appreciated, it is felt that the number of men transferred after each patrol should be partially dependent upon the length of patrol. It is not considered possible to take an inexperienced man (generally with little experience in *any* type of ship) and, within 30 days of war operations, train him to be an efficient submarine man capable of pulling his own weight in the organization, and, in fact, of training a new group of personnel.

These factors were given some weight in later patrols but, much as a C.O. liked to keep his team intact, the broader view and larger responsibilities of the force commander dictated otherwise. After all, like aircraft, submarines were an expendable weapon; the critical factor was the tradeoff in losses versus enemy ships sunk. (We had not yet learned to speak in terms of "sub-optimization," "cost effectiveness," and "system responsiveness," to which I would be exposed many years later in the MacNamara regime of sophisticated, Harvard Business School logic.) Simply stated, if crews were unchanged between patrols, the loss of any one sub would result in more than the loss of a single, skilled team; it would mean the loss of experienced seamen who could have provided the vital nucleus for several new-construction submarines.

On the material side, I was particularly enthusiastic over our prospects for this patrol. Previously our radar scope could present targets only on a single line of bearing; we had to transpose its data into a mental image as the sweeping radar antenna disclosed other targets. Now the installation of a Plan Position Indicator (PPI) would give us a continuous view, centered on our own ship, of all contacts in their positions relative to us. Our convoy training exercise had shown what great help it was in keeping track of a melee of ships.

Our group departed from Pearl Harbor on December 14, and headed for Midway to top off our diesel fuel to the maximum for the unknown number of days ahead. The three ships were essentially identical, but there was one difference which would critically affect the patrol before us. The great distances our boats had to cover, and the frequent need for high-speed running on the surface had shown the need for more diesel oil than the normal fuel tanks could carry. A relatively simple modification to No. 4 main ballast tank made it possible to use it as a fuel tank, thereby increasing fuel capacity by some 24,000 gallons. *Tullibee* and *Haddock* had this modification; *Halibut* did not. This change to No. 4 had no effect on the submarine's submerged performance; in any case, all ballast tanks had to be full when submerged. As diesel oil was consumed, seawater admitted to the bottom of the tanks took its place. This created the apparent anomaly of a ship becoming heavier as it burned up its fuel supply, since the fuel was lighter than the replacement water. On the surface the ship rode a bit lower in the water, since it was without the buoyancy of an empty main ballast tank. When all the diesel in No. 4 MBT was consumed, the tank would be reconverted to a normal main ballast tank, and the boat would proceed using the fuel in its regular fuel tanks.

As we sailed to the northwest, we conducted brief training dives and practiced group tactics, but the Pacific did not live up to its name. We lost the sun behind a low overcast; the wind turned chill; the sea was a dirty green flecked with mounting whitecaps. Driven by steadily increasing northwest winds, the swells increased in height and in the force with which they slammed against our bow. Occasionally the entire forepart of the ship would be buried underwater, even to the rim of the hatch which led to the conning tower from the bridge. Several times green water rushed down the hatch before the quartermaster could slam it shut. With most of our vital fire control and radar instrumentation located in the conning tower, the torrents of salt water could cause serious problems. And in the uneven pitching, tossing, rolling motion of our ship, many of our new men, with little or no seagoing experience, were miserable. They did their best to keep food down while they stood their watches, then collapsed into their bunks, wet clothes and all. The bunk room smelled of salt water, of sweat and vomit, of unwashed bodies. Fortunately we were far from the enemy; he could not take advantage of our temporary inefficiency.

Entering Midway lagoon was always a challenge to captains. The channel that ran north from the sea buoy was deep enough and straight, but uncomfortably narrow. A prevailing swell from the south made a ship entering at slow speed yaw widely, requiring large amounts of rudder to hold her in the channel. To keep better steering control, most of us preferred entering at a higher speed; about twelve knots would overcome the alarming tendency of overtaking swells to throw a submarine's stern about. Once inside the coral atoll, there was room to maneuver, even though this time the normally smooth, green lagoon was leaden gray, torn by whitecaps.

We remained overnight to give all hands a few hours sleep in a motionless bunk. Next morning we headed back out the channel and found the seas still rough. Turning to the west, we proceeded in a loose column formation with fifteen miles between ships. At midnight we advanced the clocks twenty-four hours, our date becoming December 21, because of crossing the international date line. But skipping the twentieth on our calendar did not save us a stormy day's passage. The wind and seas were now increasing, and to avoid punishing our ships and ourselves we had to progressively reduce our speed from fourteen to twelve to nine knots. In the mounting head seas the ships pitched heavily, causing our screws to break water and race. Throughout this first day of winter we made good a speed of only five knots. In the strong gale, winds reached a speed of forty-five knots, driving before them waves that averaged twenty feet from trough to crest, and occasionally reached fifty feet. The unobstructed sweep of thousands of miles of ocean allowed swells of enormous reach and momentum to build up.

Secured with canvas safety belts to prevent being washed overboard, our lookouts kept their cold, wet watch. Binoculars were discarded, useless in the flying spray. The officer-of-the-deck, wedged against the coaming in the forward corner, peered over the wind screen looking upward at what seemed a moving, gray hill, a mountain of dark marble veined with spume, that would surely crash down and destroy the submarine.

Making steerageway into each succeeding wall of water, *Halibut* shuddered and trembled, a deep rumble coming from the empty main ballast tanks as waves beat on them and rushed past. We could have submerged to escape the violence of the storm; 150 feet below the surface all would be serene; only a gentle roll would hint of the turmoil above. But such a gale could persist for days. In a few hours we would have to surface, our battery depleted, and be in an even more precarious situation.

As it is, no ship is better able to ride out a massive storm than is a submarine on the surface. Her circular hull, constructed to withstand the crushing pressure of the sea when submerged, is the stoutest, most rigid of any ship's. We were essentially a steel bubble, with only one small opening left for the furiously probing fingers of the sea— the conning tower hatch. Even the main engine air induction valve for the diesels was closed. It was located just below the cigarette deck aft of the bridge, and to leave it open was too risky. A massive wave overriding us could flood the engine air induction trunk and damage the engines. At the slow speed we could make, the diesels could draw all the air they needed through the interior of the boat from the conning tower hatch. Even that, at a shout from the O.O.D. as the bow plunged especially deep into a wave, would be slammed shut by the quartermaster standing below it with lanyard in hand. The temporary vacuum this drew on the boat's atmosphere, while jolting our ears, reduced the stench that permeated our sodden, tortured ship.

As the mighty regiments of the sea marched relentlessly against us, seemingly to overwhelm and push us down, *Halibut* dipped her bow, was lifted up the oncoming slope of water like a fisherman's bob, then slid into the valley beyond. The two extremes of the ship, the torpedo rooms, felt the most violent motions, the greatest pitching and heaving. Thirty-two weary men shared their berthing spaces with fourteen silent torpedoes strapped firmly to their racks. Ten other fish, fully ready, slept snugly in their own long, dark berths.

With ten years of sea duty under our belts, Jim and I had experienced such storms before. We knew that no timetable was important now, and that our total effort must go to avoiding damage to *Halibut* and injury to our men so that we might fight another day.

Mack and a few of our senior enlisted men who had also been through this before went stoically about their duties. In the after engine room throttleman Schwieso shouted to his oiler, Paul Eurich, "I'll take a good, clean depth-charging anytime instead of this."

Chief Roberson juggled the watch bill, improvising watch sections as best he could with those least affected by our violent motion. We could not have as lookout a man who could barely climb the ladder, and who was too weak and wretched to be efficient. Robbie remembered very well the tragedy of a year before. On her first war patrol, off Attu Island in the Aleutians, *Halibut* had lost one of her lookouts overboard. We wanted no repeat.

In control room and conning tower, foul-smelling buckets were wedged in place. They held the puke of watchstanders unsettled by the wild motion of inclinometer bubble or gyro compass heading. Ready to fill in anywhere was motor machinist's mate Rantz. In port, the big, likeable bachelor led timid shipmates on boisterous forays to sailors' haunts, always a step ahead of the shore patrol. At sea, he was at his best when the going was roughest. He responded with broad smile and profane good humor to whatever assignment the chief of the boat gave him. With so many men seasick, he would joke, he could at last get enough to eat.

No one's condition was being made fun of; everyone was cold and miserable. Men lay in their bunks, some cursing the day they'd chosen navy instead of army. What's wrong with lying in the mud, sinking one's fingers into Mother Earth? When summoned to watch in the dark, it's a nauseous, retching job getting down on all fours to find shoes kicked under bunks or into corners on the cold, clammy deck.

Nightfall brought no relief. With vision now totally obscured by the black night and the cold, cutting spray driven by over forty knots of wind, we brought our lookouts down from their exposed positions on the periscope shears to the relative safety and shelter of the bridge deck.

Our surface search radar was manned, but the mountainous waves and the flying spray that drenched our antenna filled the scope with a confusion of sea-return echoes. We could have passed within 500 yards of a target and been none the wiser.

We were unable to see oncoming waves. It was impossible to tell when a particularly huge one would engulf *Halibut*, sending water up around the conning tower fairwater and down the hatch. In the utter blackness, hearing seemed to become more acute. The noises of the angry sea seemed more harsh. The whine of the gale, the sound of waves gnashing and snarling, the slam of our bow into a wall of water, the rumble and roar of water through our superstructure were the dominant memory of each watch.

Our night watch procedure, from 2000 to 0800 the following morning, called for officers-of-the-deck to stand two-hour watches. Lookouts were relieved more frequently. All would come off watch bruised and battered, sometimes cut from being thrown against edges of metal. Weary, soaked to the skin, eyes reddened by salt spray and strain, they came below to hot coffee and a cigarette before crawling, still shivering, into their bunks for what rest the plunging, rolling ship might permit.

Next day was our fourth in the winter gale, which had originated in the far, northwest Pacific and was moving slowly eastward. Below decks our normally tidy ship was a shambles. Everything movable was lashed down or wedged in place. Our cooks kept hot soup and coffee available around the clock and improvised meals for those who could eat more. The ceaseless motion, the bumping of heads and shins, the tiring muscular effort of holding on, the inability to eat or sleep in comfort, made tempers short, stilled the normal, good-humored, profane chatter. The crash of breaking crockery, the clatter of a loose bucket, of tools adrift, the creak and groan of our laboring ship, the rage of unmuffled curses, took its place.

As the wind and seas shifted gradually to the north they diminished, allowing us to add a few turns to our r.p.m. as we bore to the southwest. By now, however, our pack was scattered, and some two hundred miles behind its scheduled position.

Christmas Day dawned cold and windy. The sky was a dreary gray overcast, but now cloud cover was much higher. The motion of the sea seemed gentle in comparison to the torment of the past few days. Haggard men went about the tasks of cleaning up the ship, drying her out, restowing gear, testing equipment. Our cooks, Tommy Thompson and his helpers Norman Thomas and Hugh McCracken, had been up before dawn preparing a traditional Christmas dinner, from roast turkey to mince pie and all that came between. We were now within range of Japanese planes from Marcus Island, but I decided to stay on the surface, confident in our watch topside, secure in the Power that stilled waters, and not willing to lose more time in getting to our patrol area.

Dinner was at 1400 that afternoon, and as I pronounced grace over the intercom, each man's thoughts and prayers were his own, of Christmases gone by or of the Christmas Day that had not yet dawned for loved ones back home. Married or single, we all longed for Christmas at home. Three of us in the wardroom, six others in the crew's quarters had children. The thought of young wives coping with Christmas alone was painful. Men spoke softly to their neighbors, but in our hard, masculine world at war, sentiment was not allowed to show.

Topside, O.O.D. Si Lake and his three lookouts searched the sea and sky as intensely as if their lives depended on it—as, in fact, they did.

Both crew's messroom and the wardroom were festooned with tinsel and familiar Christmas ornaments which commissary officer Jim Conant had obtained in Pearl. The wardroom table was covered with a snowy white table cloth, and two red candles dripped their wax as *Halibut* rolled. Strauther Wallace balanced carefully as he came forward from the galley bearing the huge platter on which was the turkey for the wardroom. His shining face had a great grin as he placed the platter carefully before me.

As I reached for the improvised carving set of galley knife and fork, Jack Barrett, our irrepressible Irish bachelor, reached under the table, then raised a bottle high. "Captain, I knew we'd be out for Christmas, so I smuggled aboard a bottle of sparkling burgundy before we left Pearl."

So blatant a violation of Navy Regulations needed punishment, which I took under advisement while we disposed of the contraband in the most sensible way. We drank a toast "to loved ones now far distant." Then I restricted Jack to the ship for the next thirty days.

This was the second Christmas in a row for *Halibut* at sea. A year ago Mack, Jack, and Si Lake were in this same wardroom, patrolling submerged off Hokkaido. Mack remembered the miserable conditions: poor visibility, snow, sleet, and bitter cold. They had made no contacts. The winter clothing provided for submarines sent to high latitudes was inadequate. Lookouts and watch officers suffered from cold hands and feet, and put on so much clothing it was bulky and cumbersome, endangering everyone if they had to clear the bridge in a hurry. At least this time we were heading south.

That reminded Jack, not at all distressed by his house arrest, that only a year ago he was "George," lowliest of all ship's officers, saddled with all the mundane housekeeping chores. Today he was fifth from the bottom.

When we rose from our tables in wardroom and crew's mess, stuffed in traditional manner, we gathered in succession in the control room where Chief of the Boat Roberson was also Santa Claus. Before we sailed from Pearl, boxes of gaily wrapped small gifts, one for each officer and man, had been put aboard. Ladies residing in Honolulu had thoughtfully prepared them for our lonely Christmas far at sea. When I opened my package I found the model of a Hawaiian outrigger canoe.

Twenty-four hours later, we were about 100 miles southeast of Marcus Island when our aircraft warning radar indicated a plane at eight miles and closing. Shouting, "Clear the bridge! Dive! Dive!" O.O.D. Ray Stewart jumped down the hatch on the shoulders of after-lookout Donald Noonan. Even as the three lookouts were landing on the control room deck with great thumps, I arrived in response to the two blasts of the diving klaxon. As seawater rushed into our ballast tanks, canceling the positive buoyancy which had held us to the surface, and while our radio antenna was still above water, we transmitted in our wolf pack code, "Diving for plane," to warn *Tullibee* and *Haddock*. Hardly had we leveled off at 150-foot depth when three bombs exploded, not close enough to cause damage but loud enough to tell all hands that once again we were in enemy territory. Our six weeks' respite from attack was over.

What with the heavy gale which had slowed all of us, and the need for each boat to dive occasionally to avoid aircraft patrols, it was December 29 before we made rendezvous in our assigned area and took up the search plan ordered by Brindy as O.T.C. Although we were now down in latitude 20° north, far south of Midway and west of Guam, wintry storms still plagued us. Heavy seas beat on us as we tried to maintain positions fifteen miles apart on our scouting line. At that spacing there was small chance that a surface ship could pass between us undetected by day or night. As we advanced we were sweeping a lane at least forty-five miles wide.

Nevertheless, the water coming over the bow, the flying spray, the motion of the ship affecting arcs of vision made it very difficult to keep an effective watch. I was also uneasy that our topside watch, bundled in foul weather gear in a vain effort to keep dry and warm, would lose vital seconds in getting down the hatch should we have to dive suddenly. Never could we relax our guard against the unpredictability of the sea. On December 30, when we closed to speak to *Tullibee*, we were saddened to learn that a huge wave had crushed one of her lookouts against his guard rail with such force that his binoculars were jammed into his diaphragm. Carried below in great pain, torpedoman Lawrence Kidwell died that night of internal injuries and was given a sailor's burial.

11

A Shortage of Fuel

Every time we got under way for our patrol area, our sailors hungered to learn of our assigned area, for news of what we expected to find there, and how we'd go about our job. I knew from my brief nighttime chats with crewmen topside that the more the officers and crew could communicate, the better for all hands. I tried to keep them informed of the situation when we were attacking or being attacked, although this was not always feasible.

To help satisfy the appetite for news and to relieve the pressures of shipboard life, Jack Barrett proposed that we publish a ship's paper. I thought it was a splendid idea and that we could make it not only a source of news but of humor, of praise, or of admonition if needed. Jack had been business manager of the *Lucky Bag*, the yearbook published by his 1943 Academy class. Now I appointed him editor-in-chief of the *Halibastard Herald*, accountable for all material published.

ComSubPac's nightly broadcasts often contained items we could pass to our men, but much of the paper's contents had to be developed on board. We quickly discovered much talent in our shipmates: a roving reporter, a cartoonist, even a "lonely hearts" columnist. Publication dates were flexible; we tried to hold to a weekly schedule. Production facilities were limited. Yeoman Glen Snell's typewriter was our press; he could produce only an original and two carbon copies at a time. We had no duplicating facilities. The flimsy, three- or four-page issues were eagerly awaited, read aloud at mess, or passed hand-to-hand to waiting shipmates.

In one of the earliest issues, Tommy Thompson, who had been a baker in the kitchen of a first-class hotel, poked fun at his editor this way:

In the good old days in the Argentine,
On a war patrol we drank kerosene.
No vitamin pills or chocolate malts,

We seasoned our food with epsom salts.
We had no class of forty-three,
There was no one aboard but the skipper and me.
He fired fore and I fired aft,
We raised plenty hell with surface craft.
We did a barrel roll for 65 feet,
And an outside loop to take her deep.
On a quick dive we had no trouble,
We didn't use your god-damn bubble.
On a short patrol, as I recall,
We left in the spring and returned in the fall.
Pretty rugged, I'll have you know it,
Even for a ship's cook poet.

My own effort to while away an afternoon of fruitless search produced the following:

NAI-O-BE FROM KOBE

I

In that far off island nation, lives a girl of reputation.
Famed for figure and for features, she is fairest of all creatures.
Queen of Geishas is her title, she is nothing if not vital.
It's terrific, cataclysmic, but in fact it's always rhythmic,
    When Nai-o-be shakes her obi down in Kobe.

II

You can buy her suki-yaki, with a quart or two of sake,
But, withal, she may desert you, with her Nippon-easy virtue;
She's as proud as Fujiyama of her cherry-blossom glamour.
It's an ocean of commotion, it's a typhoon in slow motion,
    When Nai-o-be shakes her obi down in Kobe.

III

Men have conquered nature's forces, tapping all her vast resources,
Save this child of humble peasants, laden down with pearls and presents.
Known to be a bit myopic, eye to eye they see one topic,
It's tremendous, and stupendous, just the thing to lease or lend us,
    When Nai-o-be shakes her obi down in Kobe.

IV

Princes of imperial blood have sought to snip this rarest bud,
Saying, this is not for masses, but reserved for upper classes.
And she asks her private Buddha, tell me if I really should-a.
Never did a torso, more so, grace a night club or stage door so,
    When Nai-o-be shakes her obi down in Kobe.

V

Soon her fame, that fragile chalice, sped her name unto the
    palace,
Summoned to the royal precincts (even kings may have those
    instincts)
By decree she now is rationed, point-for-point there's none so
    fashioned.
Now it's regal, double-eagle; it's so good it can't be legal,
    When Nai-o-be shakes her obi down in Kobe.

VI

Now there's culture, joy in Asia, even down to hot Malaysia.
Tariffs, duties, all abolished, customs now are far more polished;
Trade and commerce, how they've flourished, in that ancient art
    she nourished,
For the Spirit of Bushido has been matched with her libido,
    Since Nai-o-be shook her obi down in Kobe.[1]

The first contact in our area came on the last day of the year. In
the middle of the afternoon, as we cruised on the surface, we sighted
smoke. As we headed *Halibut* toward the telltale sign, we soon made
out masts and could tell that we had a sizable ship in our sights. When
we ran up our periscope, the lofty, magnified view disclosed twin
stacks and a large superstructure. We continued to close while we
tracked our quarry, and found that she was not zigzagging nor did she
have an escort. Then the declining sun, glinting off her white-painted
upper works, revealed why. On each of her two stacks was a large,
red cross. Comparison with our ever-ready ship identification manual

1. Forty-four years after these immortal verses were composed, I received a letter, dated
January 31, 1987, from G. Paul (Peppie) Cooke, Jr., of Kualapuu, Molokai, Hawaii, informing
me that, having been sent a copy of "Nai-o-be From Kobe" by his sister Phoebe Cooke
Fitzgerald in 1944, he had set it to music, and he and his wife Pat had recorded it. He had
subsequently performed the piece by request at numerous navy social occasions, he said,
and now, almost a half-century later, was applying for copyright in his name and mine!

showed that this was *Takasago Maru*, a properly marked hospital ship. We could only let her continue unmolested on her course to Japan.

Two days later, acting on Ultra intelligence he had received from headquarters, Brindy disposed our three ships six miles apart across the enemy's expected track, where we were to form a submerged line of ambush. Any ship which passed through our line would be 6,000 yards or less from at least one of us.

Twenty-five minutes after diving we sighted the target, a Japanese I-class submarine proceeding on the surface in the bright morning sunlight on a steady course at fifteen knots. Lying low in the water, moving fast, she was almost past us when we picked her up 7,000 yards away, and our effort to close to firing range using full submerged speed was futile. She was somewhat closer to *Tullibee*, who was still on the surface, and soon we heard and felt four explosions. These were the end-of-run explosions of the spread of four torpedoes which *Tullibee* had fired at a range of 3,000 yards. There could be no doubt as to the target's course and speed, but the long run of the torpedoes gave their intended victim time to evade. When she sighted the torpedo wakes speeding toward her, she turned away briefly, then sped on her way. We came away from this incident more than ever convinced that the safest place for a submarine was submerged.

After a week of fruitless patrolling, Brindy asked Beetle and me whether we'd be willing to leave our ships to join him in *Tullibee* to review our tactics and make further plans. I answered, "Yes," without hesitation. Although I knew of no case when this had been done with a submarine in wartime, I felt at ease leaving my ship in the wide-open reaches of our sea area in the war-savvy hands of my exec, with our embarked PCO Jim Grady backing him up. We arranged a rendezvous for subsequent meeting in case our ships were forced to dive and became separated.

Beetle was also eager to compare notes. As soon as it was dark on the night of January 3, our three ships lay-to a couple of hundred yards apart. Soon *Tullibee*'s air-inflated rubber dinghy, propelled by two strong-armed paddlers, came alongside to get me, then paused alongside *Haddock* to pick up Beetle.

The black sea was smooth, disturbed only by the swish of two paddles as *Tullibee*'s sailors stroked their way back to the dark shape of their ship. They were clearly enjoying this break in the routine monotony of submarine life. There was no moon, but on this clear night at latitude 19° north, the image of countless stars was reflected from the black surface. Beetle and I spoke quietly, exchanging news of how our ships had fared in the rough passage from Midway.

When we were about fifteen feet from *Tullibee* I grabbed the line thrown to us and we were hauled alongside to starboard just forward of the conning tower. Brindy's exec, Lieut. Comdr. Greer Duncan, greeted us as we scrambled awkwardly on board and led us to the bridge and Brindy's warm welcome.

The three blacked-out subs lay-to a few hundred yards apart. They kept a careful visual and passive sonar watch. We wanted only one radar in operation; *Tullibee*'s occasional all-around sweeps were enough. On board our ghostly ships almost 250 men waited for whatever revised plan our midocean council of war could produce.

Three skippers were soon seated around *Tullibee*'s wardroom table enjoying the special meal laid on for us. Shortly afterward, the table was covered with charts and publications as we reviewed our actions of the past few days and made plans for the future. It was apparent to us that the rationale behind deploying our wolf pack to this particular area, this enormous stretch of sea, was the scheme to exploit the excellent intelligence which our codebreakers were supplying. The near-perfect trap laid for the I-boat was a fresh example. There was little shipping along this route, but there was frequent movement of warships back and forth between Japan and her major stronghold of Truk. We were free to roam hundreds of miles in any direction, covering routes to the Marianas and the Caroline Islands. It seemed likely that we could waylay some major ships and thus assist the invasion of the Marshall Islands that was coming up. My chief concern was that this type operation required much high-speed surface running to get into successive positions of probable contact. Aside from being slightly wearing on our nerves, this procedure was extravagant of fuel.

Reassured that there was no major flaw in our tactics and that we were applying Convoy College lessons properly, we laid out our search plans for the next few days to cover what we judged would be the most fruitful routes. Signalling *Halibut* and *Haddock* by blinker tube to close in, about midnight Beetle and I returned to our own ships via the same water taxi that had brought us. Strong hands grasped me and hauled me to *Halibut*'s deck from the thin, rubberized fabric that had separated four of us from the miles of black water under us.

Over the next few days our pack continued to search according to our plan. Cruising on the surface out of sight of each other we scanned sea and sky unceasingly. With the experience of the Japanese I-boat fresh in mind, lookouts knew how important it was to watch for a periscope. Unlike our steam-turbine fish, the excellent Japanese torpedoes, fueled by oxygen, left little or no wake. Aircraft were also a threat here; *Tullibee* had been bombed by a float plane. However, in the generally clear skies they did not greatly concern us. And below decks, in our tiny, cluttered radio room, an equally alert watch was kept, straining for any sudden signal from our packmates.

When we did sight the enemy, we had only fleeting glimpses of high-speed ships hurrying southward toward the Carolines or northward to Japan. On one occasion *Halibut* got within 10,000 yards of a heavy cruiser, either *Atago* or *Takao*, escorted by two destroyers, but no one of us could close for attack. On January 11 it seemed our frustrations would finally cease. An hour before sunset, patrolling on the surface and keeping a high periscope watch, *Halibut* sighted the tops of a warship while it was hull down, seventeen miles away. Flashing a contact report to our pack by radio, we commenced tracking, using radar intermittently for ranges and our periscope for visual bearings. Such good data soon gave us the target's base course and speed, and we put ourselves dead ahead on the same course. As the range slowly closed, the heavy, pagodalike structure revealed we were tracking *Yamato*, one of Japan's two super-battleships. She and her sister ship, *Musashi*, were 70,000-ton Goliaths, built in utmost secrecy. They carried a main battery of nine 18.1″ guns, the world's heaviest naval ordnance. The largest caliber mounted in our navy was 16″.

Here was an almost ideal situation: the pride of the Imperial Japanese Navy advancing, seemingly unaware that three hungry wolves lay in wait ready to expend every one of their sixty-eight remaining torpedoes. If any one of us could hit her, and damage her enough to slow her down, we were strong enough to penetrate any screen she might have and would keep slinging torpedoes into her until she sank.

Exhilarated by these thoughts, we worked carefully in the fast-fading twilight, allowing the range to close gradually. As soon as it was dark we would press in with our attack. Since she had made first contact, doctrine called for *Halibut* to make first attack, then become "trailer" while the other boats went in. However, we were farthest off her track, and if she continued zigzagging on base course 270° she would pass between *Haddock* and *Tullibee*. With a target of such importance, we would not stand on formality; whoever could get in to attack at any time would do so.

Suddenly, just after nightfall, our periodic radar sweep showed the range opening drastically. Turning 180° and heading right for *Yamato* at full speed, we watched helplessly as her radar pip weakened and faded from the screen. Calling *Tullibee* and *Haddock* by radio we learned that neither had made contact. It was clear that our opposing skipper was clever and capable. He could not have detected our small ships by sight or radar at the extreme range at which we held our massive target. The intermittent probing of three high-power radar beams had alerted him. With nightfall imminent, he had steamed on normally so as to mislead us, then as darkness came he made a radical turn and quickly ran away from us. Here was a bitter lesson in war's unending contest of technology, of measure against countermeasure. In this case, it was a radar detector giving warning of our presence. Not before the end of June, 1944, was radar installed in all of Japan's major warships, but a ship as important as *Yamato* no doubt had it sooner.

As we continued patrolling, *Halibut*'s fuel capacity became more and more a matter of concern. Making rendezvous with *Tullibee* in the vicinity of the Caroline Islands, once more Beetle and I went aboard her to confer with Brindy. At this time *Halibut* had 41,000 gallons of diesel remaining, while *Tullibee* and *Haddock*, due to the extra amount they had carried in their ballast tanks, each had some 60,000. The day was near when *Halibut* would have to drop out of the wolf pack and return to base. To preclude this, each of the other C.O.s agreed to transfer 7,000 gallons of fuel to me, and to do it that night since conditions were favorable.

As soon as I had returned, *Halibut* proceeded with *Tullibee* to the lee of Eauripik Island some twenty miles away, while *Haddock* kept a careful radar and visual search nearby. So near the equator, we could no longer sight the reassuring presence of Polaris, but new, unfamiliar constellations mirrored themselves in the smooth, dark sea. From ashore came no sight or sound, only the sweet, sticky smell of the tropic night.

As *Tullibee* lay-to, *Halibut* eased cautiously close aboard to starboard, working party on deck ready to receive the hose through which would be pumped the diesel oil. But how deceptive was the seemingly flat surface! To our bodies, attuned to the violent motion of recent days, it seemed almost motionless, but as our ships lay side by side, using rudder and screws sparingly to keep our vulnerable sterns apart, Brindy and I peered anxiously overside only a few feet apart on our respective bridges. Here in waters miles deep, the long, slow swell of the sea, remnant of the storms we had weathered, gave our passive ships an irregular, unpredictable motion, bumping them together as they rolled or heaved unevenly. Stout as is the pressure hull of a submarine, its superstructure is light and tender. The thin plating of the main ballast tanks, their associated piping, and the bow and stern planes could be easily damaged. Quickly pulling clear of each other, we shouted new instructions and tried another tack, on a new heading. But once again the ceaseless motion threatened too much damage. As dawn approached, we headed for the freedom of the open sea.

Perhaps we had been detected during our nighttime maneuvers for in a few hours we sighted the tops of a destroyer heading our way, his sonar pinging as he approached. We flashed a contact report, then dived and closed for attack. We got to a range of 1,500 yards. Thirty-seven minutes after we had sighted our target we fired a spread of four torpedoes. In the fast developing situation we had to fire with large gyro angles; before settling on their final course the fish had to turn about 60°. The first three torpedoes exploded prematurely only a few seconds after firing. Thus alerted, the destroyer was able to dodge the fourth. The shallow, six-foot depth setting we used to avoid underrunning the destroyer, and their large turn, apparently caused the fish to broach and detonate prematurely.

Immediately after the first explosion the *Asashio*-class destroyer evaded with a drastic turn, dropped depth charges, possibly to detonate any other torpedoes, then turned back to find us. By now we were heading for the deep. Finding an excellent density layer somewhat below our test depth, we avoided the twenty-two additional depth charges he dropped. However, to get back to periscope depth we had to vent the pressure off negative tank. It had been blown empty as we neared our maximum depth, and now contained air under high pressure, about 135 p.s.i. The release of the high-pressure air into the ship made the hull a resonant instrument audible at great distance. Sure enough, each of three attempts to vent negative brought the destroyer back on us. The last time, at dusk, perhaps his ardor had cooled; we were able to get back to periscope depth.

Now we had another problem, a routine submarine problem but one which required caution nevertheless. During any prolonged dive there would be a buildup of air pressure in the boat due to leaks from the air banks, from any pneumatic mechanism, from the venting of torpedo tubes after firing, from the venting of negative tank, and from just the rise of temperature in the boat. This time the manometer in the control room indicated 4 ½" pressure above atmospheric. Normally, at the end of a long submergence we would run our air compressors and draw down the excess by charging the air banks. This had not been possible with the destroyer so close, and it would risk serious injury to personnel to open the conning tower hatch with so large a volume of high pressure to escape. The sudden release of all that air could blow a man through an open hatch, breaking limbs or cracking a skull.

With an enemy nearby we could not afford to linger with deck awash while we slowly bled down the excess pressure through a slightly cracked hatch. The alternative was to close the lower conning tower hatch, come quickly to the surface, throw open the upper hatch, and as that much lesser volume of high pressure air escaped, quartermaster Bill Henderson and I sprang to the bridge. When a careful look all around showed all clear, our turbo-blowers in the pump room were started to suck air from the boat and blow it into the main ballast tanks. When our internal air pressure was reduced to about normal, the lower hatch was opened. It took a seemingly endless two minutes for this operation as Henderson and I, isolated on the bridge, kept a careful lookout, communicating below through the intercom.

On January 17 I reported to the OTC that *Halibut* had fuel enough for only three more days if we operated with the wolf pack. We would then have to head for Midway, our nearest resupply point. On the other hand, by operating independently in a submerged patrol, we could stretch our time on station to seven days. Brindy released me reluctantly, and *Halibut* headed for the Marianas to see what she could find off Guam or Saipan.

For two days and a night we patrolled off Port Apra. In December of 1941, Guam had been the first U.S. possession occupied by the Japanese, and I expected to find them making good use of the large island and its chief harbor. However, a look inside showed only a large freighter hard aground, and no activity.

About 100 miles north of Guam was the island of Saipan, which

Japan had controlled since 1920. After an overnight run we dived off Tanapag Harbor and closed to investigate. At once we encountered heavy air and surface patrols. The planes varied from a large, four-engine flying boat to single engine, low-wing planes that looked like the famous Zebra. The surface ships were two destroyers and three smaller patrol boats. By midafternoon we learned the reason for all the activity. We sighted the smoke of two freighters standing toward Tanapag. They had two patrol boat escorts.

We maneuvered carefully to intercept them before they reached the harbor, but could get no closer than 5,000 yards. The approach on this group was unfortunate, for when we sighted a high-speed warship we were in a poor position to attack her. As we closed the range, I identified the contact as a *Katori*-class cruiser accompanied by a destroyer. They were apparently heading for Japan, zigzagging on base course 315° at seventeen knots. Once again we were not quite on the right spot, and the targets sped by 4,500 yards away.

We had an hour to go before dark. Jim Conant encoded a brief contact report which we would transmit to ComSubPac when we surfaced, giving the cruiser's position, course, and speed.

On January 23 our fuel situation was such that this would have to be our final day of patrol. We would have just enough diesel to get back to Midway, 2,200 miles away.

We headed once more for Tanapag Harbor and found even heavier ASW coverage. Two destroyers and four smaller patrol boats were patrolling Garapan Anchorage just outside Tanapag Harbor. At 1030 we were detected in the clear, unruffled tropic water, and received five aerial bombs. They were not close enough to hurt us, but they did bring a destroyer quickly our way. We went to 300 feet, but when no further countermeasures developed for a half-hour we came back to periscope depth. I was determined to find out why there was such intense antisubmarine effort.

At 1135 we discovered why. Anchored in Garapan Anchorage was a light aircraft carrier. Her profile was similar to that of the *Otaka*-class shown in our recognition manual. She had several planes on deck, and I could see no sign of damage to the tantalizing target.

By carefully plotting the carrier's position, we saw that a long-range torpedo attack on the motionless target would be possible if we could circumvent the screen of ships and planes. The sea was almost a flat calm, very clear, and dangerous coral reefs extended from the shore.

Overhead were air patrols; on the surface were antisubmarine patrols; below were jagged reefs.

Closing in from the sector with deepest water, we time our approach so as to pass astern of the ASW ships when they reversed course at the inshore end of their sweeps. During two hours of excruciatingly slow progress the boat becomes swelteringly hot; we had shut down our noisy air-conditioning and ventilation systems.

Suddenly, two near-miss aircraft bombs startle us. They seem smaller than depth charge explosions and have a different sound, not the *brr-roomp* we are all too familiar with, but a shorter, sharper *blang, blang*. The boat shakes, but I get no report of damage.

A quick look at the nearest destroyer shows him belching black smoke and swinging hard in our direction. I note that the periscope optics are dirty; some grit or dust has been shaken loose inside its barrel.

"Take her deep! Go to 300 feet! Use negative!" I shout to Si Lake at the diving station.

We've been detected, so there's no harm in taking a depth finder sounding on the way down. The bottom is barely 400 feet deep. Leveling off at 300 we find no temperature gradient to help us hide from the three ships now pinging all around us. In this poorly charted area we must work our way out to deeper water quickly. Let's do it now while they're still in doubt as to where we are. We turn seaward and use more speed. We are slowly sinking. Even with full rise on our bow planes we can't stop the steady downward creep of the depth gauge needles. Seaman 1c Dan Vogel is bow planesman; motor mac 3c Ernest Sturgeon has the stern planes. They watch their bubble and depth gauge helplessly as *Halibut* sinks deeper.

"Captain, I'll have to pump out or speed up to hold her," says Si.

I've been watching my own depth gauge in the conning tower all the while radioman 3c Don Bice on the sonar set is telling me what he hears. "No. Not now. Try to hold her as you are."

One set of props has speeded up and is coming toward us, the peculiar *zish-zish-zish* of its screws clearly audible. A depth charge explodes, first the *click*, then the *brr-roomp*. Not close.

Henderson keeps his usual tally. Pencil slashes in his quartermaster's notebook mount to thirteen. The explosions are always on our port side. I'm glad of that; they haven't bracketed us yet. Perhaps they're dropping on the knuckle of our wake.

All unneeded pumps and motors are shut down. In the stillness of the boat we hear new creaks and groans as the mounting pressure of the sea squeezes *Halibut*. The racket of a locker popping open and spilling its gear on deck seems deafening.

The search and depth charging continue. Sometimes the pinging seems right on us; the enemy screws speed up and come right at us. Fifteen more depth charges are dropped, sometimes in pairs, but we get only minor damage. A sea pressure gauge shatters, and an engine circulating water line leaks. In the control room a high-pressure air line fitting leaks. We've endured so many depth charges in the last few months that I'm not very concerned. It will take a rare combination of skill and luck to put a depth charge close enough really to hurt us. I remember, "His truth is a shield and a buckler. . . . " Do my men have the same confidence, or do they rely only on me?

By this time we have all stripped to our shorts. In the 110° temperature, sweat streams off our bodies, fills our shoes and gathers in puddles at our feet. Some men remove their shoes and pour the sweat carefully into the control room wastebasket. Our heads ache, our eyes burn, our lungs labor in the hot, foul air. My own limbs, weak and dehydrated, tremble at any exertion. I have come down from the conning tower and cling to the rungs of the ladder in the control room. I stand behind the diving officer, where I can at once see any trouble we are having with depth control. At the same time I can give course and speed orders more easily in attempts to outmaneuver our attackers.

At each depth charge explosion I add a few turns to our r.p.m., and sometimes turn to confuse the Japanese sonarmen. But we keep sinking, to 360, to 370, to 380 feet. We check the master depth gauge against others that read sea pressure directly. There is no doubt that we are still going down, deeper than we've ever been. Finally, at 405 feet the downward motion stops. *Halibut* is 35 percent deeper than her "test" depth!

The persistent hunters hang on our trail, their depth charges churning the water around us. My head aches as though a red hot poker has pierced my forehead. My eyes sting from sweat and heat. The air our straining lungs gulp is a heavy, wet compound, hot, stale, and sticky. We test it in our chemical analyzer and find that CO_2 is approaching a dangerous level. It is time to break out the carbon dioxide absorbent which we carry in large, sealed canisters. We've never had to use it before.

Mack and Roberson supervise spreading the white, granular compound carefully in a thin layer on sheets spread on bunks in the torpedo rooms and in the crews' quarters where most of our men are.

As the afternoon wears slowly on, the explosions become more distant, and we ease cautiously upward. It is sunset before we are back to periscope depth. I am so weak that I cling to the periscope handles for support. I can rotate the scope for the vital look-all-around only by leaning my weight against one handle while I stumble after it in an almost instinctive 360° sweep.

Thirteen and one-half hours after diving we surface with the black hills of Saipan looming astern. I remember this day as the most difficult, the most physically and mentally exhausting of the war for me. Its only reward was survival.

We had only enough fuel to get back to Midway. During the night we rounded Saipan to the north. At dawn we dived to give all hands a needed rest, and spent the day at 200 feet quietly heading eastward to get clear of Saipan's air and surface patrols.

The quiet of such a day was peaceful, broken only by the drone of fans and occasional footsteps in the passageway. The internal quiet of yesterday, of any day under depth charging, was anything but peaceful. When all dispensable machinery, including the air-conditioning plant, is secured, the atmosphere soon becomes one of sodden heat, compounded by the tense expression on men's faces as the few on watch go about their duties and the rest lie grimly in their bunks or gather in small, whispering groups. If anyone stubs his toe noisily, drops or accidentally bangs something, he is glared at; no words need be said. You even expect a sneeze to be heard by the Japs. Such inboard stillness makes the bedlam outboard all the more terrible. Satan's reception room must be like a submarine in the tropics in the midst of a depth charging: the sweat-soaked heat, the crash and bang of depth charges, the screams of our tortured ship, the rumble of ships passing over, the whine of their turbines, the knowledge of a hundred grinning, jumping devils overhead, the torment of uneasy consciences, and fear!

If even just a few fans can be started up, their soft purr is cathartic; the men know we're drawing away from our pursuers. When the bow planes can be shifted back to power operation, or the steering, it's still better. And if we start the air-conditioning or a pump they know we're practically sitting on the lanai of the Royal Hawaiian sipping beer. Then men move freely about the boat; voices are no longer held to a whisper; the cooks get busy at their chores; a few weak jokes are tried.

Unknown to us, the carrier we had tried to attack was *Unyo*. On January 17 she had been damaged by two torpedo hits from *Haddock*, and had taken refuge in Saipan. It was not the first time *Halibut* and *Unyo* had met. The previous July *Halibut*, then commanded by Phil Ross, had damaged the 16,700-ton light carrier in a torpedo attack off Truk. Now she escaped us once again. At the end of January she was towed from Saipan to Japan under escort of three destroyers. On that perilous 1,500 mile journey she survived attacks by our subs *Gudgeon* and *Saury*, and reached port safely. Eight months later her charmed life ended. She was sunk by *Barb* in a close-in, night surface attack.

After we left the area, *Tullibee* and *Haddock* tried for a few more days to increase our bag. Our wolf pack, which had sailed with such high hopes, had a miserable score: *Tullibee*, a 500-ton net tender sunk; *Haddock*, the 16,700-ton carrier, damaged; *Halibut*, zero.

But no, we were not quite empty handed. As we sailed dejectedly homeward, one of the nightly "family grams" brought news that Betty and newborn eight-pound daughter were in excellent condition. Thus it was that after fifty days at sea during which we had covered 11,000 miles, an event in faraway New Jersey gave us our only prize. We could paint on the wardroom bulkhead, among the symbols depicting Japanese ships sunk or damaged, the silhouette of a stork, its tiny bundle representing our minuscule tonnage for the patrol.

It was no surprise to Jim that his child would be a girl. During the frequent, long periods of inactivity on this patrol, expectant father Jim Grady, always statistically inclined, tabulated the children of all submarine officers as best we could recall, and found that 70 percent were female!

Arriving off Midway the morning of February 1, we found the channel closed, too rough for entry, and had to spend an uncomfortable twenty-four hours in the heavy seas offshore. The winter storms we had encountered hereabouts as we had proceeded on patrol had rarely abated. The coral reefs encircling the atoll in a living breakwater had been pounded by a succession of winter gales, and in mid-January our submarine *Flier* had gone aground just off the channel. In attempting to assist her, the submarine rescue vessel *Macaw* had herself struck

a reef and foundered. Her skipper, Comdr. Paul W. Burton, and four
of his crew were lost.

Paul and I were classmates, both at the Naval Academy and at Sub
School in New London. I remembered him fondly for his genial,
engaging spirit and puckish bent of humor. Trained in deep sea diving,
he was at one time Officer-in-Charge of the underwater escape-train-
ing tank at New London. To encourage the more timid to undertake
the deeper levels of escape, it was he who had life-size mermaids
painted on the underwater, inner wall of the tank opposite the airlocks
at the training depths. At 18 feet Paul had a blonde painted, at 50
feet a curvaceous brunette, and at 100 a tempting redhead. As Paul
explained, "It's easier to make the first, you know."

Leaving these memories behind, I conned *Halibut* up the wind-
lashed channel leading to the lagoon covered with whitecaps. The sad
sight of *Macaw*'s helpless hulk only deepened our gloom as we moored
alongside submarine tender *Sperry* who would give us our refit. Our
wolf pack experience had not been a rewarding one save for the fact
that we had pioneered in the form of wolf pack that was standard
thereafter.

12

"Mr. Mosley, Sir"

With our ship safely in the hands of SubDiv 101's relief crew, we moved to our breezy rooms in the Gooneybird Hotel and the enlisted barracks on the twenty-foot "high" ground of Sand Island, the western of Midway's two islands. The weather was still wintry, with sunny, warm days being followed by days of cold, blowing rain. I took a room on the sunny side of the building. It had just been vacated by Comdr. John S. McCain, Jr., C.O. of *Gunnel*. I knew Jack only by hearsay as the dynamic, profane, cigar-smoking, whiskey-drinking son of equally colorful and feisty Admiral McCain. In years to come Jack and I became warm friends whose duty paths crossed regularly.

It was nesting season for the gooneys, and one had built its nest under the window of my room. The sloping mound of sand with a depression in its top was carefully lined with needles of the ironwood trees. Inspection of the nest showed that its occupant had sustained a shower of cigar butts, razor blades, and bourbon.

Nearby, Jim Grady had adopted one of the awkward, fuzzy, scrawny little gray chicks. When its parents were absent at sea foraging food, Jim would drop vitamin pills down its gaping gullet. No doubt it grew to become king of the gooneys.

More than 300 years ago it was said, "A ship and a woman are ever repairing." And again, "Who wishes to give himself an abundance of trouble, let him equip these two things, a ship and a woman. No two things involve more bother, for neither is ever sufficiently adorned." How true this seemed during our wartime repair periods.

The refit that was to be accomplished by *Sperry* was interrupted by storm damage to our main ballast tanks as we were moored to one of Midway's exposed piers. We had to sail back to Pearl for the more major repairs this required. The loss of time for the trip to Pearl and back was regrettable, but we benefited from the material upgrading this made possible. *Halibut* received the modification which permitted carrying fuel oil in No. 4 main ballast tank (lack of which had hampered our wolf pack patrol), as well as the updating of various electronic equipment. Though our submarine weapons made only slight advances during the war, the improvements in electronics were remarkable. They gave us a decisive advantage over our foe. The advantage took various forms, most telling being the great improvement in radar performance. It was also significant in radio communications, in sonar, in depth charge and minefield detection. Each time we sailed we had greater technical capabilities; it was up to us to exploit them fully.

On March 21, 1944, we put behind us the failures and frustrations of our last patrol and sailed once more, with hopes and morale high. But whether a seasoned veteran or a neophyte submariner pretending indifference to his shipmates' taunts, every man on board found that each occasion of going to sea brought a period of adjustment. One's daily routine, one's very life had to be adapted to the larger, common life we shared in our ship. The moods and vagaries of the sea, the performance of our ship and shipmates under stress, controlled our physical and mental activity.

Such reflections were on my mind as I stook on the cigarette deck abaft the bridge and watched the green mountains of Oahu and Kauai slip into the sea astern of us. But of more practical concern was the fact that we sailed each time with a revised team. This time in port I had to transfer three top-watch standers—Barrett, Lake, and Gregerson, receiving as replacements two young officers fresh from submarine school. They were Ensign Robert J. Alexander and Lieut. (jg) Paul Mann.

Alex was a Naval Academy officer, graduated in June, 1943, a product of the shortened wartime curriculum. He was from Paterson, New Jersey, the very city in which Irish immigrant John P. Holland, developer of our navy's first submarine, had earned his living as a lay teacher in a parochial school. I asked Alex if this had influenced his own choice of submarine duty. He said no, it had not, that the actual impetus came when he was ten years old and read a book about the 1925 sinking of *S-51* off of Block Island. From then on he was determined to be a submariner, even giving up Academy leave one summer to experience submarine life in an ancient O-boat at New London.

Alex was a lively addition to our wardroom. He was a free spirit, as uninhibited in thought and speech as John Holland, and had the same Irish passion for politics. He was still a bachelor, but there was room in his life for only one girl—Mary—who would one day share his thirty-one-year navy career.

Paul Mann was a reservist who had entered the navy through one of the emergency augmentation programs. He was slim and graceful, of medium height, a dark-haired, well-tanned young man from California. He had a neatly trimmed mustache. I think he was the most dapper submarine officer I saw during the war. No doubt the fact that he and his wife had been a professional dance team had a bearing on that.

Both Alex and Paul were typical of the alert, aggressive young men who were attracted to the submarine service. For one thing, in no other type of ship would they be given so much responsibility so soon, and be in combat so early. They would stand junior officer of the deck watches during the long passage to our patrol area. By the time we reached it they would have to be ready for top watch, with the safety of ship and crew entrusted to them.

With our submarine force so dependent on naval reserve personnel, both officer and enlisted, I had many opportunities to observe them in combat and out. They were no less brave than those in the regular navy, no less capable in the specific tasks for which they had been hastily trained. On the other hand, officers and enlisted men of the regular navy, professional sailors, seemed more at ease in the unforgiving realities of war, more reconciled to the family separations and personal hardships. After all, they had chosen a way of life and made a commitment to service, knowing that their culmination could come in war. There was little concern for one's career. If anything, the challenges of combat, the greater responsibilities shouldered, were accepted as career enhancing. This was not true for the young reservist; he frequently found his education interrupted or his career in disarray. With the end of the war he would not necessarily find his job waiting or settle comfortably into a predetermined career path.

As for our replacement enlisted men, nine were making their first patrol. One of them was a ship's cook, 3c. The morning he reported on board from the squadron's replacement pool he stood perspiring in the control room, sea bag at his feet, turning his papers over to Yeoman Snell, when the exec passed through on his way to officers' country. Noticing the new man in the circle of familiar faces, Mack asked, "What's your name?"

Plucking off his hat, ill-at-ease to be the center of interest but without a change in his impassive expression, the new cook answered, "Mr. Mosley, sir."

"Glad to have you on board, Mr. Mosley. Hope we can say the same for your cooking."

Since John Paul Jones's time junior officers in the navy have been addressed "Mister," but from this day we had a ship's cook who was "Mr. Mosley," or sometimes "Ol' Man Mose." He was a stocky, burly man, homely in appearance, as slow-speaking and thinking as he was lumbering in motion. In the weeks ahead we would learn little more of Mr. Mosley's background than appeared in his brief service record. He was older than the average recruit, and a native of New Mexico, a fact which apparently influenced his cooking. Whatever he cooked he cooked to a turn—as the boys said, "Till it turned black"—and sprinkled lavishly with salt, pepper, or Tabasco.

In a submarine the cook can't be a sensitive soul. Unlike those in larger ships, his galley is not removed, denied to the ship's company, out of sight from the crew's mess tables and beyond the range of their ceaseless good-humored, derogatory comments. The submarine cook literally stands behind his product in his tiny, hot galley, only an arm's length from the shipmates seated at the mess tables in the after battery room.

We were to find Mr. Mosley equal to his testing. On our first morning under way Chief Commissary Steward Terry entrusted breakfast to Mose, who produced fried potatoes, sausage, and scrambled eggs. Almost with his first mouthful, Red Creighton, our seaman first class and gunner's mate striker, yelled, "Hey, Mose, where'd you learn to cook?"

"On the ranch. New Mexico."

"What'd you do, take a correspondence course in Mexican tamales?"

"Cooked on roundup," replied Mr. Mosley seriously, his brown eyes like a friendly puppy's, unaware that Red delighted in needling new members of the crew.

"When'd you join the navy?"

"Six months."

"Ever been on a ship before?"

"No."

"Well, do you know the difference between an order and a command?"

After deliberate reflection Mr. Mosley replied, "A command is from the captain; an order is two fried eggs."

In the days and weeks that followed we found Mr. Mosley impervious to insult, indifferent to compliment. His stolid features never varied as the boys heaped contempt on his cooking or tried to cajole information from him. Neither did his style of cooking, which was best summed up by Silvio Gardella, our firecontrolman 2c, when he said, "The trouble with Mose's cooking is he thinks that when it's burning it's cooking, and when it's burnt it's cooked." Still, Mr. Mosley proved to be great for morale among his *Halibut* shipmates as the uncomplaining butt of many pranks, the source of many hilarious episodes.

We were two days out of Pearl, proceeding to Midway, when Mose was at work in the galley making ready the evening meal. Suddenly he was startled by the voice of the messenger of the watch who leaned through the door into the messroom and yelled, "Mose, long-distance call for you in the control room."

Impassive as always, Mose reacted automatically to the summons. Wiping his hands on his cook's apron, he lumbered forward to the phone which was mounted amidships on the steel cylinder that formed the well for housing No. 1 periscope. The control room gave its usual underway, surface-cruising appearance. The section on watch was in its customary indolent but alert attitude, no one seeming to pay more than usual attention to the cook as he clumsily reached for the telephone handset. Taking a deep breath, Mose lifted the hand phone gingerly to his ear. He had just parted his lips to say "Hello" when a sudden glint of awareness came to his eyes. Replacing the handset, Mose looked sidewise and found the grinning faces of his shipmates.

With his head thrust up through the hatch leading into the pump room below, electrician's mate 3c Clyde Webb was first to break the silence. "Whatsa matter, Mose? Ain't ya gonna take the call? Maybe it's important."

"What happened, Mose? Somebody try to reverse the charges on ya?" asked Bill Henderson.

"It was probably that *wahine* reporter that writes about cookin' in the Honolulu paper that wants Mose's recipe for shortnin' bread."

"Don't you give it to her, Mose. We want to go back to Hawayah after this trip."

"Say, I went to one of them loo-ows," said Clayt Rantz. "You know, where you stuff a pig with hot rocks and bury it in the ground with a gunny sack. That's the thing to do with Mose's chow—put it in a gunny sack and bury it with them hot rocks he calls biscuits."

Mr. Mosley made no reply, but trudged back to his galley while his shipmates joked about the "long-distance call."

Back in the galley Mose found a furious Chief Terry snatching tins of black, charred biscuits from the electric oven where Mose had forgotten them. As Mr. Mosley waited for the hot, smoking mess to cool so that he could scrape it into the garbage pail, his shipmates grinned and jeered, "Aw, too bad, Mose. Just a coupla more minutes and the biscuits woulda been done."

"Jeez, Mose, if you was only pretty you'd sure make a real nice bride."

"Hell, it wasn't your fault, Mose. I bet those electricity mates screwed you. Next time don't let 'em give you D.C. juice. Tell the chief to switch on the A.C.—some o' that cookin' A.C.," said Webb.

"Look here, Mose," said Red. "You shouldn't oughta smell up the boat like that. You gotta cut out fryin' and bakin'. What you oughta serve is somethin' like cold boiled beef."

"Cold boiled beef?" asked Mose, reacting to the apparently helpful note in Red's voice.

"Sure, that's it," called Clayt. "You boil the beef in cold water. Mighty tasty."

It was clear that there had been no telephones in Mose's upbringing. He regarded them with distrust and suspicion. A tongue to speak and ears to hear—those were the only communications equipment Mr. Mosley understood or required. The roving reporter of our *Halibastard Herald* captured this fact in a scene he recorded as follows:

SCENE: Control Room, submerged.
TIME: The afternoon watch.
CAST: Mr. Mosley, Red Creighton.
Action
The phone rings.
RED: "Pick it up, Mose. Say 'Hello'."
MOSE: "Hello."
After a period of blank consideration, he hangs up.
"Shucks, I can't understand anythin' over a phone. Never could."
RED: "You've gotta learn how to use the phone, Mose. Sup-

pose you was in the forward torpedo room and wanted to pass
a word to the after room. What would you do?"

MOSE: "I'd walk aft and tell 'em."

RED: "But suppose you were in a hurry?"

MOSE: "I'd run."

—End—

While we were undergoing refit in Pearl there was a noticeable tone
of optimism in the war news being released to the public. It was
confirmed by contacts we had with ComSubPac and CinCPac staff
officers. It was clear that Nazi Germany's fate was sealed. She had
already been driven out of much of her conquered territory. It was
only a matter of time before her resistance would be crushed by the
two powerful offensives closing in—the Anglo-American drive from
the west, and the Russian from the east.

In the war at sea the once-dire threat of Doenitz's U-boats had
been overcome. In his own words, "Radar, and particularly radar
location by aircraft, had to all practical purposes robbed the U-boats
of their power to fight on the surface. Wolf-pack operations against
convoys in the North Atlantic . . . were no longer possible"[1]

The tide had also turned in the Pacific. Our naval strength had
been restored following the disaster at Pearl Harbor and was growing
steadily. The Battle of Midway in June, 1942, and the capture of
Guadalcanal in February, 1943, had taken the initiative from the Japanese.

The U.S. strategic plan for the Pacific called for a campaign of island
hopping. General MacArthur's forces were to advance northward from
Australia through New Guinea to retake the Philippines; Admiral
Nimitz's naval, air, and land forces were to move westward through
the central Pacific to the Mariana Islands (Guam, Saipan, Tinian).
Each would take islands as needed to provide air and naval bases for
further advances, but would bypass others held by Japan. By "leapfrogging" some of the more strongly defended islands, we would leave
Japan's over-extended forces to "wither on the vine." When the Philippines and Marianas had been seized they would be the springboard
for the next leap on the road to Japan, through Okinawa and Iwo Jima.

1. Doenitz, Karl. *Admiral Doenitz Memoirs* (London: Weidenfeld and Nicolson, Ltd.,
1959), p. 341.

Important to this strategy was the virtual blockade imposed by our submarines, which denied reinforcement and replenishment to Japan's beleaguered garrisons. Both her warships and supply ships had to run the gauntlet of our boats deployed across their routes. At the same time, the rapidly growing number of our submarines cut more and more deeply into Japan's lifeline of raw materials from its southern conquests.

After the correction of our torpedo problems in the fall of 1943, our rate of sinkings increased so that for the year U.S. submarines had sunk about a ship a day for a total of 1.5 million tons. By the start of 1944 we were confident that our improved weapons and equipment and more experienced personnel would vastly improve that record.

By late March, as *Halibut* steamed steadily westward on the surface in the lengthening days and shrinking nights, proceeding to her patrol area, we knew that Admiral Nimitz's forces had taken the Gilbert Islands and Marshall Islands as planned, and were neutralizing Japan's major base at Truk by heavy naval air attacks. Our aircraft carriers were also striking Guam, Saipan, and Tinian in preparation for the all-out assault in June. Meanwhile, General MacArthur's forces were leapfrogging up the east coast of New Guinea, neutralizing the important Japanese base of Rabaul, and getting into position for the return to the Philippines.

By this time the Japanese fleet was completely outclassed. It had neither the numbers nor the advanced equipment of the U.S. fleet. In the previous ten months it had lost thirty-three ships: twenty-five destroyers, five light cruisers, one escort carrier, one seaplane carrier, and one battleship.[2] The U.S. superiority in aircraft carriers and in the quality of their air squadrons was particularly significant.

With her supply of raw materials and fuel from the South Seas being severely limited, and her shipyards straining to repair damaged ships, Japan simply could not compete with the industrial capacity of the United States. Nevertheless, her martial spirit was undiminished. There was much desperate fighting ahead, and the major losses on both sides were yet to come.

2. Dull, Paul S. *The Imperial Japanese Navy* (Annapolis, Md.: Naval Institute Press, 1978), p. 299.

13

Off Okinawa

The waters surrounding Okinawa were our assigned area for this patrol, *Halibut's* ninth. Heavily garrisoned by Japanese forces, Okinawa was the largest island of the Ryukyu Islands chain, some 300 miles south of Japan proper, on the route to Formosa and the Philippines. It was about 60 miles long, 9 miles wide, mountainous and irregular, with a population of a half million. It was a long way to go, 5,200 miles from Pearl Harbor, but the additional fuel we now carried would give us 2,000 miles extra range at fifteen knots and would permit us to remain on station a reasonable time. Our operation order directed us to depart our area on May 5 if no other factor caused earlier termination.

Five days west of Midway we had consumed the fuel in No. 4 MBT. It was divided in two halves, 4A to starboard, and 4B to port. We adjusted valves and fittings to make the tanks once again conventional main ballast tanks. The residue of diesel oil in them would leave a telltale "slick" if not washed out, so we submerged and surfaced a few times to flush the tanks. Each succeeding dive would cleanse the tank walls and crevices even more, so that by the time we were close in to enemy shores there would be no concern on this account.

For the next two days we were troubled by a list to starboard; the vent valve to No. 4A apparently was not seating properly. This was a large valve at the top of the tank and located in the ship's superstructure under the free-flooding deck. When we were on the surface, such valves were shut, trapping in the ballast tanks the air which prevented seawater from rushing in the open flooding ports near the keel. To dive we had only to open all the vent valves, air would escape from the ballast tanks with a tremendous sigh, and we would quickly slide underwater, carried down both by our loss of buoyancy and by the downward thrust of our diving planes as we tilted forward.

Our problem was not a serious one. When submerged, both 4A and

4B would be fully flooded and there would be no list. On the surface, however, the leaking of 4A's vent valve permitted its tank to take in more water than 4B did. This was an annoyance, for it interfered with rapid, safe movement about the ship and hampered work such as the routine maintenance of torpedoes, the watering of batteries, and engine repairs. Soon we would learn to what good purpose our valve leaked.

On the night of April 4 there was a bright moon and calm seas. These were good conditions for working topside, but I was uneasy. We were crossing the routes which Japanese warships would take in their movements between Japan and their South Pacific bases. To make repairs we would have to slow our speed and send men to work in the cramped space between the pressure hull and the topside deck. Could we get them out in time if we were detected and forced to dive? Wouldn't we be a sitting duck in this position? Still, it was better to take the risk out here rather than closer to the enemy shore.

As soon as it was dark, after blueprints had been studied, tools made ready and instructions given, we slowed to one-third speed and headed down the moon streak to minimize our silhouette. On call, Jack Allison, who was chief of our auxiliary gang, Bob Chalfant, and Dick Kelly came up the conning tower hatch, clambered down on deck, and went quickly aft on the wet, slippery surface.

I stood on the bridge quietly, not betraying my anxiety. The first section had the watch. Joe Galligan had the deck; his lookouts were Gene Oakey, Don Noonan, and Bill Austin. Little "Obie" O'Brien was quartermaster, and Silvio Gardella had the wheel in the conning tower. Just a few feet behind and to starboard of him, Ray Welley hunched over the dimly luminous PPI scope.

At slow speed on the surface our bottom-mounted sonar could be effective, so that too was manned, searching underwater for screw noises as carefully as radar scanned the surface.

Mack Butler had passed word throughout the ship as to our problem, and that three men would be topside working in the superstructure. Lookouts on the bridge, and radar and sonar operators silently intensified their search.

It was a still, clear night, the moon lighting a bright, silvery road down which we were traveling. The only sound of the sea was the soothing swish of water gently lapping along the curved sides of our ballast tanks. Everything was so peaceful it only magnified my fears. Here we were in the position I dreaded most—proceeding slowly on the surface in an area where enemy subs might be lurking.

We could not speed up or zigzag. That would complicate the already difficult task of our working party. If an enemy sub had detected our approach and dived before we saw him, we would join the lengthening list of those boats "overdue and presumed lost."

I didn't trust the tranquillity with which we were moving slowly down the moon streak. In my uneasiness the thought recurred: would we have to dive to save our ship at the cost of shipmates trapped topside?

I glanced aft. There was room in the superstructure for only two men to work. Chalfant crouched on deck, his head ducked down the opening of the hinged deck grating where Allison and Kelly were working. Brief gleams from their flashlights, the clang of tools on metal, seemed to shriek our presence in the clear, calm night. Would the work never be completed?

In response to my call, Chalfant said, "We're almost done, captain. Just a couple more minutes."

As our men scrambled back to the bridge to go below, radar reported contact, dead ahead at 7,100 yards. The pip was small when first seen, but now radar technician Ray Welley shouted up the hatch, "Big pip! Saturation size!"

Simultaneously, starboard lookout fireman Gene Oakey spotted the target. Looking where they reported, I saw the dark bulk of a sub-marine surfacing across our track. In the bright moonlight visibility was excellent, but our small silhouette up-moon from the enemy, who was in the rather blind and deaf transition stage—neither fully surfaced nor submerged—meant we might be able to dive and close for attack before he detected us.

Diving at once to radar depth, *Halibut* began her approach to torpedo range. Sonar had made contact almost as soon as radar, and reported the resonant sound of high-pressure air blowing main ballast tanks. Searching on radar's reported bearings I tried to locate the target in our night periscope. As we turned toward the target, we made our tubes ready. Here, for the Japanese, was the situation all submariners dreaded—caught on the surface while an unseen enemy waited, waited for his slowly turning periscope to mark the correct bearing before sending torpedoes on their way. Or so it seemed until the steady bearing, the speed-up of screws, their fading away signalled that our quarry had been alerted and fled.

Late that night as we reviewed events over the chart table in the dim, red light of the control room, Chief Roberson asked thoughtfully, "What if we hadn't had that trouble with No. 4? Suppose we hadn't stopped to fix it? We'd have crossed dead ahead of him in that bright moonlight, with him still submerged."

Repeating the Ninety-first Psalm before I dropped off to sleep that night, I found new reassurance in the words of the psalmist: "Thou shalt not be afraid for the terror by night. . . . "

Proceeding onward to the island chain, we were to find our area uncomfortably small and confining. It measured ninety miles in latitude and about three times that in longitude, but the part of use to us, the watery part, was much reduced by the numerous islands, large and small, scattered athwart it. Unlike our previous patrol, when we had many thousands of square miles of open ocean to roam in, we were now always close to Japanese islands, called by them Nansei Shoto, and surface patrolling was a bit chancy.

For this patrol we had changed our coloration. Because of the divergent views on this subject, ComSubPac gave some leeway to skippers in the camouflaging or color of their ships, not insisting on a standard. When the war started we had believed most of our operations would be submerged, and prewar tests indicated that an overall black color was best in reducing the likelihood of being sighted. I had preferred to retain the black when we sailed in the wolf pack with *Tullibee* and *Haddock*, but they had shifted to gray, with highlights of even lighter color about the bridge. Because of the numerous rendezvous we made, opportunities for comparison, both by day and night, were frequent, and I soon became a convert to gray camouflage. On several occasions, closing in on one another on the surface at night, *Tullibee* and *Haddock* could see *Halibut* well before we sighted them. The knowledge that we were in gray was reassuring on this patrol as we scoured the interisland channels of our restrictive area.

Reading every scrap of information we had on board concerning Okinawa, I found even the U.S. Hydrographic Office "Pilot" covering these islands fascinating. Reporting that Okinawa Jima was largely rough, rocky, and infested with deadly snakes, it went on to say that, in addition to these reptiles, on the three northernmost islands "there is also a creature, about one foot in length and the shape of a lashed-up hammock, with black stripes, that is most virulent." This was probably the *habu*, and it did cause concern when our amphibious forces landed there a year later. However, at the time we were there, I wanted the enemy to learn that there lurked offshore in these waters a creature over 300 feet in length, the shape and color of a shark, that was also most virulent. Perhaps they knew that, which accounted for our dearth of contacts.

Our track in the area became a maze of crisscrossing lines on our chart. Submerged by day, we hugged the prominent capes; at night we prowled through the island channels on the surface, favored by dark nights and our excellent radar. Late on the night of April 12 we finally found targets, several ships heading westward close inshore through the channel between Amami O Shima and Tokuno Shima. Slipping astern of them and gradually closing, we followed warily through the channel. The steep, black hills coming down to the water seemed almost as confining as the cliffs of a Norwegian fjord. Turning north, our targets went behind some small islets. We waited at the far end for them to come clear. Suddenly we sighted a freighter coming down from the north, smoking heavily. This bird in hand was all the more tempting, since its escort of three small patrol craft indicated a target of some importance. She was only 15,000 yards away and we had to work fast before she got by.

We went first to radar depth, then eased down to periscope depth. At exactly 0200 we fired a spread of three torpedoes, the central one hitting squarely amidships, the others missing fore and aft, indicating that our target was smaller than we thought. She turned out to be *Taichu Maru*, 3,213 tons, and the one hit was enough to send her to the bottom.

When one of her escorts detected us and turned toward us as if to ram, we went deep. All three escorts commenced dropping single depth charges at about one minute intervals, just right for testing our newest gadget—the depth charge indicator, or DCI. This had been installed during our refit at Pearl by an engineer who had come out from the Navy Underwater Sound Laboratory at New London, where the DCI was developed. It consisted of a series of blastphones mounted in our superstructure. They would sense depth charge explosions and activate lights on a panel in the control room, indicating whether the explosion was to port or starboard, ahead or astern, above or below.

The intent was to be of assistance in evasion, giving an indication of the pattern the enemy was dropping.

As a seasoned recipient of depth charges I was skeptical that the device could determine the depth or direction of a depth charge explosion by sound alone. In our experience to date, we had done pretty well by use of our submariner's ears. This time a total of eighteen depth charges was dropped, and the flashing lights checked closely enough with my own estimates. I became convinced they were useful, at least psychologically. Obviously a depth charge close enough to hurt or sink us needed no indicator lights, but as long as they could see the flickering lights, men seemed reassured that we were doing a good job of outsmarting our pursuers.

In between the depth charges we could hear the more satisfying crackling and banging noises of our target breaking up. When the depth charging stopped and the escorts started pinging we came back to periscope depth. One hour after our attack we came to the surface in the black night and quickly outran the one escort near us, much to the delight of all hands below. The two other escorts were busy picking up survivors in the flashing beams of their searchlights.

Turning back to the north we searched for the convoy we had been trailing, but they had vanished in one of the several channels open to them. At daylight, close in to the islands, we had to dive.

After the night's activity, the enemy certainly knew we were in the area. We sighted numerous planes and small patrol vessels hunting for us. Perhaps they glimpsed us now and then in the next few days. Even if they couldn't pin us down close enough to attack, it was enough on a given day to know which side of the island chain we were working. It was an easy matter to route their shipping in and out among the islands so as to avoid us. At any rate, following our one attack, two weeks of maddening, tense but fruitless patrolling ensued. The part of our area west of Okinawa was the East China Sea, the *Tung Hai*, and we figured it should be the more productive, so we spent most time there. When our close-in, submerged patrolling of likely focal points produced no targets, we moved offshore to enlarge our search by surface patrol. I knew it was risky, but acceptably so since it was our job to find targets. By zigzagging at moderate speed and keeping an extremely alert lookout, I was confident no harm would come to us.

When we did this, there would be noticeable tension in the crew. Aside from the planes we frequently sighted, the memory of our recent brush with an enemy sub was vivid. The relaxed shipboard atmosphere of submerged patrolling was missing. There was more movement about the boat. Men did not seem content to sit still and read, or to play acey-deucey, cribbage, or pinochle, or even to lie in their bunks. It was as if they could not concentrate on even those simple diversions, and had to release nervous tensions by moving about among shipmates. Since we were on the surface there was no restriction on smoking; the smoking lamp was lit. Men who smoked lighted one cigarette after another, and the big coffee urn in the mess room needed frequent replenishment. Any man coming off watch from bridge or conning tower was quizzed as to what he saw, what the weather and visibility were, what the captain or the O.O.D. said.

In the control room Red Creighton, our homespun Arkansas philosopher, sat on the blueprint chest, which was also the seat for the bow planesman. Should the diving alarm sound, Red would at once rig out the bow planes. He was not yet a petty officer, but was struggling to become gunner's mate 3c. He was an uncomplicated young man, well liked for his invariable good nature, simple, country humor, and native friendliness. Shipmates were comfortable with Red, whether on shore leave or on board. I knew it did not take much liquor or beer for Red to become playful and boisterous ashore, but he was so obviously a morale asset on board that I would forgive his little escapades.

When James Dowling, one of our new, young seamen, came down from his hour's stint as lookout he eased into position next to Red. In a little while he spoke in hushed tones intended only for Red and asked, "Do you ever get scared on the boat?"

"Shucks," boomed Red so loudly that I heard him even as I was stepping through the door from officer's quarters, "I'm scared from the time we cast off until we tie up again."

Helping fill the apprehensive hours of our crew were two schools: "school of the boat" for the thirty men not yet qualified in submarines (nine of whom were making their first war patrol), and "Professor Alexander's Academy of Mathematics." Perhaps inspired by the daily applications of math to submarine life, whether in Mack's navigational computations, in Jack Hinchey's diving book, in fuel usage rates, in torpedo fire control problems, or whatever, a number of the crew showed great interest in mathematics. We started a class which met each afternoon in the forward torpedo room. Young Alex was the obvious choice as instructor. Not only was he our "George," but he was the one with most recent academic experience. He was a good choice; he liked teaching and was good at it.

In order to connect his pupils' math with their daily work, Alex gave them problems such as: how many seconds will it be before you hear the explosion of a torpedo that hits 1,800 yards away; how many cubic feet of air do our engines burn per minute if they're running at 60 r.p.m.?

Alex had eight regular, earnest pupils. One was cocky Stedman Stone. As he came through the passageway in officers' country after school one day he saw Mack in the wardroom. "Well, Mr. Butler, it won't be long till I'm right up here eating in the wardroom."

Located where we were, midlength of a vast archipelago that stretched from the Kuriles through Japan, the Ryukus, Formosa, the Philippines, and down to Indonesia, there were countless birds to complicate the problems of our lookouts and of our radar as well. Overflying the seabirds of the region, winging northward high and fast, were huge flocks of ducks, no doubt returning from their winter sojourn in the rice paddies of Formosa or the Philippines. How incongruous it seemed in a world at war to recall similar migrations watched with wonder in boyhood days half a world away. But this time we'd watch uneasily, straining through binoculars to clarify—was it a plane, was it a bird? Not pushing our luck too far, waiting for the right conditions, we did get in the better part of three days of surface running. The first time we were forced down by 1030; the next time noon; the third day it was 1600.

Our fruitless nighttime searches left much time for our one-way link with home. The broadcast receivers in the wardroom and the crew's mess were almost continually "ON," tuned to San Francisco as we tried to keep abreast of the war's progress. Changing time zones as we did, five hours as we moved from Pearl Harbor to Okinawa, our favorite shortwave programs would come at odd hours. There was much repetitious news, and not enough of what we liked, entertainment programs such as "Command Performance," "Musicale Americana," "Your News from Home," or just sweet music with a nostalgic flavor that often reminded our boys of that last high school dance.

The high ratio of "news" to entertainment was partly due to the effort to enlighten and propagandize the peoples of the Pacific and Asia, so we would turn, as well, to the propaganda of the other side. We could easily receive Radio Tokyo and the program of "Tokyo Rose," who broadcast in colorless, flat English. She received a high entertainment rating from submariners, chiefly because of her bold exaggerations and clumsy propaganda. How many times did we listen to lurid tales of sea battles in which numbers of our carriers were "instantly sunk," "sunk," "heavily damaged," "damaged," "slightly damaged," "destroyed forever," and so on! The fine distinctions were sometimes hard to follow.[1]

The Japanese propaganda effort involving our subs seemed particularly inept. Perhaps it was intended not for submarine consumption but for those at home in the United States. They might have been considered gullible since they lacked official, detailed information of our submarine operations. The need for strict security in submarine operations meant that news of our actions was greatly curtailed; even daringly successful exploits were generally released only long after the event. All our outgoing personal mail was censored as well. As much for these reasons as from our own need to restrict communications to preserve stealth and secrecy, our submarine forces were dubbed the "Silent Service."

The crew of *Batfish* was particularly amused at Christmastime. Sitting down to the traditional sumptuous feast, though this time close to the shores of Japan, they listened to Tokyo Rose tell of "scores of U.S. pirate subs sunk," and that our crews "were now reduced to eating rats and cockroaches." As *Batfish* skipper Wayne Merrill told me, his boys were not slow in passing their plates for more "rats and cockroaches."

1. Actually, there was no one person named Tokyo Rose. She was a composite of several female announcers who broadcast English language programs intended to undermine the morale of our forces fighting in the Pacific. It was the GIs who coined the nickname Tokyo Rose. Nevertheless, in a still controversial 1949 case, the U.S. government brought to trial for treason the embodiment of Tokyo Rose in the person of Iva Toguri D'Aquino. She was a Los Angeles–born graduate of the University of California at Los Angeles. She had gone to Japan for family reasons in 1941 and was trapped there by the outbreak of war. Drafted to be an announcer on Radio Tokyo, it was she who came to be identified as Tokyo Rose and became the subject of the longest treason trial in U.S. history.

At times we could also tune in Russian broadcasts, and "Moscow Mary" became a favorite of mine. She had a rich, pleasing, contralto voice, and it was easy to fantasize over the disembodied personality far away. I wondered what she looked like, but as pleasing tones recited words of war, I wondered even more what she felt. The bloody, always to-the-point Russian communiqués went like this: "Today the Red Army forces liberated 60 populated places, killed 5,000 Hitlerites, captured 2,000 machine guns, 300 cannons, and shot down 90 aircraft." And so on in each broadcast to the ringing finale—"Death to the German invader!"

14

Sampan Convoy

O ur long days and nights empty of results ended with a bang, the crash of exploding warheads and the crack of depth charges. In six hours we fired thirteen torpedoes, damaging one cargo ship and sinking two. The total of depth charges thrown by the frantic Nips in their several futile counterattacks was near 200.

To leave no accessible corner of our area unsearched, I decided to work our way through the ten-mile-wide passage between Iheya Retto and Okinawa Jima. Following a brief nap, I went to the bridge at 0030 on April 26 to be ready for any eventuality. This was not like peacetime, when the less an O.O.D. saw of the captain on the bridge the better he liked it. I knew that watch officer Jim Conant would prefer having me immediately available. It was a pitch-black night, with rain clouds drifting down from the northwest. Navigator Mack was in the conning tower carefully checking the picture on the PPI scope against the chart. Only that made it possible to navigate the unfamiliar, winding channel in total darkness. As we moved silently across the black surface at ten knots, the eerie glow of phosphorescence persisted about our bow and in our wake.

About 0100 radar picked up pips other than the rocky shores, and, sure enough, at last we were started on the exciting game of stalking our prey. After two hours of tracking to learn our targets' course, speed, and formation, we moved in to attack. From what we could see and what radar showed, I estimated that we had three medium-sized freighters and at least four, possibly six, small escorts.

I wanted to fire at a range between 2,000 and 2,500 yards, that range being to our advantage at night, but had to fire at just under 3,000 when the escorts came close. We fired three torpedoes at each of two freighters, and watched their luminescent wakes streak toward their targets. Two of them hit, starting a weird spectacle such as might appear on a darkened stage to simulate a scene of horror or night battle. Whistles were blowing; lights were flashing; guns were firing and depth charges exploding, adding not only the din of their concussions but also their dull, green flashes to the scene.

While this was going on, it was with great satisfaction that we eluded the frantic escorts and roared off into the darkness at full speed on the surface. One escort hung on our tail for a while, but we could make over twenty knots when needed, and we soon shook him off before working back to see if we could attack again. It was disappointing to be able to claim only damage to one ship. Could the brilliant tracks of our torpedoes in the phosphorescent sea have alerted our targets in time to evade?

After our attack the convoy had scattered, but we soon picked up a lone ship plodding its fearful way toward Japan. This time, with no escorts to annoy us, we closed to 1,300 yards, and two hits soon sent *Genbu Maru* to the bottom. By this time dawn was breaking and it behooved us to put some miles between us and the scenes of action. Off we sped to the northward, passing closeby to three lifeboats filled with survivors. They would have no trouble getting to the nearby shore.

As expected, the determined hunt for us was not long in coming. After we had dived and were trying to close on some puffs of smoke we'd detected, loud pinging disclosed someone searching for us. Soon he came over the horizon, looking like a small destroyer or torpedo boat. The steady bearing on which he came, the constant small angle-on-the-bow he presented, and the strength of his supersonic ranging led me to believe he had contact on us and that a depth charging would soon follow.

Taking matters into our own hands, we went to battle stations and, after a brief, seventeen-minute approach, fired four stern tubes at a range of 900 yards. I did this with some misgiving; the target's obvious shallow draft would make it easy for torpedoes to underrun him, as had happened to us before.

Not so this time. In less than a minute two hits literally tore apart the coastal minelayer of 570 tons. Her mainmast snapped off and fell over the side. From our identification manual we could tell she was either *Tsubame* or her sister ship *Kamome*. The first name means "Swallow" and the other "Seagull." The sea did the swallowing. As the forepart of the ship filled with water, the large down angle tilted her stern clear of the water. I could see crew members scrambling uphill to the fantail where rudder and screws were now exposed. There had been no time for them to launch the lifeboats that now dangled crazily in a tangle of lines. With nothing else in sight, here was a rare chance for our men to get a satisfying look through a periscope at one result of their efforts. Each man could have only a few seconds' look at our victim who still clung to the surface, with survivors throwing overboard anything that would float. While all hands in the conning tower took their turn at No. 1 periscope, Mack kept a careful, all-around search with No. 2. We had just called below for men from control to take their look when a twin-engine bomber arrived on the scene. It was followed shortly by a trawler-type patrol boat. This fellow was a little too small to attack with torpedoes, and when the plane dropped a bomb close to us it was time to duck.

As we were passing 150 feet going deep, another bomb or depth charge shook the boat considerably. Once we reached 300 feet our attackers lost us. I put the sound of the patrol boat's screws astern, and we pulled away. An hour later we came back to periscope depth. I could see the patrol boat three miles away with the plane circling overhead. All afternoon we worked our way clear of them and of a second patrol craft that joined the hunt. Between them they dropped some ninety depth charges on false contacts, for none was close to us.

In getting clear we knew we would be intruding some thirty miles into the area assigned to *Spearfish*, commanded by my friend and classmate Joe Williams, and the fact that our usually reliable radar chose this time to go out of commission gave me much concern when we surfaced. I was sure that Joe was as eager to find targets as we were, and I hoped he would not be trigger-happy that night. Fortunately we surfaced in a driving rain, unable to see even our own bow except during occasional flashes of lightning. We ran speedily back into our own area, while in the dimly lit conning tower Ray Welley took apart our radar and sweated over wiring diagrams that were not always accurate.

Since we'd had no lunch during the depth charging and couldn't have supper until after surfacing, by 2100 we were all ravenous. I liked soup of all kinds, especially onion soup, and for weeks I had been after commissary officer Paul Mann to have our cooks brew up some real onion soup—thick, pungent, heavy with croutons and cheese. The initial efforts produced thin, watery concoctions, which I rejected. Chief Terry had no recipe, just a description of what I wanted, and he persisted. This night, perhaps because of the prolonged simmering under depth charging, he hit it just right, and we had a sturdy brew. It was a night that also deserved the tot of brandy I broke out for all hands.

The next morning at breakfast, after our routine predawn dive, as Mose busied himself in the shining, stainless steel galley, the conversation once more took the old, familiar turn. Chewing vigorously on a piece of fried ham, Red Creighton called out in a hurt tone, "M-i-s-t-e-r Mosley, down in Arkinsaw where I come from no self-respectin' hawg'd let hisself get in this condition. Great balls o' fire! What'd you do to this meat?"

By now fully aware of the comradeship always underlying Red's words, Mose was encouraged to reply, "Guess it got burnt a little. Shucks, it ain't right to cook with ee-lectricity. Sure wish I had my own fryin' pan on a wood fire."

"Well, there's only one way to cook ham, my Aunt Effie alluz sez. You gotta boil it with black-eye peas. That makes good eatin'."

"Aw, what's an Arkinsaw hill-billy know 'bout good eatin'?" chimed in "Doublegut" Marsh, the boat's leading chowhound. "I drove through that country when I was sellin' hardware, and before I could get out I had indignation so bad they had to feed me on Ozark Mountain plasma for a month, intro-venally, too."

"Oh, yeah? That musta been in north Arkinsaw. Down in Saline County we got another way to feed you city slickers."

But the day was a restful one, with peace and quiet throughout the boat. We ran along at periscope depth, keeping a careful watch well off shore. Men were catching up on their sleep, taking sponge baths, enjoying the quiet in well-fed contentment. That afternoon Mr. Mosley, who had shown an unexpected talent for barbering, had a waiting list of customers.

When I learned of his special skill (and inspected a job or two of his) I had him give me a haircut. He came to my cabin to do the job privately. Though he approached the task very diffidently, I was pleased with his work. He never took money for his work, though he could have made a tidy sum on a long patrol. There was ample precedent. Mess boys, particularly Filipinos, often did barbering on the side, charging their shipmates twenty-five cents a head.

On our previous patrol we had no one to call our official barber, but hair had to be cut. In the tropics, in the heat of our confinement below decks, long, shaggy hair was uncomfortable, even dangerous in some work. I had Jim Grady crop my head, and then I clipped him. Fortunately it was a long patrol; by the time we reached port we were fairly presentable.

We now had eight torpedoes remaining, but only seven days in which to use them before we had to start homeward in compliance with our operation order. At this stage of the war Japanese shipping was becoming scarce. By the end of 1943 Japan had lost 675 merchant ships totaling almost 3 million tons.

With our time in the area rapidly running out, and lacking shipping targets, we looked for other ways to inflict damage. We passed submerged close along the northern shore of Kume Shima and reconnoitered for shore targets worth attacking with our 4″ gun. Two warehouses at the head of a pier jutting out from the island seemed suitable. Calling gun pointer O'Brien and gun trainer Jack Perkins to the conning tower, I showed them their targets through the periscope. Meanwhile Mack saw to it that battle surface stations were properly manned, with ammunition broken out from the magazine under the crew's messroom.

We made our battle surface just before dusk. From periscope depth to first shot away took less than sixty seconds. Water still cascaded from the bridge and superstructure when the first of our shells hit home. At a range of 3,000 yards our single 4″/50 caliber gun sent fifty high explosive shells into the wooden structures before we sped away.

However, we were not alone in searching our area for targets. During the night's driving rainstorm our radar picked up two targets some miles apart. To see if they were worthy of torpedo attack we had to close to sight contact. At 3,200 yards we identified the first as an antisubmarine craft too small for a torpedo, so we went after the other. In the black downpour we had to close to 1,300 yards before we could see that she, too, was a small patrol boat. Our bombardment had brought visitors, in this case, small boys trying to do a man's job. But we passed them by. We could not use our guns effectively in the conditions existing.

Two days later we were patrolling submerged off the eastern coast of Okinawa when, in the middle of the afternoon, we sighted a group of eighteen large, motor-driven sampans. Many of them also had sails rigged. They were about 150 feet long, very sturdily built of wood, and displaced perhaps 250 tons. At first this seemed to be only a fleet of fishing vessels, but closer inspection revealed no fishing gear, and their compact formation, led by a larger, trawler-type vessel, was suspicious. We trailed them as they passed just east of the island of Okinoyerabu and headed south.

I knew that at this stage of the war Japan was hurting badly in her overseas shipping capacity. She could not replace the tonnage being lost to the increasingly effective attacks by our submarines. In addition, our carrier air strikes were reaching more and more of her once-secure island bases, sinking many ships caught in harbor. Unlike the secrecy in which our submarine operations were held, announcements were promptly made of successful air attacks. We knew that at Truk alone the February air raids sank fifteen naval vessels, nineteen cargo ships, and five tankers.

Trying to cope with these losses, the Japanese began using their submarines to carry cargo, and now this pitiful convoy of wooden sampans was further evidence of their desperation. The total capacity of all eighteen was not equal to that of even one medium-sized freighter. Nevertheless, it was our job to find and destroy their shipping, and if we couldn't do it with torpedoes we'd have to use our guns.

The formation was drawing ahead of us and soon faded from periscope view, but I was not concerned. Once on the surface we could easily overtake the plodding little ships. Visibility was good and the sea was calm—good conditions for a gun action. Even after sunset there should be enough light for the gun crews to pick out their targets. My plan was to open from the coast until out of its sight, then surface and overtake the convoy shortly after dark. I did not know what armament the sampans mounted, but it could not be heavy. If the escort stayed in the lead we could approach from the rear, and at short range take two of the sampans under fire at a time. We would smother one with our 20 mm. and .50 caliber machine gun fire while our 4″ eliminated the other. We would sink or disable as many as we could before the escort could interfere. From my *Sculpin* experience I knew how hard it was to sink such wooden craft. We might even be able to board one or two to learn what cargo they were transporting and take a prisoner or two.

Shortly before dark we surfaced and took up the pursuit. In two hours we regained contact. There was plenty of time for all gun crews to adjust their vision to the night. Gunner's mate Fry was gun captain of the 4"/50 mounted on deck forward of the bridge, and he had all his men going through a dummy firing run as we closed in for attack. Stone was in charge of the forward 20 mm.; Black had the after; Davis and O'Connell manned the .50 caliber machine guns. When gunnery officer Ray Sterwart reported all in readiness, with ammunition at each gun, we closed in to 1,200 yards and opened fire on the two trailing sampans.

The streams of 20 mm. and .50 caliber tracers carved fiery arcs in the sky and soon got many hits on their target, starting a small fire. The more deliberate fire of the 4" began slamming hits into its target when small caliber return fire hit two of the gun's loaders, quartermaster Ffrench and torpedoman Marchant. The two men made their way painfully below to the crew's mess and chief pharmacist's mate Robert McClain, our in-house doctor. Doc McClain had so impressed me by his work on previous patrols that I had recommended his promotion to the warrant officer grade of Pharmacist. We all hoped the appointment was awaiting our return to port.

The 4" continued firing deliberately. Suddenly her target exploded violently with a huge billow of yellow flame. Metal fragments struck *Halibut*, wounding lookout Joe Marsh in the right hip.

Smoke with a very strong odor of gunpowder hung on the sea and was drawn into the boat by our ventilation system. The violent explosion they heard and the acrid fumes of gunpowder made our men below decks think our gun had exploded or that *Halibut* had been holed by enemy fire. But in my mind there was no doubt that the sampans were hauling munitions to Japan's beleaguered island garrisons.

The sampan fleet was now fully alerted. When a report came from below that Ffrench's wound was serious, I ordered "Cease fire!" and turned away. Going below, I found Doc McClain with a worried frown on his normally carefree face. Willard Ffrench, our young quartermaster, had lost a good deal of blood, and was in considerable pain before a shot of morphine quieted him. His duties in the conning tower and on the bridge brought Ffrench into frequent contact with the O.O.D.s and myself, and we all had a special liking for the soft-spoken, hard-working young man with the ready smile. Two small caliber bullets had hit him just under the left lower ribs. Doc's fear was that they had damaged lungs or liver. The wounds of Marchant and Marsh were superficial.

Our chief petty officers quickly volunteered their bunkroom as a sick bay for Doc and his patients. The CPO bunkroom was located in officers' country on the port side of the forward battery compartment, immediately aft of my own cabin. It contained bunks and lockers for six men, and was the off-duty lounge and rest area for our chiefs. Ffrench was placed as tenderly as possible in the most accessible lower bunk.

I told Mack to set course for Midway; we would leave our area one day early. Our men's lives were more important than the chance of finding worthwhile targets in the next twenty-four hours. When well off shore we sent a message to ComSubPac reporting our situation. I requested that a doctor and suitable medical supplies be placed aboard an outbound sub for rendezvous with us.

In a couple of days we used up all of the blood plasma and saline solution we had. One of Ffrench's lungs had been pierced, but no other vital internal organ was hit. Doc tended him constantly; when he needed rest himself, Mr. Mosley took over. Somewhere in the background of that strange man, a past that he never spoke of, Mose had acquired some experience in caring for sick or wounded. He showed a skill and tenderness that were unexpected and incongruous in so burly and inarticulate a fellow.

My own role was that of medical consultant, based on an expertise quickly acquired through reading all medical publications on board. Doc needed only moral support and encouragement. Before the war brought him into the navy he had worked in the first aid dispensary of a Pennsylvania steel mill as a step toward acquiring a medical education, but never before had he had singlehanded responsibility for men's lives. Stopping in the bunk room one night, I found Doc frantically working with bloody hands to stop a hemorrhage that sent blood spurting from Ffrench's side. I could give no professional help, only encouragement.

Ffrench's condition and progress were closely followed by his shipmates, with medical bulletins published in the *Halibastard Herald*. When Doc permitted brief visits, men would pause in the narrow passageway, pull aside the green drape, and give words of encouragement to the pale, thin figure under the blood-stained sheet. We quickly found that any loud or unusual noise greatly disturbed the wounded man, so we dispensed with the diving alarm and turbo-blowers on our daily trim dives. The weather was excellent, and we made all possible speed eastward, not even zigzagging. Because our low platform and small silhouette were not visible at great distances, high speed was a better safeguard against submarine attack than any zig plan.

Mack outdid himself in the perfection of his navigation; the engineers coaxed maximum efficiency from our Fairbanks-Morse diesels; and all hands did what they could to give Ffrench comfort and assistance. On the sixth day of our high speed, trans-Pacific run, within five minutes of Mack's predicted time of rendezvous, a tiny speck showed dead ahead. It was the new *Perch*, outward bound on her first patrol in a wolf pack with *Peto* and *Picuda*. Our rubber boat was inflated and ready. We quickly brought on board Lieut. (jg) L. E. Ramey, a young doctor newly graduated from the University of Virginia Medical School. Flashing "Thanks. Good luck." to *Perch*, we continued our dash for Midway.

Dr. Ramey's small bag of personal effects and the kit of medical supplies he brought were passed down the hatch after him as he went below on the most unusual "house call" he would ever make. After he had examined Ffrench carefully and quizzed Doc McClain as to treatment given so far, Dr. Ramey gave Ffrench intravenous injections and dressed his wound before moving on to our other two wounded men.

After he came to the bridge to give me a report on our patients, Dr. Ramey remained topside. He had just gotten adjusted to *Perch's* motion, but now, on a different ship moving at higher speed on an opposite course into moderate swells, he had to start all over. We fed him soup and crackers as he huddled on the bridge almost every waking minute of the next seventy-two hours. Doc McClain gave him regular reports of Ffrench's condition and vital signs.

It was no disgrace to get seasick in these boats. *Gar* had recently brought in to Midway eight aviators she had rescued after their strikes on Palau. Although the fly-boys were overjoyed to see her when *Gar* picked them up, they were almost as happy to see the last of her. And this very night, the ComSubPac nightly news reported that *Tang* was bringing in twenty-two downed aviators she had rescued off Truk! By war's end 504 U.S. Navy and Army Air Force flyers would owe their safe return to submarine rescue.

When we arrived at Midway on May 11 senior medical officers examined Ffrench, prescribed treatment, and recommended that we leave him just where he was, since we were proceeding that very day to Pearl. To bring him out of the boat would have meant manhandling him through a watertight door, then passing him vertically up through the torpedo room hatch, a procedure that was certain to be both dangerous and painful.

All in all, this arrival at Midway was an event happier than usual. Not only did we bring our wounded men (and their doctor) safely back, but everyone was in high spirits. This was the first stop of a trans-Pacific voyage that would take us to San Francisco for a major overhaul. The few married men on board looked forward to reunions with their families; the bachelors knew that the navy's favorite liberty port would bring unaccustomed pleasures and delights.

The May sun was brilliant on the lagoon, and the battle flag and pennants the men had made to show our successes fluttered proudly from our raised periscope as we moored alongside *Sperry* once more. After giving the highlights of our patrol to our squadron commander, I returned to my cabin with delicious anticipation. Stacked on my desk was a seven-week accumulation of mail. The first order of business was to arrange the letters in chronological order of postmarks, to be read in sequence. Simply fingering the envelopes, sensing their bulk, eyeing the familiar handwriting of loved ones, wondering what sweet or sad words lay within, prolonged the pleasure.

The ship was eerily quiet; most machinery was stopped; the rhythmic noises of *Halibut* working in a seaway were stilled. Men sat on their bunks or squatted in odd corners reading letters from home. In his bunk just six feet from mine, Ffrench lay dozing, tired from the prodding and ministrations of Midway's top medical talent. As I slit the first envelope I was thinking already of the sweet reunion to come in New London, where Ginny and our girls awaited me.

It was over a year since a young wife and two small children had faded from my sight on a station platform. As I hungrily scanned the latest batch of snapshots, I saw the changes of that year. Joy and Vivien were so much taller, their pudgy arms and legs were longer and leaner, with telltale bandaids on knee or elbow showing how active they now were. Ginny was slimmer, too. The problems of singlehandedly caring for two lively children, a house and yard, while coping with wartime shortages and rationing, were real. There was news of welcome visits by relatives—my father, her brother, my sister—as well as by skippers who were returning from the Pacific to take command of the new boats now coming down the ways so frequently at the Electric Boat Co. shipyard across the river in Groton. They gave what news they had of me when last they saw me in Pearl or Midway. It's what one expected in the close-knit, fiercely loyal, yet unemotional submarine community, but Ginny was beginning to wonder when my turn would come. In her letters were always words of faith in divine protection, words of courage and confidence which inspired and bolstered my own.

We had traveled less than half the vast ocean that lay between Okinawa and California, and there were many days on which our mail would be read and re-read, but as we cast off the mooring lines that afternoon we knew that each turn of our screws was taking us closer to Frisco, to leave, and home. In days ahead we would learn, too, both the glad and the sad news which the mail had brought to ship-mates: one heard of a $29,000 inheritance; one learned of the loss of his mother; another, the death of a brother fighting in Europe; but, cruelest of all, two of our chiefs got letters from their wives, announcing they were leaving for someone else.

Our stay in Pearl would be brief. Once again the medicos examined Ffrench and declared it unsafe to bring him up the hatch. It was best to attend to him in his bunk until arrival at San Francisco, when we would transfer him to Oak Knoll Naval Hospital. Meanwhile, Marchant and Marsh were fully recovered, proud possessors of their Purple Heart medals.

After forty-eight hours in Pearl we were under way once more, heading northeast into brisk trade winds on the final 2,100-mile leg of our trans-Pacific dash. By this time the Japanese Navy was too badly mauled to be a threat in the eastern Pacific. Even their submarines were no longer a major concern. Except for the December 7 raid on Pearl Harbor, when five I-class submarines carried five midget two-man submarines close to Oahu, Japan's subs were never operated imaginatively or aggressively against our fleet or shipping. (All five midgets were lost.) Still, recurring attacks on our boats by our own air and surface forces showed that the danger from mistaken identity was real. To minimize this danger we were routed to be always at least thirty miles south of the shipping lane from California, and we kept strictly to the prescribed fifteen-knot speed of advance.

The weather was good; we were clean and well fed; we were going home. For three months we would sleep in beds that didn't roll or bounce, and there would be no depth charges to count. There was reason for the high spirits and hilarity on board. We had off-loaded our unspent torpedoes at Pearl, and the torpedo rooms seemed cavernous. Routine ship's work was quickly attended to so that the card games, cribbage, and acey-deucey tournaments could resume. Mack and I had our nightly chess match without fear of interruption. I knew I would have to detach him for his own command when we reached port, and I needed to win two games to be sure of a draw. We never played chess for money, but in cribbage Mack was a few dollars up on me.

Alex was in especially good humor. In time I would find out why. He was Jack Hinchey's assistant engineer and electrical officer, and the two men had a running battle of wits, with Jack generally in the lead. He had assigned Alex the keeping of the battery record book. This required daily, cumulative entries. If a mistake was made one day it carried forward and all later entries would be in error.

Early in our patrol Jack saw an error, and told Chief Electrician's Mate Allan Braun, "Alex made a mistake in the record book, but I won't tell him until we reach Frisco. It will take him three days on board to correct."

Chief Braun had taken a liking to the unconventional, good-humored young officer and privately tipped off Alex. Thereupon, Alex hatched a plot of his own. He kept a double set of books—one with the error, and a second, hidden book all corrected.

Sure enough, shortly after we reached San Francisco Jack said, "Alex, I have bad news for you. You made an error in the battery book a couple of months ago and now all entries have to be corrected. Don't go ashore until that's done."

Alex pretended consternation and confusion, protested, pleaded for more time, but Jack was adamant. Grabbing the book, Alex stormed out and pretended to get on with the corrections. Fifteen minutes later he broke out the secret second set of books and presented it to Jack. "Here you are, Jack, all corrected."

This was incredible; Jack couldn't believe it, so he spent hours checking the figures while Alex gloated. It was in such playful mood that we passed under the Golden Gate Bridge on May 24 and threaded our way through the shipping in the busy harbor.

To my great disappointment we had been assigned for overhaul not to one of the naval shipyards at Mare Island or Hunter's Point, but to the private, commercial ship repair basin of the Bethlehem Steel Co. This was a yard with primitive facilities and not much experience in submarine work. Its chief attraction was that, located at Sixteenth Street in south San Francisco, it was not far from the fleshpots and other entertainments which for so many years had lured seaweary sailors to this port.

The first order of business was to get Ffrench safely to the ambulance which waited on the pier to take him to Oak Knoll. He was pale and shrunken, barely able to stand after twenty-one painful days in his bunk. He moved slowly, step by step, to the ladder in the forward torpedo room. The climb would be very trying, but a stretcher was ready for him topside. He gripped the ladder with bony, white-knuckled fingers. Gathering his strength, he climbed, rung by rung, painfully upward to where willing hands of shipmates assisted him out the hatch and onto the stretcher.

Next, Jack and I met with the navy's resident Supervisor of Shipbuilding for the San Francisco area. He was Comdr. F. C. (Kraut) Dettmann, a highly competent engineering specialist whose technical and managerial expertise guarded the navy's interests at Beth Steel. While we reviewed the work lists we had sent on ahead from Pearl, and found out what alterations would be made to upgrade *Halibut*, all hands proceeded to strip ship. A two-story barge moored outboard of *Halibut* would provide living facilities for our personnel as well as stowage space for everything we removed from on board. Like a steady stream of ants our men moved from our hatches across one brow to the barge, then back on another, as they removed the thousand and one items which made our ship habitable and operable.

Meanwhile Mack had laid out a watch bill appropriate to our overhaul status, and specified an orderly leave program for all officers and men. We already had in hand orders for Mack to proceed to Manitowoc, Wisconsin, where he would take command of the newly constructed *Lizardfish*. After trials in Lake Michigan, he would take her down the Mississippi to New Orleans, then on to Panama and the canal, and thence to Pearl Harbor. I hated to lose him, but Mack had fought a hard war, from the loss of S-27 through nine war patrols in *Halibut*, and was eager for his own command. He would have John Dempster as one of his officers. Our former yeoman and battle stations talker was now an ensign.

One of the war's great success stories was Manitowoc Shipbuilding

Company's performance in building submarines. That shipyard on the shore of Lake Michigan was chosen to augment our submarine building capacity, using Electirc Boat Co. plans and procedures. It was not long before the hard work, ingenuity, and craftsmanship of Manitowoc's workers produced submarines that were more sought after than those from any other yard. I was glad that Mack would get so fine a ship, and one that was a "thick skin," or heavy hull boat with an operating depth of 400 feet. Though *Halibut* was a "thin skin," 300-foot boat, and had safely endured much depth charging, I was not among those who believed that the thinner, more flexible hulls were preferable. The theory was that the lighter hulls would dimple or absorb shocks more readily than the stiffer, more brittle hulls, which might fracture. But there *had* been too many times when we had had to exceed our prescribed operating depth.

After three days *Halibut* rode high in the water with gaping holes in her skin where "soft patches" had been removed. Her storage batteries had been taken out, her magazines emptied, her periscopes and guns taken to the shops at Mare Island. Her battered hull, obscenely stripped bare, lay helpless as a shell-torn soldier under a surgeon's knife. She no longer lived. I could do nothing to help her; I was ready to go on leave.

Doc McClain brought word from Oak Knoll that Ffrench wanted to be in a hospital near his home on Long Island, New York. Although not yet out of danger, he was strong enough so that the doctors would permit him to travel across country by air. I was going home to New London, and we quickly arranged that I would take him with me on the same airplane. What a joy it was to deposit him safely in St. Albans Naval Hospital on Long Island! It had been a long, painful journey for him—confined in a submarine bunk for 7,000 miles across the Pacific, then 2,500 more in a plane across the country.

15

Repair and Reunion

When we were plebes at the Naval Academy, not all hazing was physical. There was much taxing of our mental capacity as well in the memorizing of sports results, of historical facts, and of poetry, to be recited at Sunday evening meal in the mess hall. The first classmen at my table were especially fond of *To the Ladies* by Rudyard Kipling, and *The Laws of the Navy* by Rear Admiral Ronald A. Hopwood, R.N. More than once I had been directed to recite one or the other as I sat bolt upright at table, enjoined to keep my "eyes in the boat."

As the morning train from New York City made its slow way through the Connecticut countryside, my eyes were not in the boat. They feasted on the unfolding New England springtime, and I recalled from *The Laws of the Navy*:

When the ship that is tired returneth,
　　With the signs of the sea showing plain,
Men place her in dock for a season,
　　And her speed she reneweth again.
So shall thou, lest, perchance, thou grow weary
　　In the uttermost parts of the sea,
Pray for leave, for the good of the Service,
　　As much and as oft as may be.

I would be home for thirty days; that seemed little enough after thirteen months. Was that too long? So much could happen in thirty days at sea. But I forgave myself. My ship was laid up; she needed rest, too. We would both be better when we sailed again.

The click-click I now heard signaled only the lengths of steel rails passing beneath our wheels, not the explosion of distant depth charges. Stamford, Bridgeport, New Haven came and went, like ships slipping over the horizon. Now the towns were fewer. We passed Niantic, and

I took down from the overhead rack the one bag that carried all I needed. Two small packages held the gifts I had bought for the children in Grand Central Station. Had they outgrown the toy and doll I'd picked? I brought no gift for Ginny. She had enjoined me to hurry home, to forget such nonessentials.

The train whistled its approach to New London. In a little while the river came in sight. A sleek new submarine was heading downstream. Was it sailing off to war, or was it just going out to the sound for trials? But now we were rolling to a halt, and I scanned the platform eagerly, hungry for that first glimpse of my family. Waiting to board the train were ten or a dozen blue-clad, playful young sailors with seabags at their feet. Perhaps they were sub school graduates on their way to join submarines at the shipyard in Portsmouth, New Hampshire.

There they were! At the corner of the ornate, old-fashioned red brick station, out of the stream of passengers coming and going, Ginny and the girls waited anxiously. I hurried to them and clasped Ginny in a long, wordless embrace. When I stooped to kiss Joy and Vivien, their wild hugs knocked my cap to the ground.

On my first morning home I lay half-awake wondering where I was. Why was *Halibut* so still? No sailor had rapped on my bulkhead and said, "Captain, it's five o'clock." Had I forgotten to specify a morning call in my Night Order Book? There was no hum of motors, no creak of springs, no motion to my bunk. I lay naked between cool, clean sheets, alongside someone who slept on with slow, measured breaths.

As sleep drained from my mind and early morning sunlight flooded unfamiliar walls, I remembered. I was home, safe in my family's snug harbor. I did not need to flop heavily on top of my bunk, fully dressed in damp, sweaty clothes. I did not need to bathe out of a messy, slopping wash basin; I could take a shower whenever I pleased. I could feel my wife beside me, take her in my arms. I could play with my children and hear them laugh—not be all day with tired, sweaty men and their heavy humor, no matter how loyal. For many days the war would be out of sight, out of sound, though not always out of mind.

An important, pleasant task of the first few days at home was to deliver messages from husbands to anxious wives, or news of how they fared. With patrols taking up to fifty days, there were long periods between letters sent home. And even if a recent letter was in hand, it was reassuring to a wife to speak with someone who had actually seen and talked with her loved one. How did he look? Was he all right? What did he say?

The first lazy days were followed by busier ones. There was much to be done about the house: binding doors and sticking windows to be freed; dripping faucets to adjust; furniture to repair; storm windows to be replaced with screens; a car to tune and clean; a hedge to trim; a vegetable garden to prepare. How did women alone cope with these things? But even as I went about these tasks I wondered how *Halibut's* repairs were proceeding. A weekly telephone report from Mack or Joe Galligan kept me informed.

Summer comes slowly to New England. The waters of Long Island Sound and Thames River were too cold for bathing, but the rocky shores and sand beaches were collecting the sun's heat. Our house was on Glenwood Avenue, not far from Ocean Beach and Pequot Beach. Depending on the wind, we would choose one or the other. The children loved warm afternoons on the beach where they played at the water's edge or involved me in ambitious sand construction while Ginny sunbathed nearby. Joy was almost six years old, Vivien almost four. Of those years I had been home no more than half the time. This would be a month to treasure, a snapshot of childhood so quickly outgrown.

There was little social activity in New London. The submarine community is one of relatively young people. Most of the navy wives living there were busy with the care of their children, bravely trying to make life as normal as possible for them. Sadly, the cost of our silent, wet war was rising. By June 1, 1944, we had lost thirty-one submarines, and New London was home for a good many of their officers and enlisted men. All of us shared the loss of close friends. There was no mood of frivolity or escapism, only the quiet acceptance of duty to be performed. The special nature of submarine duty, the awareness that ship and crew are a single entity, is implicit in our language. In submarine warfare ships die with their crews; rarely are there survivors. We do not speak of men and submarines separately. When we say *Seawolf, Tang, Albacore* we know we speak of the men who live and fight in them.

The civilian community was sympathetic and supportive. Almost every family had a husband or son in one of the armed forces. When Ginny told our butcher that I was coming home on leave he promised a special cut of beef. And the owner of the combined drug-liquor store saved for us that rarest of wartime commodities, a fifth of scotch.

The days of my leave counted down. The children were now fully at ease with my constant presence. They loved rough-and-tumble play with father. Their parents preferred a more tender tumble, and made plans for Ginny to come to San Francisco for three weeks. To make this possible, my unmarried youngest sister would come from Chicago to New London to care for the children.

Tickets for air travel between New York and Chicago were relatively easy to obtain, but from Chicago to the West Coast and back it would be necessary for Ginny to go by train. With my military priority I was able to fly all the way.

San Francisco was a bustling, crowded city, enjoying the wartime boom in its shipping, commerce, and industry. Men of the army, navy, marines, and coast guard prowled its streets and savored its cosmopolitan nightlife. Its Barbary Coast and Chinatown provided comfort and reassurance to those awaiting transport overseas, and consolation and forgetfulness to those just returned. It was not easy to find reasonably priced accommodations, but in a few days I settled for a tiny kitchenette apartment in the Gaylord Hotel.

By the time I returned to San Francisco, Mack Butler had been detached to take his own thirty-day leave en route to his new command. To replace Mack as exec and navigator, I was lucky that I was able to get another highly competent, war-experienced officer, Lieut. Comdr. Guy F. Gugliotta. When he heard of that, Alex irreverently but rightly exclaimed, "Jeez! Galantin, Gugliotta, Galligan, and Hinchey. That sounds like the Notre Dame backfield."

By coincidence, both Mack and Guy had survived wartime patrols in obsolescent, worn-out pigboats which ran aground in poorly charted, desolate reaches of the Pacific and had to be abandoned. I knew what problems they had faced. My own wartime apprenticeship had been as navigator in such a boat, *S-24*, patrolling out of the Panama Canal Zone.

Guy was from a large family in New Jersey. He had graduated from the Naval Academy in 1938, and after two years' service in surface ships had opted for submarine duty. As for so many of us, sub school offered Guy and his young bride a pleasant prolongation of a honeymoon, although by that time the accelerating buildup of the submarine force had shortened the course from six months to three.

By the end of 1940 dependents were no longer permitted on the Asiatic Station, so when Guy was ordered to the Philippines he had to leave Bobette, his very pretty, dark-eyed bride of six months, in California. In Manila Guy reported to Lieut. James W. (Red) Coe, skipper of S-39. Red was one of our finest submariners, a daring leader whose laid-back, self-deprecating, good-humored style was perfect for the arduous, dangerous pigboat navy. Guy would forever speak of Red with affection and admiration.

In August, 1942, S-39 was on her fifth war patrol, en route to the Solomon Islands from Australia, when she ran hard aground on a submerged reef and had to be abandoned. Her new skipper was my Naval Academy and sub school classmate Francis E. Brown. All hands survived the disaster and were picked up by the Australian corvette *Katoomba*. Frank then took command of S-44, but was lost with his ship in the Kuriles in a gun battle with a Japanese destroyer.

By 1944 Guy had his own command, S-28, at Pearl Harbor. Her job was to train enlisted personnel and to act as target for our ASW forces. Two weeks after Guy turned over command of his ship, she sank from unknown cause while operating south of Oahu. There were no survivors.

With these tragic experiences behind him Guy came to *Halibut*, happy to be reunited with Bobette for the remaining few weeks of our overhaul, and pleased to be at last in an up-to-date fleet boat. It was a good time for Guy to learn all about his new ship, but his first sight of her was not reassuring. "Do you think she can ever be put back together, captain?" he asked with a smile in his always soft-spoken, low-key style.

It was a good question. There is nothing more seemingly disorganized or dirtier than a submarine undergoing major overhaul. Could we remove the grime, the oil, the dirt and dust which now fouled our once immaculate ship? Could all those pipes and components lying helter-skelter in shops and on the pier ever be fitted together again? Would the scattered and disordered pumps and motors once again become the intricate, finely tuned mechanism we had lived and fought in? There were large openings in the pressure hull, either from the removal of soft patches or from holes deliberately cut to facilitate removal of machinery. We wondered if *Halibut*'s reworked skin would ever again be the tough shield it had been during so many depth chargings.

With combat performance and their own safety so dependent on their ship, submariners paid more attention to the details of construction and material condition of their ship than did other sailors in general. A boat was not simply turned over to a repair facility for overhaul or refit. It was traditional that submariners be their own inspectors of material, following closely the progress and quality of work in shop and on board. When we sailed in her again, when we dived *Halibut* once more, we would know her more intimately than before. And if she was to satisfy us in capability, we must be able to satisfy her in our own performance.

Our days were filled with examination and study of every installation in *Halibut*, critical review and test of every component. The combined efforts of shipyard workmen and ship's company were bringing her slowly (too slowly, I thought) back to fighting trim. But there was more involved than emphasis on material condition. The other parts of the combat equation were our own knowledge, skill, and state of training. To remove the rust of many weeks on the beach, and to learn the capabilities of the new equipments we were receiving, there were regular visits to Mare Island and Hunters Point. At those navy yards, toward opposite ends of the great bay, the navy had installed training aids and simulators for submarines, as well as schools for instruction in many practical aspects of seagoing. Our new shipmates would have some familiarity with our equipment by the time we took our ship on sea trials.

It was a time for training in more ways than one. In Alex's quick progression from Annapolis to New London to submarine war patrol off Okinawa, he had not had time to learn the ways of wily, hard-bitten chief petty officers. Chief Electrician's Mate Braun sensed this. An officer's signature was required on chits to draw alcohol from the navy yard supply department. Braun presented Alex his requisitions for one gallon of grain alcohol "to clean generator brushes."

Alex signed a weekly requisition for grain alcohol until, after six weeks, the supply officer called him in. "Son, I see all these requisitions for grain alcohol. Do you have any idea how many generator brushes can be cleaned with one gallon of grain alcohol?"

"No, sir, I don't know the exact number."

"Well, one gallon will clean all of the brushes for all SubPac boats for one year."

Alex stopped signing the chits, but he told me years later that he never lost his admiration for Chief Braun and all he meant to our boat.

Rest and recreation—R & R—was not yet the organized, scheduled fringe benefit it was to become in later years. Much still depended on the initiative, ingenuity, and primal urge of the individual. These qualities were not lacking in submarine sailors. My *Halibut* men were not satisfied with the plentiful but generalized and expensive pleasures offered in San Francisco. They developed a more personalized outlet. The Bethlehem Steel ship repair basin was not many blocks from the heart of the city. There, on Powell Street, was Lefty O'Doul's Bar and Grill. Lefty was a colorful baseball figure. He had been an outfielder of more than passing fame in the major leagues, then manager of the San Francisco Seals in the minors. Now he presided over the pub which bore his name.

By common consent Lefty's bar had become the unofficial home port, the snug harbor for *Halibut* enlisted men in their off-duty hours, and the convivial rendezvous with friendly landlubbers of the area. Lefty himself was always good for a loan. Any *Halibut* sailor needing a little cash to tide him over to payday had only to deposit his IOU in the box kept on the bar. So routine a fixture did *Halibut* sailors become in Lefty's that on busy evenings it was not unusual to find O'Bie O'Brien, our likeable little quartermaster, tending bar.

It was here, also, that we acquired our mascot "Skeeter," the little patchwork dog of confused ancestry who would endure future depth chargings with us. Edie, the big-hearted, buxom hostess who kept the boys happy and laughing, gave him to us.

Skeeter liked beer. He would lap it up from a dish while he sat at the bar on a stool alongside his newfound shipmates. As he waited patiently for his ration one evening, he was the innocent cause of a small brawl. A civilian habitué of the place eased up to the bar and ordered his usual. Seeing that the regular barkeep was about to serve the newcomer, O'Bie spoke up. "Now wait a minute! Skeeter was here first." With a little affirmative action, the rights of seadog minorities were upheld and order restored.

The affection and attachment between sailors and Skeeter were so obvious that I permitted signing him on as a crew member complete with service record. The only black mark his record acquired came when he instinctively lifted his leg alongside one of our CPOs. When he was presented at Captain's Mast for this offense, his counsel, torpedoman Jack Perkins, offered in extenuation that when Chief Terry slipped going down the engine room ladder he had barked his shin, thereby leading Skeeter to believe he had a wooden leg. I did not consider that a suitable excuse.

Our officers were motivated by the same forces which moved our men. I returned from my leave to find that our wardroom officers had established themselves on high ground of their own. Their more sophisticated tastes and greater means led them to Sutter Street, where their favorite nightly rendezvous was "The Forbidden City," a nightclub which featured oriental dancers. The star was a dainty Chinese girl, Mai Tai Sing, who added the exotic lure of the East to the less subtle movements of the western fan dance. In time, the regular table of *Halibut* habitués became a routine stop for the young ladies of the company.

One evening the high-water mark in acquiring the ancient lore of the orient was reached over bottles of California's best champagne, which our young bachelors thought a suitable exchange for their submarine pay. (By this time in the war, the extra pay for the hazards of submarine duty had been raised from 25 percent to 50 percent of base pay, equaling that allotted to aviators.) In the midst of lively banter with one of the pretty Asiatic girls, the question suddenly popped forth. Motioning back and forth with his palm down, one of our boys asked the smiling, dark-eyed dancer, "Tell us, Mai Sing, is it true that things are different in China, that oriental girls are not like western girls?"

"Oh, that! You mean our pussy is different?"

"Yes. Horizontal like."

After a pause, "Well, it all depends on how you look at it."

Armed with such Confucian wisdom, our young men returned to their duties relaxed and at ease. Our ship was scrutinized horizontally and vertically; our training proceeded on course; officers and men prepared themselves for our deployment.

The inevitable personnel changes had been made. Guy had taken over as exec and navigator from Mack Butler, and our fifth officer, Lieut. (jg) Mann, had been detached for duty elsewhere. To fill our normal complement of seven officers I obtained big, smiling naval reserve Ensign William N. Kidwell. Bill was a native of San Francisco but had grown up in nearby San Jose. He was a 1943 graduate of San Jose State University and had aspired to be an architect. However, since he was enlisted in the navy's V-7 program for reserve officers (just as Ray Stewart had been at the University of Florida), the navy had first call on his services. He was sent to the Midshipman Training School at the Chicago campus of Northwestern University. The impression that Bill's forthright, manly character and six-foot, three-inch stature made on the officers in charge resulted in his designation as Battalion Commander of the 3,500 young men in his class.

Bill had never seen a submarine, and had no fixed ideas as to what duty he'd prefer. Just at this time Lieut. Comdr. Slade Cutter came to Northwestern. During his brief respite from war patrols he was one of the outstanding young submariners that the navy sent on motivational and recruiting tours. So impressive was Slade's appearance and record, so inspiring his character and leadership, that over 400 midshipmen volunteered for submarine duty. Bill was one of the seven selected for sub school. From school he was sent to Mare Island to await assignment to a sub, and it was from there that I got him.

We assigned Bill as Assistant Torpedo and Gunnery Officer, Assistant First Lieutenant, Commissary and Recreation Officer. He quickly showed his eagerness to learn and accepted with good grace the mundane tasks that come to a boat's most junior officer. Alex was grateful to be relieved of his position as "George," and the two became close friends. Their fertile minds made regular contributions to the *Halibastard Herald*. The two young men could always see humor in the foibles of the human race and express it, Alex with Irish wit and eloquence, Bill with his talent as a cartoonist.

Bill quickly shouldered his responsibilities as Recreation Officer. Our other four bachelor officers were pleased to take advantage of his knowledge of local entertainments and diversions. It was he who led the way to The Forbidden City, the nightclub where he had played in the orchestra during his college years. Under his friendly, sophisticated guidance Jim Conant achieved a new maturity, one more in keeping with the twenty-one years he had just attained. To this point girls had played no part in Jim's life. Now he was so entranced by a pretty Chinese girl of the chorus line that, on sailing for our next patrol, he presented her with his hard-earned "dolphins," the submarine qualification pin.

Bill also showed his business acumen. Through private, somewhat irregular channels in San Jose he obtained a refurbished ten-cent slot machine. This was installed on the support barge assigned to *Halibut*

24. Double exposure, taken through periscope, of sinking *Eihuku Maru* following attack by *Halibut*, off Bungo Suido.
25. The 9,500-ton *Heiyo Maru* is shown on fire, through periscope of U.S.S. *Whale*, February, 1943.—*U.S. Navy*

24

25

26

27

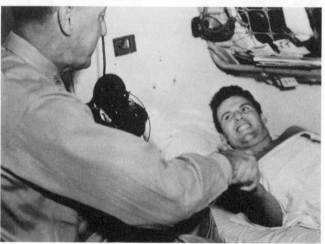

28

29

30

26. Stern of Japanese ship going under following torpedo attack, photographed through periscope.—*U.S. Navy*

27. "Deerslayer" Mack Butler, Phee Fitzgerald, and Jack Hinchey on Molokai.

28. Willard Ffrench, on board *Halibut* at Pearl Harbor, receives the Purple Heart Medal from Vice Admiral C. A. Lockwood, Jr. Because of his wounds, Ffrench was not removed from the submarine until he reached San Francisco.

29. Admiral Lockwood presents Purple Heart medals to Joe Marsh and Lee Marchant.

30. Spray breaks across the prow of *Halibut,* en route to Japanese waters.

31. The *Halibut's* mascot, Skeeter, on watch topside.

31

32

33

34

35

32. Japanese lifeboat, adrift at sea.

33. *Halibut* returning to Pearl Harbor on May 15, 1944, after her ninth, and next-to-last, war patrol. —*U.S. Navy*

34. Ship's party, San Francisco, August, 1944. Seated, left to right: Bobette Gugliotta, Ginny Galantin, Emma Cunningham. Standing: Galantin, Lt. E. S. Cunningham, LCdr. Guy Gugliotta.

35. *Halibut* "plank-owners," the men of her original commissioning crew still on board after the final war patrol. Left to right: Bob Chalfant, Clayton Rantz, John Perkins, Jack Allison, Dave Roberson.

36

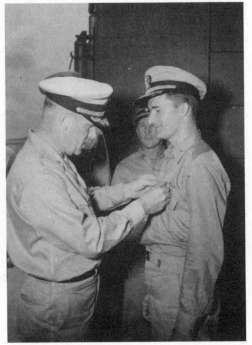

37

38

39

36. The crew of the U.S. Fleet Submarine *Halibut,* upon return to Pearl Harbor after the final combat patrol, December, 1944. Standing amidships, left to right: Lt. Hinchey, LCdr. Gugliotta, Comdr. Galantin. CPOs and officers, from left: seated on rail, CPhM Griffen; crouching, CCS Terry, CRM Lawrence, Lt. (jg) Stewart, CTM Soulis, Ens. Alexander, CMoMM Schwieso, Lt. Galligan, Ens. Kidwell, CMoMM Chalfant, CMoMM Roberson; seated on rail, CEM Braun; standing behind Chalfant, CETM Welley. Not pictured: Lt. (jg) Conant, CQM O'Brien, CEM Whittaker.—*U.S. Navy*

37. Galantin receiving Navy Cross from Capt. Willis A. Lent, July 10, 1945.

38. Submarine skippers engaged in roundtable strategic conference at Lido Club, Panama, Sept. 29, 1945, en route to East Coast. From left, clockwise: Benny Bass, unidentified, Vince Schumacher, Bill Kinsella, Frank Lynch, Herm Kossler, Galantin, Bill Winter, Droop Hawk.

39. Postwar award ceremony, Submarine Base, New London, when *Halibut* was awarded the Navy Unit Commendation. Left to right: Rear Admiral John Wilkes, Galantin, David Roberson.

40. Admiral I. J. Galantin,
June 15, 1967.—*U.S. Navy*
41. Visiting the U.S.S.
Nathan Hale, Navy Yard,
Charleston, S.C., 1977.

40

41

and moored alongside. Its lure was irresistible to the civilian yard workmen. In one month they enriched our recreation fund by $1,700. With a fine appreciation of the importance of preventive maintenance, Bill had sent two of our crew to "slot machine school" in Oakland. They learned how to service our ancient machine and how to ensure that no major jackpots were paid.

We put the slot machine profits to good use. The farewell party we gave as our San Francisco days drew near their end was the finest all-hands ship's party I'd ever attended. Cost was no problem, so we went first class. We rented the auditorium on the top floor of the Mart Building, and Bill engaged a portion of the Warfield Theater's stage show, including dancers and musicians. Our invitation list was comprehensive; it included parents, wives, other relatives, girlfriends, key shipyard workmen, and others to whom we were indebted. We had only two wardroom wives, and both Ginny and Bobette were on hand. Not to be outdone, our bachelors, officers and enlisted, brought their own attractive ladies. Though I looked carefully all around, as a sub skipper should, I did not sight any of the girls from the Forbidden City.

The party was also the occasion for unfurling our new battle flag. Again Bill Kidwell had exploited his local knowledge to our advantage. He persuaded two girl students in the Art Department of San Jose State to design and fabricate a flag which would display *Halibut*'s record. The handsome, deep sea-blue silk flag showed many small fish in silver, representing the ships we had sunk or damaged, about to be swallowed by a large, fierce fish that, incidentally, looked nothing like a halibut.

The girls and the flag came to our party and were the highlight of the evening. The flag now hangs in the Submarine Force Library and Museum at Groton, Connecticut.

When the busy, final days of overhaul and test were upon us, Ginny was once again on her transcontinental train trip, and I moved back to my room aboard ship. It was there that the submarine career of Ensign Kidwell, so auspiciously launched, came very close to foundering. He had become acquainted with a very attractive young lady, the daughter of a navy captain then at sea in command of an aircraft carrier. Bill had invited his girlfriend and her mother to dinner. In the course of the evening they expressed admiration for the men who fought beneath the sea. Carried away by his pride in his service, he invited them to "come see my boat" then and there.

When they arrived at the Beth Steel repair basin, Bill escorted the two ladies across the brow and was greeted by the deck watch, seaman 1c Richard Schoenlaub. "Good evening, Mr. Kidwell." Schoenlaub was surprised by the unexpected nighttime visitors, but was not about to impede the progress of an imposing, self-assured ensign.

"I'm taking my guests below for a quick tour. We'll be going back ashore in a few minutes," said Bill.

By this time our boat was tolerably neat and clean, and the proud young officer led the ladies on their exciting tour. As they passed my room I heard the female voices and Bill's explanation of the officers' living quarters. The heavy, green drape was drawn across the entrance to my sacrosanct stateroom, and I sat out of sight at my desk, wearing only underwear and sandals.

When Bill assisted his guests in their awkward passage through the door to the forward torpedo room, he found torpedoman 2c Bertheau stripped to the waist, tattoos showing from shoulders to wrists, and torpedoman 3c Tudor Davis doing some work on the tubes. Eager to assist the new young officer who had not yet mastered the intricacies of torpedo firing, Bertheau volunteered, "Mr. Kidwell, do you want me to fire an inboard slug?"

Without really knowing what was involved, Bill impressed his ladies with a confident, nonchalant, "Yes. Carry on."

An inboard slug was an exciting exercise at any time; in the night-time stillness of the boat, it was a spectacular event.

Bertheau charged one of the impulse air tanks, had Davis open a breech door, manipulated various valves, said, "Standby! Fire!" and tripped the firing valve.

The resounding blast of air from the open torpedo tube into the torpedo room had hardly abated when there appeared at the door from the forward battery compartment an astonished sub skipper dressed only in underwear and sandals. I was intent only on appre-hending the idiot who seemed bent on wrecking the boat.

Ensign Kidwell quickly recovered from his momentarily stunned surprise. "Captain, may I introduce Mrs. Johnson and her daughter, Louise?"

"How do you do? Mr. Kidwell, I'll see you in my cabin at nine in the morning. Good night."

Years later Bill confided that my coolness under the fire of such unexpected events, and in such informal costume, convinced him I would be safe to go with on war patrol.

I was greatly concerned by the poor performance of the shipyard. Jack Hinchey and Joe Galligan were finding more and more delay and inefficiency in the repair and reinstallation of components for their departments. We found material in our reduction gear casings that looked suspiciously like sabotage. The main electric power control cubicle was being shock mounted, and the insulation of some of its wiring was strangely damaged. Welding was often improper; numerous flaws had to be chipped out and reworked. Pumps were not meeting their test requirements. An overhaul that should have taken no more than 90 days was clearly going to run over 100. When I turned to Kraut Dettmann for help he put all the pressure he could on management, but to little avail. The company's ship superintendent seemed powerless to get cooperation from the foremen of the various trade unions.

It was the last straw when Ray Stewart reported that we had almost sealed a workman in our forward fresh water tank. Fortunately he had looked inside before the manhole cover was bolted in place. A yard workman was in the tank, sleeping blissfully amid fumes of alcohol.

My frustration and bitterness overflowed in a letter I wrote home: "It has been one discouragement and disappointment after another. In peacetime we used to gripe about overpaid civilian workmen and their workmanship, but those days were bliss compared to these. The power, the selfishness, the indifference, the lack of patriotism the unions now show is nauseating. It is disheartening to see what contemptible selfishness we are fighting to preserve. If the same slow, inefficient labor prevails throughout the country as here, think how many days the war is being prolonged, how many lives are being thrown away."

As our days in the yard counted down there was impatience and eagerness to be done with shop visits, with pressure tests, with measurements and inspections. There was only desire to trade the noise, confusion, and dirt which had overflowed *Halibut* for the quiet, orderly, clean life of the sea.

Within the limitations of our original design we received what modernization and improvement were feasible. In an already jam-packed hull, space was as critical as weight. Inevitably, new equipments meant further encroachment on the space available for those who must live and fight in the submarine. Nevertheless we eagerly sought any alterations or additions that meant greater offensive capability, better sonar, quieter or more reliable operation.

The major improvements *Halibut* received were lengthening of the conning tower to accommodate an automatic plotting table; shockmounting the main electric power control cubicle; installing a more powerful, quieter trim pump; adding another passive sound set; and installing a 40 mm. rapid-fire gun in place of a 20 mm.

Admiral Lockwood allowed considerable leeway in the gun armament skippers chose, and the gun change was in partial response to what I had written after our last patrol:

> At its very best, use of submarine guns against shore targets is of little effect and not much more than an irritant to the enemy so that this use should have little weight in considering the size of submarine armament. Furthermore, a single 3″ or 4″ gun has such a slow rate of fire and, with our platform and means of fire control, such a low HPGPM (Hits Per Gun Per Minute) when used against shipping that it overexposes the submarine to counterfire. Since these small guns cannot get hits below the waterline, but rely chiefly on setting internal fires and riddling the hull and superstructure, it is open to question whether the fire of a quadruple 40 mm. would not be more effective.

I didn't get the four barrels I wanted, but the single barrel 40 mm. was a big improvement over the 20 mm. gun it replaced.

Twenty-three of our seventy-three enlisted men were new to our ship and new to submarine duty as well. In spite of this turnover we were as well off in experienced submarine personnel as most boats at this stage of the war. Before we returned to action in the far Pacific we would have the 2,100-mile trip to Pearl and subsequent lengthy voyages to Midway, Saipan, and beyond in which to restore and refine our operating skills.

The first, fumbling return to operation came in postoverhaul tests in San Francisco Bay, initially on the surface, then in careful slow dives in the shallow water of the bay. Everyone's spirits rose; we were once again a team, and *Halibut* responded to our orders.

At last we were ready for a deep dive test. We proceeded out the Golden Gate to the submarine operating area. Would the shipyard work we were so critical of pass this test? Four Beth Steel workmen were with us, not as the "surety deposit" Chief Braun called them, but to take readings and assist in expected minor adjustments.

The order "Rig for dive" sounded through the boat as we passed under the bridge and our bow lifted to the slow swells rolling in from sea. It was raw and cold topside in the briny, foggy air, but I stayed on the bridge so that O.O.D. Joe Galligan would not have to concern himself about keeping me informed. There was always traffic moving in or out of port: freighters, warships, fishing boats, even sailboats. Each had to conform to the Rules of the Road, but always there was risk, the chance that a signal would be misunderstood or a course correction misinterpreted. Submarines operated so little in the company of other ships that it was reassuring for young officers of the deck to have the skipper on hand. Even the General Prudential Rule, that "common sense" rule which every midshipman memorized early in his plebe year, left little leeway for action. In the years since, how often had I rehearsed it in my mind? How did it go? "In obeying and construing these rules due regard shall be had for all dangers of navigation or collision and for any special circumstance which may make a departure from these rules necessary in order to avoid immediate danger." Or words to that effect.

When was danger "immediate"? Was it like a depth charge sinking slowly toward you, or like a torpedo speeding your way? To avoid immediate danger out *there*, the best rule was: "Don't get detected."

Guy had prepared our diving message, leaving only the time of dive to be filled in when it was transmitted by radio to the base. We gave three hours as the duration of dive. That should be enough to go slowly to 300 feet and back, checking machinery and fittings as we went. If we did not send our "surface" message within thirty minutes after our three hours were up, it would trigger "Event 1,000," the search for an overdue submarine and rescue of its people.

At the sound of the diving alarm Chalfant, who had recently been promoted to chief petty officer and operated the hydraulic manifold, closed the main engine air induction valve and the hull ventilation valves. Rantz and Schwieso shut down their engines and secured their hull valves. When his panel of indicator lights—the "Christmas tree"—showed only green, Chalfant reported, "Green board."

Jack watched intently the needle on the barometer mounted above the diving station. He tapped the glass face lightly, making sure that the blast of high-pressure air being released into the boat was indeed raising the pressure.

When he reported, "Green board. Pressure in the boat," it was safe to dive.

"All ahead two thirds. Go to sixty feet."

Chalfant pulled the levers which opened the main ballast tank vent valves. We could hear the air rushing from the tanks.

Jack leaned over Noonan and Austin, watching their use of bow and stern planes. When he had a fine trim at slow speed, we went down in 50-foot increments. At each level we paused long enough for each compartment to inspect carefully for leaks or distortions. In the control room Yeoman Burgess logged the reports they sent over their sound-powered telephones. When I was satisfied that there was no serious problem, we went down to the next level. Our fathometer chirped cheerily as we descended, finding a bottom that varied from 400 to 500 feet.

At 150 feet the packing gland of No. 1 periscope leaked badly. We tightened it to slow the leak, but that bound the scope to the point that we could not use it. Other stuffing glands and flanges leaked as we went deeper, but they were all manageable. The hull compression measured at the battens rigged in key locations was within tolerance. The new Gould trim pump and all important auxiliaries worked properly at all depths. At maximum depth we exercised the bow and stern planes from hard rise to hard dive, and worked the rudder to its full limits in both power and hand operation. All in all, it was a very satisfactory deep dive test.

We returned happily to port, confident that the next time we passed beneath the Golden Gate Bridge we would be heading for Pearl Harbor and a return to action.

When on another gray, chilly day we did sail out the great bay, we passed the Farallon Islands abeam and took departure for Hawaii. As *Halibut* rose and fell to the ground swells, neophyte sailors ate little and hurried for their bunks. On our last patrol Ensign Alexander had difficulty adjusting to the constant motion of his new home. Now, seasoned veteran that he was, he helpfully assured anyone interested that if only catsup sandwiches were consumed during the first three days at sea, seasickness would be avoided. He failed to explain to those like Kidwell, who did not normally become seasick, that the sight of catsup sandwiches could provoke the malady.

Good news awaited me when we reached Pearl on September 20. I was in the group being promoted to commander. That meant a pay increase of $94 a month. This sign of confidence in their "Old Man" reassured my crew, and they presented me with the cap symbolic of the new rank, a cap whose visor glittered with its "scrambled eggs" of gold thread.

The mood in headquarters at Pearl was almost euphoric. The summer had seen great gains in the Allied military position, and massive new operations were getting under way. The Japanese were being progressively driven back toward their home islands. General MacArthur's forces had advanced to the western tip of New Guinea and had seized the island of Morotai. Their next jump would be the return to the Philippines—the invasion of the island of Leyte. Meanwhile Admiral Nimitz's forces had taken Saipan, Tinian, and Guam in bloody fighting. The two advancing forces, from the southwest Pacific and the central Pacific, were now in position to support each other directly in a final push to Japan. From its air bases in the Marianas, the United States was now able to bomb Tokyo heavily. The government of General Tojo, which had started the war against the United States, resigned.

In this situation, with fewer and fewer ship targets, our submarines were chiefly deployed in wolf packs. This would give wider, more efficient search of assigned areas, and would also provide greater concentration of torpedo fire against the naval ships which were now the more likely targets. Our few days of underway training off Oahu concentrated on group tactics, and we were once more ready for the long run westward.

16

The Battleship that Wasn't

H *alibut, Haddock,* and *Tuna* formed the wolf pack called "Roach's Raiders." Comdr. John P. Roach, in command of *Haddock,* was our task group commander, and Comdr. Edward F. Steffanides, Jr., was skipper of *Tuna.* I was happy to be with Beetle Roach again. He was an aggressive, determined leader, with a warm, engaging personality. We were completely at ease with each other, with a feeling for how each would react in given situations. I had not seen Beetle since our midnight rubber boat rides the winter before, when we were teamed with *Tullibee* in that very disappointing patrol near the Caroline Islands. Now *Tullibee* was gone, declared "overdue and presumed lost." After the war her sole survivor, gunner's mate C. M. Kuykendall, was rescued from a Japanese prison camp and we learned what had happened. In March, 1944, *Tullibee* made a night surface attack on a convoy north of Palau. She fired two torpedoes. One failed to settle on its course and made a circular run. Her own torpedo struck *Tullibee* and tore her apart with a terrific explosion.

"Steve" Steffanides was an interesting person. He was from Milwaukee, Wisconsin, and had graduated from the Naval Academy one year ahead of Beetle, two years ahead of me. He had excelled in two rugged sports, football and crew. Now, thirteen years after his athletic days, he was still slim, tall, blond, and handsome. He had resigned from the navy shortly after graduation to enter the business world, but returned to active duty in time to go to sub school and get wartime action. This would be his first patrol in command. *Tuna* was one of the earlier fleet boats, commissioned before the war, and had an operating depth of only 250 feet. Her record to date under her three previous skippers was mediocre. Steve was determined to improve it.

For this patrol our torpedo load was different. For the first time *Halibut* carried the new, electric-propulsion fish. The navy's Bureau of Ordnance had half-heartedly pursued the development of an electric torpedo since World War I, but it was not until electric torpedoes used so successfully by German U-boats in World War II fell into U.S. hands that a vigorous development program was mounted.

In 1942 the Westinghouse Electric & Manufacturing Co. was given the task of producing a reliable electric torpedo, and by 1943 a few of the Mark XVIII torpedoes were issued to our boats. Once the "bugs" in the early production models were rectified, the new fish became increasingly popular with submarine skippers. The early, optional use of electric torpedoes, and the mixed loads of steam and electric fish, gave way to enthusiastic adoption of the electric model.

The chief advantage of an electric torpedo is that it is wakeless; there is no telltale stream of bubbles or trail of turbine exhaust smoke to alert the target and point back to the location of the submarine. In the frequently calm, clear waters of the South Pacific this was a price-less asset during daylight attacks. Neither did the Mark XVIII have the depth-keeping and exploder problems which had plagued the steam torpedoes for so long.

Nevertheless, there were disadvantages as well. Most serious was the slow speed produced by the limited capacity of the compact storage batteries. When first introduced, the Mark XVIII could make only twenty-eight knots (versus forty-five for the Mark XIV steam torpedo), and even that would be reduced by stowage in cold temperature torpedo tubes or running in very cold water. This slow speed, some 900 yards per minute, made accurate determination of target course, speed, and range all the more important. Furthermore, the electrics needed frequent, at least weekly, withdrawal from the tubes for re-charging, and their maintenance procedures were onerous. On bal-ance, however, the tactical advantages outweighed the drawbacks. Chief Torpedoman Jim Soulis and his torpedoman's mates soon learned the tricks of pampering the silent, strange, new shipmates who now shared their space.

We sailed from Pearl on October 8, this time bypassing Midway and taking the 3,650-mile great circle course for Saipan. Possession of that more advanced base meant we no longer had to "top off" at Midway. The ten-day passage in good weather was used for intra-pack communications training and practice approaches, using each other as targets. Our daily "school of the boat" continued for our new men. We had a happy ship and one eager to get back into action.

The forward torpedo room, which I occasionally looked in on, was a lively place. Mounted between the torpedo tubes was our trusty slot machine. A can of dimes hung below it, its supply of free coins waxing or waning as men off watch amused themselves with the "one-armed bandit."

Bill Kidwell had brought his violin to sea, and on some nights the men who lived in the forward room would be entertained by his popular tunes. His "Nocturne for Six Bow Tubes" was not well received, not even by Skeeter, a regular attendee who would sit quietly in Perkins's lap.

No other submarine went to war with a six-foot-three ensign playing the violin, a ten-cent slot machine, and a dog qualified in submarines.

By this time the Pacific Ocean east of the Mariana Islands was virtually an American lake, freed of the Imperial Japanese Navy. However, there was excitement as our pack approached Saipan's harbor of Tanapag. In the lead, *Haddock* suddenly made a radical zig to the south and commenced blinking her signal lamp furiously. This meant that either a torpedo or a periscope had been sighted. *Halibut*, too, zigged widely and increased to full speed. Simultaneously, Radio relayed the urgent message from our sister ship, "Sighted scope. Evade."

Perhaps the location of our "Safety Lane" approach to Saipan had been compromised. At any rate, a Japanese sub was in the vicinity looking for targets. All three of us successfully evaded her and reached port safely only an hour behind schedule.

Saipan, one of the Mariana Island chain only 1,400 miles from Tokyo, had been taken by U.S. forces in the bloody assault of June, 1944. By the time Roach's Raiders arrived on October 19, the harbor had been transformed into a bustling replenishment site for our submarines with the tenders *Holland* and *Fulton* on station. The island itself was fast becoming a massive airdrome from which B-29s would roar off to bomb Japan.

As Japan's defensive perimeter progressively crumbled and contracted, the loss of the Marianas made the collapse of the homeland inevitable. Admiral King called Saipan "the decisive battle of the war." Not only did Saipan and its sister islands provide an excellent base for our air and surface forces, it greatly increased the efficiency of our submarine campaign. The advance bases we now had at both Saipan and Guam meant we had a much shorter run to our patrol areas after topping off with fuel and provisions. We could run at high speed on the surface with less concern for fuel expenditure, and were much closer to repairs and replenishment.

As we entered Tanapag Harbor and I stood silently on the bridge watching Joe Galligan conn *Halibut* alongside *Holland*, I mused on the last time we had been to Saipan. In January the island was a key stronghold for Japan, and as we tried to penetrate the anchorage to attack *Unyo*, we had nearly met disaster. Now, nine months later, as we moored alongside pioneer submarine designer John Holland's namesake, we were greeted by a U.S. Navy band and the warm welcome of old friends.

Ashore we found the chaos of frenzied construction on the site of utter destruction. The awesome firepower of battleships and dive bombers had left only piles of rubble. One structure alone deserved to be called a building; its reinforced concrete shell at the harbor landing now served as the U.S. Navy Port Director's headquarters.

The waterfront was never still. Ships were unloading; hundreds of trucks roared dustily by; new roads were being bulldozed; foundations were being poured; steam shovels and cranes groaned and screeched; huge piles of lumber grew as we watched. Everywhere dirty, sweaty soldiers and Seabees were at work with what seemed an equal number of indigenous laborers. Nightfall brought little change; powerful floodlights drowned the shadows until the hot sunlight poured once more over the eastern hills.

A hundred feet or so above sea level, on the hill overlooking the harbor, a Quonset hut posed as the Naval Base Officers Club. Sipping warm beer or raw bourbon and water were our resident warriors of all services, as well as a few of the eighty-six nurses attached to the army hospital located a short distance upland. We soon heard of a particular resentment borne by the army and shore-side navy. The enticements that the officers of the submarine tenders could offer the weary, sunburned nurses—a hot shower, clean towels, good food, a gallon of pea green paint to pretty-up drab quarters—were considered unfair in the continuing competition for female companionship.

Toward the southern end of the island, the occupation authorities had established a stockade to confine the native population who were not employed on construction projects. On a flat, dusty, scantily wooded area, 18,000 men, women, and children passed their days, trying to maintain family life while they stoically awaited their fate under the wanton aggressors and murderers they considered our forces to be.

Lieutenant Berry, USNR, was civil affairs administrator. With his permission, Beetle, Steve, and I toured the encampment, under escort by an anemic little U.S. Navy officer interpreter. Japanese made up the majority of the inmates, but the Chamorros (native to the Marianas) and Koreans also had their own fenced-in sections. Each racial group appointed a number of their members as police to maintain order and to patrol its perimeter. But provision for physical and material security was matched by concern for spiritual comfort. Each group had salvaged some sacred objects from their church or temple, and these were now installed in little, open-air chapels or shrines. Here on a sunbaked tropic island, the prayers and supplications of devoutly Catholic Chamorro, disciplined Shinto Japanese, and patient Buddhist Korean surmounted barbed wire to satisfy a common need.

Commerce and industry continued. Along one street of the Japanese sector extended a building subdivided into blacksmith, carpenter, machine, paint, and other shops. There was even a sewing establishment, where women sat on lauhala mats turning out gowns equally as colorful and revealing as Schiaparelli's but much more reasonably priced. At the officially operated central store, essential materials could be purchased at cost. In addition to having their sen redeemed by the United States at twenty to the dollar, the internees could work for the American construction forces and earn fifteen, eighteen, or twenty dollars a month, depending on their particular skill.

From our escort we learned that, by-and-large, the Japanese still believed they would win the war, and that they would be liberated by the Emperor's avenging forces. More than one oldster plainly hissed at us as we proceeded politely but curiously through the camp. As an experiment in enlightenment, copies of the Japanese language *Hawaii Times*, printed in Honolulu, were posted for anyone to read.

Great quantities of Japanese army supplies had been captured, so food was plentiful. Most was prepared in community kitchens, but, outside their corrugated iron and board huts, some of the more individualistic or fastidious families had their own smoky wood fire over which a pot or two bubbled.

No scrap of salvable, usable material was wasted, and, considering the crowded conditions, the entire area was tolerably neat. The inhabitants, including the children, were clean. The several communal baths—here just circular, concrete pads some thirty feet in diameter with overhead showers—were regularly filled with the lean, nude, muscular bodies of all ages and both sexes.

The sight of families working together, clinging to their values and customs even in prison camp, brought memories of home and children ten thousand miles away. Most poignant were those evoked by the black-eyed, black-haired, little girls who skipped rope just the way my own did, played their versions of hopscotch and jacks, and grinned just as infectiously.

Even more moving was the scene at the orphanage, a spick-and-span, wood-floored building about twenty-five feet square where some thirty children from two to eight years old lived under the supervision of girls themselves only ten or twelve years of age. We arrived just at suppertime. Sitting cross-legged on the mats spread along the four walls, each child was busy with his chopsticks and bowl of rice, fish, and vegetables. The silence was incongruous; there was none of the happy chatter we were accustomed to hearing from children at mealtime. Was this because of shyness before the fair-skinned, blue-eyed giants watching them, or brooding remembrance of the horror and suffering they had seen or endured? But childlike trust and curiosity overcame shyness and fear. As I stood before the windowlike opening of the building, my head came to the same level as that of some small boys within. Attracted by the gold braid on my cap, my collar marks, and the gold submarine pin on my shirt, they pointed to them, traced them with their fingers, and made little, low-voiced comments to each other.

By now weary from our long, dusty walk in the hot sun on unaccustomed terra firma, we gratefully climbed into our borrowed jeep for the ride back to the harbor. There was little conversation. Even Beetle, the likeable, loquacious Texan, was strangely silent as he drove Steve and me through the wreckage of Garapan to the boat landing in Tanapag harbor. Each of us was preoccupied with his own reflections on the day's events: nearly waylaid by an enemy sub; the welcome of old friends; the escapism of American men and women in the war zone; the suffering and tragedy of innocent women and children caught in the blind brutality of war.

Because of the long passage from Pearl, it took forty-eight hours to complete the lengthened list of voyage repairs and the replenishment of our three ships. On October 21 we were ready for sea once more.

While we three skippers were in the Task Group operations center in *Holland* receiving intelligence and operations briefings, our execs readied our ships to get under way. The crews were mustered and sailing lists made final. For *Halibut* the stop in Saipan had brought the return of an old shipmate. When we had entered overhaul in San Francisco in May we had to transfer Ray Welley to another boat. Now, after making a patrol in *Tambor*, he was in the relief crew aboard *Holland* awaiting our arrival. I was delighted to welcome back newly promoted Chief Electronics Technician Mate Welley. Soon the maneuvering watches were stationed; phones and engine order telegraphs were tested; all gear was secured for sea; mooring lines were singled-up; last minute letters were passed to *Holland's* post office.

At 1400 we cast off our last line, backed clear of *Holland*, turned our bow for the channel, and headed out to sea once more. A small patrol gunboat escorted us until dark. It was to be a fateful patrol for *Halibut*, her tenth and last.

Refreshed by our two days in port, we sailed in high spirits for our assigned station in the strait between Formosa and Luzon. We were eager to take part in the actions then in progress and impending. The war in the Pacific was going well for the United States. Everywhere our forces were advancing, bypassing some islands, leaving their Japanese garrisons to wither for lack of logistic support. As part of that strategy, on October 20 the massive U.S. invasion of the island of Leyte in the Philippines had been launched. At our intelligence briefing we had been alerted to the fact that the Leyte landings would trigger major fleet engagements, and that we might be diverted to a new position.

Our surface passage across the Philippine Sea was routine, enlivened only by the sight of much more wreckage than we'd ever found before. The ocean was strewn with flotsam of every sort: oil drums, lifeboats, life belts, kegs, bales, boxes, wrecked sampans, whole sections of ship's woodwork. Miles beneath us, the black floor of the sea must have been littered with the bones of men and ships.

As we proceeded warily at fifteen knots, we listened almost continuously to news broadcasts of the progress of the invasion and of the naval actions it had provoked. On the morning of October 25 our three ships reached the patrol stations that Beetle Roach had assigned. Four hours later, in response to radio information he received from

ComSubPac, he ordered us to new positions. We were now sure that the longed-for chance to pick off Japanese ships retreating from Leyte Gulf was near.

All hands were alert, eager for the action that must surely come, and we pushed *Halibut* at full speed over the almost flat calm sea. Topside our lookouts swept the horizon for planes, for masts of ships, for puffs of telltale smoke, and searched the nearer surface for a periscope or dreaded torpedo tracks. But it was from below decks that we had our first warning of targets. Within the steel drum of Halibut's hull we began to hear the blurred but unmistakable thud of distant explosions, the sound carried for miles through the seawater. Whether this was from aircraft bombs or submarine torpedoes we could not tell.

Late that afternoon we reached our new station and headed due south toward the tip of the island of Luzon. Our boats were spaced thirty miles apart on an east-west line, *Halibut* to the east, *Haddock* in the center, and *Tuna* to the west. Shrewdly deducing that the explosions we were hearing were bombs being dropped by our carrier planes, Jim Conant, our communications officer, had instructed Chief Radioman Kelsie Lawrence to search through the voice channels on our VHF (Very High Frequency) radio receiver. Sure enough, Lawrence soon heard the cryptic jargon and excitement-charged voices of our dive bomber pilots. Quickly Jim called me to the radio shack, that lightly partitioned section in the port, after corner of the control room.

Under the date of "25 October 1944," *Halibut*'s official war patrol report reads:

> About 1700 commenced hearing conversations of our dive bomber pilots who were in contact with enemy forces apparently close by. Hoped to get sufficient information to enable us to close. The flight or squadron leader could be clearly heard describing the contact as a Jap battleship with two cruisers near her, and said that another group of enemy ships was in sight to the westward. The calls of two of the planes in this flight were "BRONCO 99" and "REBEL 13." While the air group commander gave the plan of attack and retirement, considered trying to break in by VHF to get their position, when one impatient and

eager birdman said, "Let's get going and get this over with." The answer was, "I will make my attack in one minute," and soon thereafter a plane could be heard going into a power dive, followed by the word, "There goes your bomb." At this moment the commanding officer was called to the bridge by smoke in sight, but other personnel enjoyed the unique and thrilling experience of listening-in on a dive bombing attack on Jap forces that we would soon engage ourselves.

1725 A puff of brown smoke was now in sight bearing 150° T. Commenced closing at full speed and at

1732 Sent smoke sighted report to HADDOCK and TUNA. A huge splash appeared at the smoke, verifying "Bombs away" reports coming in on VHF. One pilot reported, "Yippee, I got a battleship." Soon heard the order, "All right. Let the battleship alone. Line up on the cruiser."

Now sighted a heavy AA barrage over the smoke, and could hear the concussions of distant rapid gunfire. The high level barrage showed as many black bursts with two purple ones, while the lower level was of white bursts. Three small planes were seen retiring to the westward. At least one of our planes was damaged in the attack, as one pilot was heard to report his tail was hit. Other planes said they would escort him home. More smoke was seen to the southwestward.

1739 Sent position and repeated contact report to HADDOCK and TUNA. TUNA had receipted immediately for both reports, but did not know whether HADDOCK had received them.

1742 SHIPCON #2. TORPEDO ATTACK No. 1. Sighted top of ship dead ahead. Through the periscope, identified this target as a battleship's pagoda. The radar range was about 31,000 yards, when the target became visible from the bridge deck level (horizon distance 10,600 yards) and a considerable portion of the pagoda could be clearly seen with binoculars. The top looked massive, just as the pictures of Jap BBs indicate, and particularly noticeable was a heavy cross arm, from this top, probably a rangefinder. Started sending out an amplifying report, but with the range closing fast, to avoid detection, at

1743 Dived for approach. The decision to dive at this time was made because of a previous experience this vessel had with a Jap battleship. On that occasion, radar tracking resulted in detection of the HALIBUT by its SJ radar interference, or by a possible radar pip, and the target evaded successfully.

Tracking showed that we were 13,000 yards to starboard of the track, but by using much speed managed to keep ahead of the target. No smoke or damage was evident on the target, but its speed of fifteen knots, by turn count, indicated probable damage from the air attack. As the range closed, detected two other smaller ships, bearing about 60 and 300 relative from the large ship believed to be a battleship, distant about 3,000 yards. While the light was still good, only the large ship's pagoda could be seen, making positive identification difficult. It was getting dark quickly, and by the time the target presented a fairly large angle on the bow at a moderate range, the visibility was poor (sunset 1814). The commanding officer was struck by the height and straightness of the pagoda structure. The escorting ships were seen dimly and briefly. The one to the battleship's starboard was apparently a light cruiser of the YUBARI class, while the one to port was a destroyer. During the approach, the destroyer began to smoke heavily. At

1842 Gained attack position about 5,000 yards ahead of target, 400 yards off his track to port. The smaller ships would pass well clear on either side. Anticipated firing 6 bow tubes on a small track, then swinging right for stern shots, when the starboard screen was seen to signal by yardarm blinker. The target then made its first substantial zig, changing course to the right. This gave us a chance for a much better track, but increased the torpedo run greatly, and it was necessary to fire almost at once, as the target would soon be going away. As the periscope was up almost continuously in the rapidly failing light, it is possible that it was detected by radar, the sea being practically flat.

The large last minute zig away gave the best opportunity for identification of this target. The light was poor, and own ship was being swung while introducing final attack data, but it can be definitely stated that this ship was not one of the heavy cruisers of which pictures are available in ONI 41-42, its pagoda being too straight, too high, and only one straight stack was seen, fairly close to the foremast. As this ship zigged, opening more of its length to view, no mainmast was seen, but the commanding officer laid this to the failing light which would make a stick mast difficult to see, and concentrated on getting accurate angles and bearings. From the above visual evidence the decision was made that this target was probably the YAMASHIRO. But in view of not seeing a mainmast, the ISE was also a possibility. The possibility also exists that this was the IBUKI for which little identification data is available other than ONI 222-J's statement that it may be either a CA or CB.

1843:36 Started firing forward tubes; small gyro angles, about 95 port track, 3,400 yard generated torpedo run, 6 torpedoes spread for 100% coverage, depth set 20'. The importance of keeping the poppets open a full 5 seconds had been so well stressed in training that the torpedomen not only swallowed the bubble but a bit of the ocean for good measure and we became heavy forward. With the last look, the destroyer was seen with a zero angle bearing 70 relative. Unable to see, at

1845:30 Went deep. It is believed I erred in not firing the stern tubes on sound as we went deep. Although the bow set-up was excellent the four stern shots, even on an unfavorable track, could well have been fired in view of the importance of the target. Destroyer passed close astern. Tracked torpedoes to target.

1847:50 First torpedo explosion.

48:08 Second torpedo explosion.

:53 Third torpedo explosion.

49:30 Fourth torpedo explosion.

50:10 Fifth torpedo explosion.

1850:37 Moderate explosion.

50:44 Moderate explosion.

51:44 Very loud triple explosion followed by prolonged heavy reverberations. Did not hear any explosions that were definitely depth charges.

1853 Heard many explosions of lighter intensity and sounds
–1925 similar to ship breaking up. Headed for source of noise, while coming to periscope depth. Only two sets of screws were audible all this time, and these alternately stopped and started, speeded up and slowed, moving back and forth in a manner indicating picking up survivors.

1945 At periscope depth; nothing visible.

1950 Surfaced. Sighted distant blinker lights ahead in direction of enemy's track. Sighted large target on last sound bearing of target noises. Commanding Officer and lookout described this as a very large mound, no superstructure visible, strongly resembling the hull of a large, capsizing ship. Maneuvered to close target with small silhouette.

1951 Radar contact on this object, range 12,300 yards, strong pip with broad base, unlike any seen before.

1952 Men below decks reported explosion.

1954 Target faded from radar screen and simultaneously disappeared from view. Visibility very good in light of bright half moon. Set course 030° T at full speed to close ship that had been signalling. Many gunfire flashes could be seen over the horizon to southward, but thought it better to try to overtake the late battleship's escorts (whose speed at time of attack was only 13 knots) than to get mixed up in an all-out naval battle. We were ahead of the main enemy force, in direction of their probable retirement, and if own contact failed to materialize could always drop back on the other enemy units. As we pursued to the north, star shells or flares over the horizon lighted up the scene of the engagement to the south. Passed through strong odors of gunpowder (magazine explosion!?).

2200 Received TUNA contact report. With very indefinite data of own to go on, and no prospects of regaining contact, decided to try for TUNA's contact. Headed to intercept at full speed.

2252 SHIPCON #3. Radar contact bearing 306° T, range 32,000 yards. Commenced tracking.

2255 Sent contact report to HADDOCK and TUNA. Soon sighted two very large ships, probably battleships, then one smaller, but radar indicated total of 5 ships, 2 large, 3 smaller. Continued tracking and found that though initial enemy course was 200° T, they kept working around to left (east) until base course of zero, speed 19 was reached. By successive zigs away to keep us astern, they succeeded in pulling slowly away.

2345 Sent amplifying contact report.

2400 Sent same contact to JALLAO, PINTADO, ATULE.

26 October 1944.

0030 Sent amplifying report.

0108 Lost contact, last range 32,000 yards. Targets on course 000, speed 20.

0130 Sent poor contact report to subs patrolling to north.

0245 Sent HALIBUT Serial 1 to COMSUBPAC reporting newest contact and last night's attack.

Continued chase all night and until reaching Latitude 23°—00' N., Longitude 126°—30' E.

Morale in the boat was sky-high; our sailors were exuberant. Our patrol was hardly started, but it was already successful. After months on the beach, out of action, our first attack had sunk an important enemy warship. We were convinced we had fulfilled every submariner's dream, what no U.S. submarine had ever accomplished—the sinking of a battleship. All evidence we had pointed that way. We lacked a survivor to confirm our kill, but we had hit a ship with five torpedoes of six fired, and had seen a capsized hull sink.

As we steamed warily on the surface to rejoin our packmates, we found the ocean littered with hundreds of empty ammunition boxes and every sort of flotsam. The cedar, tin-lined box we picked up in hopes that it would yield a clue as to our victim had lettered on it in Japanese, "25 mm. machine gun ordinary ammunition container, Quantity 40, Japanese Steel Works, Hiroshima Mfg. Co."

We could not foresee the bitter disillusionment that awaited our return to port and ultimate, postwar analysis. Instead, we celebrated that night by breaking out the beer. By this stage of the war it was permissible for subs to sail with a ration of two bottles of beer per man, to be issued when the skipper desired. How good it tasted after sweaty, hot days and nights of action. How reminiscently and lovingly each man fondled the smooth, chilled bottle, prolonged its drinking, then reluctantly tossed it into the messroom GI can. Smashed by the mess cooks, the amber glass fragments made excellent ballast for the sacks of garbage heaved overboard, weighing them down for the long, dark journey to the bottom of the sea.

Our log was full of data that supported our belief that our victim was a battleship. Our point of aim was the largest of three dissimilar warships. Assuming an average speed of twenty-eight knots for our electric torpedoes, the torpedo run generated by our data computer checked with the timing of warhead explosions. The fish were set to run at a depth of twenty feet. They would underrun the lesser ships, and their contact exploders would not detonate. Furthermore, the accepted figure of depth variation for the Mark XVIII at such deep setting was zero. The visual sighting and strong radar return of the capsized hull also indicated a ship of substantial size.

We did not reach Pearl Harbor and turn in our patrol report until December 1. Shortly thereafter I received a note with Admiral Lockwood's private comments. It was by this means that the admiral liked to give skippers his personal reaction, praiseworthy or critical, to their war patrols. In this case he wrote as follows:

Excellently planned attack on what you report as a BB[1] on 25 Oct. Believe this was a CA and that you got him. Jap Northern Force contained only two BB's and these, which you also saw, were seen later by other subs.

Excellent report on suspected new Jap A/S device. Will give this much study.

Fine handling of your depth charge damage. I am very proud of your valor and determination which saved your ship.

C.A.L., Jr.

There is no doubt, as Naval Intelligence knew by the time we returned to port, that the two battleships in the Japanese Northern Force survived the battle off Cape Engaño. *Ise* and *Hyuga* returned to port almost unscathed. The light cruiser *Oyodo*, which had become Admiral Ozawa's flagship after the carrier *Zuikaku* was put out of action, also returned safely, as did the light cruiser *Isuzu*. They would be sunk months later by U.S. Navy air attacks. What, then, did we sink in the Battle off Cape Engaño?

This is what I finally pieced together as the story of our "battleship." The ship we had sighted and identified as either *Yamashiro* or *Ise* was actually the latter, a hermaphrodite battleship-carrier. Following their defeat at Midway in 1942, and in an attempt to replace their severe carrier losses as quickly as possible, the Japanese had converted the old battleships *Ise* and *Hyuga* to aircraft carriers of sorts. They had removed the mainmasts and after gun turrets of these 30,000-ton ships and installed small hangars and launching decks with a capacity of twenty-two aircraft each. Improper planning and coordination prevented these ships from receiving their complement of planes, and they never operated aircraft. Instead, for the climactic battle for Leyte Gulf, they were deployed with the main body of Japan's First Mobile Fleet, commanded by Admiral Ozawa, to give surface and air protection to the fleet's four aircraft carriers. This force, consisting of the four carriers, two converted battleships, three light cruisers, and eight destroyers, sortied from the Bungo Suido on the afternoon of October 20, and headed south on its hopeless mission. The task of this patchwork fleet was to decoy and lure American task forces to the north, away from the landing operation they were supporting, and thus permit

---

1. BB is a navy abbreviation for "battleship," while CA stands for "heavy cruiser."

the central and southern Japanese fleets, approaching from the west and south, to pounce on the vulnerable transports, landing craft, and auxiliary ships committed to the landing in Leyte Gulf. Even though he deliberately made lengthy radio transmissions and launched his own air strike of some eighty planes against the U.S. fleet, Admiral Ozawa despaired of attracting the attention of Admiral Halsey's Third Fleet. However, late on the afternoon of October 24 a lone, U.S. carrier-based search plane was sighted. Its radioed report of the discovery of enemy carriers was intercepted by Ozawa's force, giving renewed hope for the success of the decoy operation.

It was at this juncture that Admiral Halsey made perhaps the most controversial command decision of the Pacific war—to take his fleet of fast battleships and carriers northward, away from Leyte, to locate and destroy the relatively harmless Northern Force of almost empty carriers and emasculated battleships. The next morning his search planes reestablished contact, and soon this Japanese fleet was under intense air attack.

After U.S. carrier planes had sunk or crippled the four carriers, *Ise* and *Hyuga* became the principal targets of our naval aviators as they pressed home dive-bombing and aerial torpedo attacks. It was the day's last air attack on *Ise* on which we had eavesdropped on the evening of the twenty-fifth, as she was retiring toward Japan in company with the light cruiser *Oyodo* and a destroyer.

Since the "fog of war" encountered through a submarine periscope at dusk must approach that which envelops airmen diving through intense ack-ack, I am most sympathetic when reading the reported results of that day's air attacks on *Ise* and *Hyuga*:

A careful tabulation of hits scored on the two heavy ships during all the strikes of the day, which attempted to eliminate duplication of claims, arrived at the figure of twenty-two direct hits on one battleship, fifteen on the other. Ten of these were torpedo hits. Near misses were not counted. The conclusion reached by one air group commander would be familiar to anyone who followed the naval air war: "Japanese warships," he said, "can absorb an incredible amount of punishment before sinking."

From the best Japanese sources available after the war it is learned that only one direct hit was made on the HYUGA and none on her sister ship. Near misses damaged the blisters of the

ISE, but no direct hits were made on her. Captain Toshikazu Ohmae, Chief of Staff to Admiral Ozawa, inspected both ships after their return from the battle and reported "very slight" damage which "did not hamper navigation." "I was witnessing the bombing," said Ohmae. "I thought that the bombing of the afternoon wasn't so efficient."[2]

In all fairness, I must say that Captain Ohmae could have made the same remark about many submarine torpedo attacks.

Although we did not know it at the time, the enemy forces *Halibut* sighted and tracked at 2255 that night were the same two battleships, *Ise* and *Hyuga*, and their screening ships, the cruiser *Oyodo*, and the destroyers *Shimotsuki* and *Wakatsuki*. We had visual contact on the large ships, but our radar had also detected the two destroyers.

Departing from his role as decoy, Admiral Ozawa had boldly turned back to the southward in an attempt to find and make a night attack on the U.S. ships which had been pursuing his force. Our wolf pack had detected his ships, but they evaded us. However, the U.S. submarine *Jallao*, part of a wolf pack to northward of our own, did waylay and sink the light cruiser *Tama*, which was limping homeward alone after being damaged by carrier aircraft that morning.

According to the Joint Army-Navy Assessment Committee (JANAC), the official agency charged with assessing enemy naval and merchant shipping losses, the following ships of Admiral Ozawa's original seventeen-ship Northern Force were sunk on October 25:[3]

carrier *Zuikaku*—sunk by aircraft
light carrier *Zuiho*—sunk by aircraft
light carrier *Chiyoda*—sunk by aircraft
light carrier *Chitose*—sunk by aircraft and surface craft
light cruiser *Tama*—sunk by aircraft and submarine
destroyer *Akitsuki*—sunk by submarine (probable agent)
destroyer *Hatsuzuki*—sunk by surface craft (probable agent)

Clearly, we had missed *Ise* with our torpedo salvo. Neither had we hit the light cruiser *Oyodo*, who was steaming on *Ise*'s starboard hand, for she also reached port unharmed. The large zig to the right by *Ise*

2. From Woodward, C. Vann. *The Battle for Leyte Gulf* (New York: The MacMillan Co., 1947) p. 156.
3. Total losses by the Japanese in the four days of battle for Leyte Gulf were twenty-six combatant ships compared to six American; 305,000 tons versus 36,000.

and her screening ships just before we fired probably brought the destroyer across the track of our torpedoes streaking for the battleship. Fish running at twenty feet depth would not normally hit a destroyer, but the ship could have been drawing more water from prior damage or other cause. Thus, by process of elimination and some cross-check with Japanese data, our own and ComSubPac's estimates were disallowed; our victim was said to be *Akitsuki*.[4]

But doubt would persist. JANAC was not infallible. Its postwar report contained demonstrable errors, though it had done its best in interviewing survivors, collating records, and reviewing official reports. The melee of a battle in which our own aircraft and submarines, as well as surface ships, were engaged, could easily result in confusing, sometimes conflicting, claims. To complicate matters further, submarines could not generally turn in their reports until weeks after an engagement, when judgments may already have been made or opinions hardened.

An error seems to have been made in this case. The official, postwar compilation of Japanese Navy loss prepared by Japanese officers from Japanese data credits the sinking of *Akitsuki* to carrier air attack, not to submarine. The same record lists *Hatsuzuki* as "disappeared" on the same day, place and cause unknown. This tabulation of a ship's sudden disappearance from unknown cause is consistent with our attack and later sighting of a capsized hull.

---

4. Only one Japanese battleship was sunk by a submarine in World War II: *Kongo*, sunk by *Sealion* on November 21, 1944.

17

Luzon Strait

Returning to the patrol station in Luzon Strait that had been our original assignment, our wolf pack resumed its antishipping patrol. We operated in loose coordination. Keeping apprised of each other's general location, *Haddock*, *Halibut*, and *Tuna* had considerable freedom of movement and action.

Luzon Strait is the deep body of water between the Philippine Island of Luzon and the southern tip of Formosa (now Taiwan). It connects the waters of the South China Sea and the Philippine Sea. The 200 or so miles between the two large land masses has two main passages, Bashi Channel and Balintang Channel, leading through the Batan and Babuyan Islands. These generally low-lying, rocky islands were of constant concern because of the unpredictable currents, tide rips, and overfalls in their vicinity. We had to be especially careful in our navigation, and Guy took advantage of every chance the cloudy skies yielded for a "fix." Our surface search radar was now balky and erratic in spite of almost constant ministrations by our radar technicians Ray Welley and Richard Burns.

Keeping a good trim on the boat was very difficult. The variable currents averaged three knots, and the swells were of such scope that *Halibut* seemed at times to heave under us. To keep from broaching, Jack Hinchey, as fine a diving officer as I've ever seen, trimmed the boat heavy with a 3° down angle. It was also of some help to run our electric freshwater distillers while we were submerged; the water we made helped keep us heavy. The nature of the ocean here—currents, temperature, salinity—was such that below sixty-five feet we'd be exceptionally heavy, above sixty exceptionally light. The men on the bow and stern planes had a tough job controlling our depth and angle. Frequently they would have to shift their planes rapidly from 20° dive to 20° rise in order to keep reasonably close to the ordered depth. Two hours made an exhausting watch for diving officer and planesmen. At times, for no apparent reason, *Halibut* would start up, gathering momentum that could be halted only by going "all ahead full" and flooding negative tank.

U.S. submarines were now operating more and more boldly in an ever-tightening ring around Japan. Air patrols, never a major factor in Japan's ASW campaign, were becoming less and less of a threat to our boats operating on the surface. The heavy Japanese losses of aircraft and pilots and the great shortage of fuel due to tanker sinkings reduced the efficiency of the Japanese air effort. Taking all into account, when close to enemy air bases, I preferred not to use our omnidirectional air search (SD) radar. Its unreliability was amply proven, and it could be a homing beacon for enemy planes. Although the threat from the skies was diminished, inevitably our lookouts, some of them new, inexperienced in the suddenness with which a lovely, blue Pacific sky could become the source of hideous fury, would be taken by surprise.

Early on the morning of October 28, as we cruised on the surface in Balintang Channel, I was on the bridge helping keep a careful, uneasy lookout. It was a bright, sunny day, with only occasional fluffy white clouds. Jack Hinchey had just relieved the morning watch, and I was discussing with him the problem that on this patrol our Fairbanks-Morse main engines were smoking, something they never did before their recent overhaul. The brown, low-lying exhaust they left streaming in our wake considerably increased the hazard of surface running. But even as we talked, our eyes were never idle; all hands knew that whenever on the bridge their eyes must be kept moving, scanning surface and horizon. Fortunately, I was following my own preaching.

Just at eight o'clock I spotted a twin-engine Mitsubishi bomber about five miles off heading directly for us. Shouting, "Dive! Dive! Take her down fast!", there followed the longest sixty seconds of my life.

The periscope was already up, being manned by an additional lookout. Taking it over as soon as I leaped into the conning tower following Jack and our three lookouts, I watched the fast approaching plane.

We kept our course; to turn at this juncture would impede our dive, slow our rate of descent when it was imperative that we get underwater fast.

Would *Halibut* ever get under? The seconds seemed like minutes. I saw the bomber adjust its lead angle toward us as the pilot detected our act of diving. A small, black dot separated from the plane and came toward us. There was nothing we could do but "Rig for depth charge!" Calmly as I could I said, "Here comes the bomb."

As the trajectory arched toward us I felt only curiosity, a fascination with the three-dimensional geometry, the relativity in time of submarine, plane, and bomb. There was no time for fear; everything was happening too fast. Just as the fully extended periscope went under, its lens cleaving the ocean with a quick burst of spray, the bomb exploded, less than a hundred yards from our starboard bow, shaking the ship but causing no damage. It was less than a minute since I had sighted the plane and my shout had caused signalman 3c Gene Jarzencska, on watch in the conning tower, to sound the diving alarm.

As our lookouts tumbled through the hatch and down the ladder to the control room, one of them fell in a heap. As Jesse Griffen picked himself up from the deck he stammered to no one in particular, "It was a t-t-t-two en-en-engine b-b-bomber."

That was the caption on Bill Kidwell's cartoon which appeared in that night's edition of the *Halibastard Herald*. It accompanied an effective editorial on the duties and responsibilities of lookouts, which asked, "Why should the skipper be the first to detect the plane?"

Sobered by this experience, we prowled cautiously among the island passages and probed the anchorages which enemy ships might use as hideouts. By the battles for Leyte Gulf the Japanese Navy was virtually eliminated as an effective fighting force for any major action. Nevertheless, this was a costly time for U.S. subs. In this very period we suffered our highest rate of loss—eight boats in six weeks. With our great successes to date, perhaps their skippers were overconfident, taking too many chances, or perhaps their deployment, now much closer to Japanese bases, permitted more concentrated ASW search and attack by the enemy.

Although the most dramatic sinkings by our subs were yet to come (in this very month Eli Reich would sink the battleship *Kongo* with *Sealion II*, and Joe Enright would sink the huge carrier *Shinano* with *Archerfish*), by November, 1944, we had passed the highwater mark of submarine activity. It had become an aviator's, not a submariner's, war. The growing number of new carriers, protected by fast battleships, and able to operate from more forward bases, now harried the remnants of a once-dominant navy from port to port and struck repeatedly at the Japanese homeland.

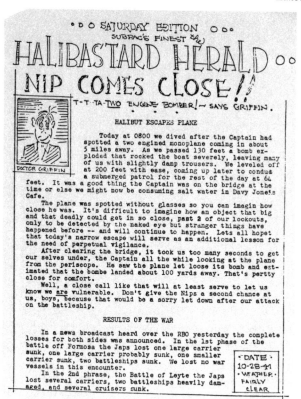

° □ ○ SATURDAY EDITION ○ ○ °
SUBPAC'S FINEST &

HALIBASTARD HERALD ° °

NIP COMES CLOSE!

T-T-TA-TWO ENGINE BOMBER! ~ SAYS GRIFFIN.

DOCTOR GRIFFIN

HALIBUT ESCAPES PLANE

Today at 0800 we dived after the Captain had spotted a two engined monoplane coming in about 5 miles away. As we passed 130 feet a bomb exploded that rocked the boat severely, leaving many of us with slightly damp trousers. We leveled off at 200 feet with ease, coming up later to conduct a submerged patrol for the rest of the day at 64 feet. It was a good thing the Captain was on the bridge at the time or else we might now be consuming salt water in Davy Jone's Cafe.

The plane was spotted without glasses so you can imagin how close he was. It's difficult to imagine how an object that big and that deadly could get in so close, past 2 of our lookouts, only to be detected by the naked eye but stranger things have happened before -- and will continue to happen. Lets all hope that today's narrow escape will serve as an additional lesson for the need of perpetual vigilance.

After clearing the bridge, it took us too many seconds to get our selves under, the Captain all the while looking at the plane from the periscope. He saw the plane let loose its bomb and estimated that the bombe landed about 100 yards away. That's pertty close for comfort.

Well, a close call like that will at least serve to let us know we _are_ vulnerable. Don't give the Nips a second chance at us, boys, because that would be a sorry let down after our attack on the battleship.

RESULTS OF THE WAR

In a news broadcast heard over the RBO yesterday the complete losses for both sides was announced. In the 1st phase of the battle off Formosa the Japs lost one large carrier sunk, one large carrier probably sunk, one smaller carrier sunk, two battleships sunk. We lost no war vessels in this encounter.

In the 2nd phrase, the Battle of Leyte the Japs lost several carriers, two battleships heavily damaged, and several cruisers sunk.

· DATE ·
10-28-44
· WEATHER ·
FAIRLY
CLEAR

The Japanese merchant marine had been devastated. By this time she had lost 1,504 ships totaling 6,225,781 tons, the great majority to submarine attack. The scores of ships damaged and immobilized for varying periods added to the certain strangulation of Japan's war-fighting power. Shipping still moved in a desperate effort to keep up essential imports and to support the forces still holding out in the shrunken overseas empire, but it was hard to find.

We ran surfaced when we could, submerged when we had to, and for three days we wallowed in heavy seas. Low, black clouds, heavy rains, wind-driven spray made visibility poor both day and night. Even in the normally still depths at 100 feet *Halibut* rolled 10°, gently but firmly attesting to the great force of the typhoon nearby. At periscope depth we had to take a course which put the seas abeam in order to avoid broaching; no other heading permitted depth control. Whenever we came to the surface we took great amounts of water down the conning tower hatch. Frequently soaked to the skin, irritable from the constant buffeting and pounding we were taking, we anxiously watched wind and barometer and moved as best we could to keep clear of the storm's path. Submerged patrol in these conditions was very inefficient, but so near to Jap air bases it was too risky to stay long on the surface under such cloud cover. The mountainous seas would prevent any fast dive. Our extended periscope was alternately fully exposed or totally submerged as huge swells rode over us. Only chance could bring us a ship contact, but it did. Late one afternoon a large ship was suddenly upon us. Calling all hands to "Battle stations, torpedo," we turned to close her track. She was not "zigging," and soon I could see why. She was a properly marked hospital ship proceeding toward the Philippines. Dejectedly, we let *Hikawa Maru* pass.

It was a dreary, fruitless time, endless hours and days of the kind that drive sailors to life ashore. Even our bunks gave little rest; it took effort to keep from being tossed out as our ship pitched, pounded, or slid down the mountainous slopes of sea. Sleepless nights were followed by painful days of bumps and bruises. The foul air and violent motion brought seasickness to many who mistakenly thought that our 7,500 mile journey from San Francisco had conditioned them to the worst the sea could bring.

The submarine war had become very complicated. Instead of large, open ocean areas free for each boat to roam in, the increasing use of coordinated attack groups in a combat zone contracting around Japan required great care. This was true in working with our own packmates, as well as being a concern lest we become entangled with boats in adjacent areas, all of us pressing to exploit any contact. Still, it was comforting to have friends close by. When our surface search, SJ radar failed and we did not have the critical spare part on board, a radio plea quickly brought Beetle's reply: *Haddock* had the spare part and would give it to us.

Making rendezvous at 0400 of a pitch black night, we could not see our sister ship. But with her own radar working well, *Haddock* coached us in by voice radio until we could make her out. After I conned *Halibut* close alongside on a parallel course, Beetle and I conferred by megaphone while we received our needed spare via messenger line and sent *Haddock* a repair part in return.

A few days later we would again find help close by when needed, for on November 14 the war almost ended for *Halibut*.

18

Hell Below

During the night of November 13 we observed an unusual amount of Japanese air activity, enough to force us down for a brief period. Clearly the area was being swept for some important traffic. Diving in Bashi Channel at dawn we patrolled along the most probable shipping route. It was a beautiful Pacific day, a blue, almost cloudless sky embracing the deeper blue of the sea whose moderate swells had only an occasional whitecap. Visibility was excellent.

Just before noon we heard the pinging of distant sonar. Speeding up and heading for the contact thus disclosed, we soon made out the tops of a northbound convoy. It was a group of at least four ships, one large modern freighter and three smaller ones. On our side of the convoy were four small escorts; there were probably others out of sight on the far side. To get close enough for an attack we had to use high, submerged speed, a noisy six knots, with only occasional brief looks through the scope. As we closed, the freighters were seen to be in two columns, zigzagging frequently. The track angle for our torpedoes was good, and the gyro angles small, but we would have to fire at long range or not at all. The torpedo run of 3,100 yards was the best we could get. Unfortunately, the three minutes it would take the fish to reach the target would give it time to zig at least once more.

At 1320 we fired four torpedoes at the largest ship. I was glad to see that a freighter in the far column overlapped our target. We swung rapidly to the right with full rudder to bring our stern tubes to bear. During the turn I kept an eye on the escorts; their sonars were pinging rhythmically and they gave no sign of being alerted. Jim busied himself with the new setup on the TDC, and Chief Quartermaster O'Brien, with stopwatch in hand, marked the time of torpedo run. "Mark! They should be there!" But there was no explosion until two more minutes had passed.

I swung the periscope quickly from the escorts to the freighter in the far column. She was making black smoke and dropping astern.

The sound of another torpedo explosion came through the water and, soon after, a strange, loud, fast buzzing noise unlike any we'd heard before.

Men in the crew's mess reported they heard this sound pass over us four times, approaching from starboard which was the direction of the escorts as well as the direction our fish had been fired. Men in the forward part of the boat thought it crossed over us three times.

Woodrow Burgess was our new yeoman and telephone talker. "Ask them what it sounds like," I told him.

It was variously described. To Ship's Cook 2c Thomas it was high speed screws; to Chief Griffen it was a torpedo; to Chief Terry an airplane flying low. To me in the conning tower the sound came as a fast, low-pitched buzzing, increasing in loudness and then decreasing for an estimated total of forty seconds. I heard it only once. I had no impression that it circled our ship, but men both forward and aft were positive it did.

As the sound faded a heavy explosion, similar to a depth charge, occurred close to port. I was puzzled by the strange noise and fearful of a new antisubmarine weapon. "Take her deep! Use negative and full speed!"

Whatever we heard, it could not be one of our torpedoes running erratic. It was too improbable to suppose that six minutes after being fired it would seek us out, pass over us several times, then explode close aboard. Neither would its turning circle permit it to pass overhead more than once.

Four more heavy explosions lit up the DCI. They detonated close to starboard but above us as we leveled off at 325 feet. They did not have the characteristic "click-brr-roomp-woosh" of depth charges.

For seventeen minutes we ran quietly, trying to slink away. Two escorts could be heard overhead, one on either quarter, their sonar echoes bouncing off our hull. All seemed to be going well. We had been in this situation many times and I felt no special concern. We were rigged for depth charge and I took my usual seat on the deck at the top of the ladder from control.

Suddenly all hell broke loose. Simultaneous with the tremendous concussion of a depth charge close by, I saw the cork lining of the hull crack and yield, pushed inboard by the deformation of the hull. The radar transceiver and the periscope hoist motors were knocked askew. Glass shattered and gauges broke. The sonar went dead. It was time to abandon the conning tower.

Pulling the lower hatch shut behind us and pounding its dogs, or latches, firmly into place, we were now all locked within the ship's main pressure hull. There were eighty of us, but we were split into small groups in the eight separate compartments of our ship. Each group was sealed from the next by the heavy watertight doors which had been slammed shut when rigging for depth charge.

When the depth charge explosion wrecked the conning tower, the light bulb which illuminated the TDC had popped out. Jim Conant grabbed it in instinctive reaction and somehow scrambled down the ladder without breaking it. He stood now in the control room tenderly cupping the bulb in his hand, as though the safety of our ship depended on that fragile glass globe.

For two minutes all seemed calm, save for the sharp probing of the Japs' active sonar beams now bouncing off our hull at a quicker pace. A few hundred feet overhead, Japanese sonar operators watched intently on their oscilloscopes the greenish blob which denoted our presence, or listened carefully to the sharp, metallic echoes which our hull returned. The rapidity of the pinging clearly indicated they had solid contact on us, were not in doubt as to our position and movement. We had survived many depth chargings in the past, and had no doubt we would do so again, but it was clear this was a more professional ASW performance than any we'd experienced in the past. Surely the near miss that had driven us from the conning tower was a lucky shot that could not be repeated in the complex problem of space and motion that stood between us and our enemy. Its solution would bring both triumph and disaster, one to the hunter, the other to the hunted. Would our pursuers gauge properly our course, our speed, our depth, the sinking time of depth charges? On our part, we had no weapons with which to attack or ward off our enemy. In a close-in engagement with shallow-draft, maneuverable ships our torpedoes were useless. If we were forced to the surface we'd have only the fire of our modest gun armament to divide against the more nimble surface craft. Here, deep under the ocean, lay our best protection; but would we choose the best depth, turn at the proper time, speed up or slow down at the right moment? These were not discrete thoughts racing through my mind, but this was the aggregate of intuition and reason that now guided us.

Suddenly several close depth charges, very loud, shook *Halibut* violently. These came so nearly together that it was not possible to count them accurately. I was standing in the control room, one hand gripping the ladder to the conning tower, watching the depth gauges over Jack Hinchey's shoulder, when I saw for my first and only time a phenomenon other skippers had reported. I saw, or rather had the sensation of, a greenish glow in the room, much as a lightning flash will illumine a dark night. Did I see it or did I imagine it? It was like "seeing stars" after a violent blow to the head. Was I merely stunned or frightened? But there was no time for speculation. It was 13:46:24 by Tokyo time, forty-six minutes and twenty-four seconds after one o'clock in the afternoon, civilian time. That was the moment at which our control room clock, our master, daily timekeeper, stopped. When we got back to Pearl, one of ComSubPac's scientists would offer the dubious explanation that the bluish-green flash was caused by sound waves of a frequency so high that they approached the speed of light.

The tremendously loud explosions, the disintegration of familiar equipment around us, the vibrations of the ship as if she was a giant fish trying to shake off a hook, had stunned and frightened me momentarily. Was this the way it would end?

No one spoke or uttered a sound. No one seemed hurt. Jack leaned over the shoulders of his bow and stern planesmen, Vogel and Sturgeon, as all three grimly concentrated on holding our depth.

We were below our safe operating depth when the depth charges exploded. The enormous concussion had driven *Halibut* 100 feet deeper. We were now at 420 feet. The explosions just a few feet over the forward battery compartment had forced us down as though a giant hand was pushing a toy boat underwater. But better down than up. Explosions beneath us would have blown us toward the surface and, if we could not keep from broaching, our presence on the surface would have drawn a storm of enemy gunfire.

Chalfant on the hydraulic manifold, Allison on the air manifold, Emmett on the trim manifold stood silently awaiting instructions. Their grips on a familiar valve wheel or lever gave them reassurance. Chief Roberson looked around the room, appraising everyone, ready to help where needed.

I broke the silence. "Jack, can you hold her?"

"I could use more speed, captain," Jack was as calm and casual as if this was a routine, morning dive to get a BT trace.

The high speed we had used to get within torpedo range of the convoy had consumed much of our battery capacity, and there were several hours of daylight before we dared surface. The submariner's instinctive hoarding of his battery, his miserly expenditure of amperes—the very life blood of his ship when submerged—made us jealous of every amp expended. As long as we could hold our depth or inch upwards it was better not to increase our r.p.m.

"You're doing fine. Try to ease up to three-fifty."

I was cool and confident once more. We'd received no more depth charges. Our sonars were out of order, but we could hear no screw noises overhead.

All around us was a shambles. There was much minor damage; everything that had been loose was displaced and thrown about. Most glass was shattered. Oil and water fittings leaked. The master gyro was knocked out. Personnel seemed stunned, but went about their tasks quietly as if this was just another damage control drill.

Guy manned the sound-powered phone which linked us to all compartments. He received their damage reports and gave instructions. In every compartment men struggled to control damage and stop leaks. By the action and attitude of our ship I knew we had no catastrophic fracture of the hull. We would be on our way to the bottom by now if that were true.

Suddenly word came over the phone: "Chlorine gas in the forward battery!" The dread report, most serious of all the problems we faced, hit me with chilling effect which I did my best to hide. We would have to handle it as only one more of the difficulties we were struggling with. We were still drawing power from the forward battery, and the boat was not getting noticeably heavy forward. There could not be a major rupture of the hull. The best we could do now was to keep the deadly gas confined to the sealed-off officers' country. Stationed in that compartment when we had rigged for depth charge were Lieut. (jg) Ray Stewart, Ensign Bill Kidwell, and our two steward's mates, Strauther Wallace and John Phillips. Wallace was an experienced submariner, a big, burly, likeable man. Phillips was a neophyte sailor, much younger, slighter, and more articulate. They were the only black men in our crew.

Even before Guy could give them orders to secure the compartment and evacuate, the handle on the heavy watertight door which led to officers' country began to revolve. Pulling open the door, Ray and Bill leaped into the control room and slammed the door shut behind them.

They had ordered Wallace and Phillips to go forward to the torpedo room and to seal that door behind them.

"Chlorine gas" was not a casualty that could be rehearsed realistically. None of us had been exposed to it. The navy had not developed a harmless, substitute gas with the same odor to use in drills. We had only described it, warned of its danger, and specified how to secure the battery compartment where it generated.

The young officers were flushed and agitated, but fully in control of themselves. In the room full of men grimly concentrating on their jobs, Ray waited for me to have time for his report. Bill braced himself against the housing of the master gyro. His shirt was wet with perspiration, and his face showed bewilderment at all that he was experiencing on his first war patrol.

Guy recalled that Bill's father had visited our ship during overhaul in San Francisco. At lunch that day Mr. Kidwell had said of Bill's forthcoming duty, "Submarine duty would be a good experience for a young man."

Guy looked at Bill and said in his calm, laconic, deadpan fashion, "Good experience for a young man."

It was the perfect remark to break the tension. I grinned along with everyone else.

From Ray's report I gathered that the tremendous concussion of the depth charge barrage, which sounded to him like a thousand sledgehammers pounding the hull, had thrown all four men off their feet. They were showered with cork from the lining of our hull, with paint flakes, and with dust from the ventilation piping. Fittings from bulkheads and deck were broken loose, and light bulbs were shattered. The books of the wardroom library spilled from their cupboard on the forward bulkhead. Drawers and lockers in officers' and chiefs' quarters were flung open, and loose items strewn about. China and glassware in the officers' pantry were smashed. There was a sharp, hissing sound, as if water under pressure was squirting through a crack. A strange, pungent odor filled the room. To two junior officers the combination was convincing evidence that the battery compartment beneath the wardroom deck was filling with deadly chlorine gas. Somehow saltwater must be reaching the sulphuric acid electrolyte of the main storage batteries. With no means to control this, the battery ventilation ducts were sealed and the compartment abandoned.

Running silent was no longer a major concern. The enemy knew where we were. We could do nothing about the banging and rattling from topside damage, and the noisy squealing coming from propeller shafts and screws. In the control room Jack worked with his bow and stern planesmen, trying to ease our ship gradually up to 350 feet. Complicating Jack's problem was the fact that our regular depth gauges were bent or shattered. He had to rely on small sea pressure gauges and convert their "pounds per square inch" to "feet" of submergence. The reading of 176 on a sea pressure gauge meant that we were at a depth of 400 feet.

Orders to the main power switchboard in the maneuvering room went by telephone. Should there be trouble there, we needed to know at once. Under the savage pounding of our hull and the intense shocks given any equipment mounted on the hull, it seemed a miracle that we had no fire in the main control cubicle or in the batteries.

Chief Braun and his two main power controllermen, electrician's mates Arthur Grisanti and David Else, were locked in the confined, sweltering maneuvering room. Braun was a strong character, a tough-minded, practical sailor who could be counted on to "tell it like it is."

In reply to a question he said, "Mr. Goolyotto, it's OK back here. Both batteries read OK. We can give you what you want."

What we wanted was a few more r.p.m. Vogel had his bow planes on hard rise but we hung at 400 feet.

"Guy, tell Braun to build up ten turns slowly, but to watch his voltage carefully."

There was no compass heading for quartermaster 2c Henderson to steer by. "Just leave the rudder amidships," I ordered.

The course we made good was of little concern. We were in the deep ocean, well offshore, in no danger of running aground. We could no longer hear anything overhead. There was no need to twist and turn. It was just as well to hold a steady course and not make Jack's job even more difficult.

We were still not sure what really had happened in the forward battery compartment. By now I knew we could not be taking serious amounts of water, but what had caused the gas? What were conditions in the battery well?

Chief Roberson had been thinking hard. He read the gauge on the forward bulkhead of the control room, which measured the pressure in the officers' quarters and the battery compartment under them. The air pressure was 52 pounds per square inch!

If the pressure hull was ruptured, the pressure in the compartment would be the same as the sea's. At our depth the pressure gauge would then read 176 pounds per square inch. Besides, if the compartment was flooding from sea we could not hold our depth; we would be heading for the bottom four miles below.

There could be only one explanation for the sudden rise in the air pressure of the battery compartment. No. 1 air bank was located in the forward battery well, its heavy, steel bottles secured to the pressure hull to either side of the battery. These interconnected flasks stored air compressed to 2,500 pounds per square inch, which we used to blow main ballast tanks when surfacing. Each night we topped them off with our air compressors as religiously as we recharged our batteries. Somehow the air pressure in the bank must be released.

In time we would learn that the violent explosions over and around our ship had deformed the hull and caused the copper piping leading from the air bank to pull out of its silver soldered joints. Released into the volume of the whole compartment, the air from the flasks raised the compartment pressure to 52 pounds per square inch.

Forward of the control room, watertight doors were hinged so that they swung aft to close; those abaft the control room were opposite. This meant that the compartment pressure acting on the door leading aft to the control room made it impossible to open. Conversely, the pressure on the door giving access to the forward torpedo room was restrained only by the strength of the dogs which held that door's rubber gasket firmly against its knife edge. It was essential that we know whether we indeed had chlorine gas to cope with. There was only one way to find out. The forward torpedo room would have to ease up gradually on their door and sniff carefully for gas.

Since his battle station was the forward torpedo room, Ensign Alexander was senior man in the compartment. Guy got him on the phone and explained what we wanted done. "Caution him to be very careful, Guy. There's lots of pressure on that door."

I waited grimly. If it really is chlorine, I thought, we'll keep it confined in the forward battery compartment until we can surface and ventilate.

The control room was unnaturally quiet. The bow and stern planes had not been put out of commission; we could still operate them in "power." The only sound was the occasional click of their control switches as Vogel and Sturgeon worked to hold us at 350 feet.

Braun reported no problem with main power. He was drawing normal current from the forward battery; it could not have serious damage. A fire there would be devastating. Jack now had good depth control, so we took off the extra turns we had used. Every amp was important.

Jim Conant became aware of the light bulb in his hands. Firecontrolman 2c Silvio Gardella, who took care of the TDC, was standing beside him. "Here, Gardella, you take it," said Jim sheepishly. Then he shambled to the radio room where Chief Lawrence and radioman Joe Janus were trying to protect the badly damaged sets from the water dripping from the flooded antenna trunk.

Guy spoke into his phone, "Control, aye aye." As he listened his face was expressionless as always, his only sign of more than usual emotion being the nodding of his close-cropped head.

"Are you sure?" A pause. "He does?" Then, "That's good." Guy never used three words if two would do.

In his flat, matter-of-fact tones, almost as if passing chit-chat, Guy reported. "Alex says he doesn't smell chlorine. He had Soulis check it, and he agrees." (Chief Torpedoman Jim Soulis was the senior enlisted man in the compartment.) "It smells funny, but they don't know what it is. The door is secured again."

As long as the forward battery compartment retained its high pressure our ship would remain divided in two parts and we could not assist our men struggling with the damage in the forward torpedo room. With 52 pounds per square inch acting on it, the control room door was sealed as firmly as if it were welded shut.

I felt older. I realized I really *was* "the Old Man," the skipper my men were counting on to make the right decisions. But I was confident, too. Eight years of submarine duty and many emergencies had prepared me for this. For more than a year *Halibut* had responded to every demand I placed on her, escaped every attack made on her. Now she had survived the most violent, most accurate blows the enemy could deliver. With every second that passed, I was more certain that we could handle our problems.

I ordered the doors abaft the control room to be put "on the latch," and sent Joe Galligan aft to learn first-hand what problems we had. Men could now move from room to room to assist in the inspections and repairs required.

The first step in lowering the pressure in the forward battery compartment was to let it expand into the torpedo room. Torpedoman Ed Bertheau slowly backed off the door locking mechanism until high-pressure air whistled through the crack under the rubber gasket. Finally the pressure in the two rooms equalized at 28 pounds.

Now able to enter the battery compartment, Alex and Soulis made a quick inspection. They found many cracked cell tops and all ventilation ducts disconnected, but a battery that still functioned despite the leakage of electrolyte. A later, more detailed inspection would disclose that 10 cells of the total of 126 were completely dry, and that many others were cracked and leaking.

The source of the strange odor was clear. Everything loose had been flung about. Glass bottles and containers in the chiefs' and officers' bunkrooms had been shattered or spilled. The contents of the wardroom pantry and its refrigerator were on the deck. The combined, indefinable odor of sweat, shaving lotion, hair tonic, shoe polish, medicine, vinegar, salad oil, coffee, food and sulphuric acid had meant to our men that the emergency we had so often drilled to handle— Chlorine Gas in the Forward Battery!—was at hand.

I was reassured by the more complete reports now being telephoned from forward, but our shipmates were still separated from us by a heavy steel door which the cumulative pressure of 28 pounds per square inch bound shut. Somehow we would have to equalize the pressure on both sides of the door. There was no provision for this in the design of the ship, no interconnecting pipe or valve we could open. The bulkhead flapper valves in the ventilation supply and exhaust lines were themselves held fast shut by the same pressure.

I discussed possibilities with Guy, Jack, and Chief Roberson, but it was Chalfant who came up with the solution. From its manifold in the control room, the trim line ran to the variable (trimming) tanks in the forward room. By sacrificing its normal use and removing valve bonnets, we could interconnect the two rooms and thus bleed the pressure into the control room. From there we could release it into the rest of the boat.

Jack had a good trim and said he could do without the trim line if we didn't move too many men back and forth.

As soon as we'd instructed Alex what to do, Emmett proceeded to unbolt the heavy, corresponding flange on his manifold. In the pump room below us, motor mac Warren Easterling monitored the trim pump and the maze of other vital auxiliaries. He had so many leaks from sea, distorted pipes, and misaligned shafts that he called for help. Chief Roberson jumped down the hatch for a quick look, then sent for Paul Eurich to give Easterling a hand.

As the valve bonnets were loosened, the foul-smelling air from forward began to whistle past the flanges. The volume of air we had to release through a four-inch pipe would make this a long, noisy process.

Meanwhile, in the heat and pressure to which they were exposed, our men in the forward room were working to exhaustion. The room had been particularly hard hit. The skids on which the 2,000-pound torpedoes were strapped had jumped one foot under the violent downthrust given the boat. The deck plates were dislodged and men were thrown into the bilges. Sea valves had spun open, admitting much water. Tank tops and hull contours that had been level or smooth were wrinkled and deformed. Numerous bolts on manholes and flanges were sheared or bent. A steady stream of water came from the breach of the signal ejector, and water dripped from the forward escape trunk. It was flooded and useless. With all the excess weight we'd gained forward, no wonder we'd had trouble working our way up.

Gene Oakey, an intelligent, very likeable, powerful young fireman, was a member of the torpedo reload crew. When the enormous shock and deafening explosion hit, he was knocked into the bilge. He was convinced that he was going through the bottom of the boat. He would swear to me that as he grasped wildly for support he saw in the after corner of the room, in a brilliant white light, the figure of the Madonna with outstretched arms. To this day he remains convinced he was not hallucinating.

Chief Soulis and his gang reacted instantly to the chaos in their space. They closed valves, tightened hatch dogs, took up on loose bolts, cleared away loose gear, and searched for damage. While most struggled to control damage, other men took turns rotating our sonar heads by hand power. The sonar receivers and amplifiers still worked, but the training motors had been knocked out and their shafts bent. The slow, straining rotation of the sonar domes by hand gave a sketchy audio picture of activity on the surface. It seemed strangely quiet and ominous.

Were our hunters lying low, waiting for some false move on our part? We were certainly making enough noise with our squealing shafts, singing propellers, topside banging, and internal racket to announce our location and invite more barrages of depth charges.

But they didn't come. I reasoned that, desperately short of shipping as they were, the Japanese had instructed their ASW commanders not to leave a convoy unguarded, prey to another submarine of a wolf pack, while they worked over one that was in no position to harm their flock. Whatever the reason for their lack of persistence, the knockout punch was not delivered. We crawled away battered and bleeding, victims of only a long knockdown count. Every minute we were left unmolested, painfully climbing back to 300 feet, struggling to control and repair damage, our chances of escaping, of surviving to fight again another day, increased greatly.

The process of bleeding down the excess pressure from the two forward compartments into the rest of the ship continued. Finally the pressure that had been 52 pounds in the forward battery, then 28 in both forward compartments, became 12 when released throughout the entire ship. When the pressure on both sides of the control room's forward door was equalized, we opened it and sent men forward to assist those isolated and exhausted in the torpedo room.

A careful catalog of damage would be made later, but under the direction of their chief petty officers, all hands were inspecting, testing, or repairing the machinery and equipment they were responsible for. It was a subdued, continuous, all-hands evolution as we gradually eased toward the surface.

Cautiously we eased up on the dogs of the conning tower hatch. When no water appeared, we threw open the hatch and re-entered the conning tower. It was dry, but a shambles of distorted hull, misaligned or wrecked equipment, broken glass, shattered cork insulation. Both periscope hoist mechanisms were out of line, but we were able to raise the scopes. No. 2, the slender attack scope, was useless, its interior optics damaged. No. 1 was barely usable, internally dirty and foggy, but three hours after the last depth charges exploded, its objective lens pierced the surface. With Quartermaster Henderson leaning on the handles to help me push the damaged periscope around, a look around showed all clear.

It was 1645; the sun was still high, and it would be two and a half hours before it would be dark enough to surface. We needed all that time. We desperately wanted our SJ radar, not only to alert us to enemy forces, but to help locate our own subs in the vicinity. Our radio transmitters and receivers were knocked out. If we could get the radar back in operation it would serve both as I.F.F.[1] and as a communication link to our sister subs. Ray Welley was crouched on the conning tower deck, his wiring diagrams, tools, and instruction books spread out around him. Ignoring the wreckage and confusion about him, he went through his meticulous check-off procedure, isolating faults. Never one to waste words, not naturally an optimist, he promised nothing except, "I'll do my best, captain." That was good enough for me.

1. Identification, Friend or Foe—an electronic device that received coded, high-frequency radiations which identified friendly forces.

19

"Need Help"

While all hands bent to their tasks about the ship, I had time to consider another problem. The unusually high air pressure in the boat made it dangerous to fling open the conning tower hatch in normal fashion and spring quickly to the bridge for that first, vital, quick look all around. The sudden release of the enormous volume of twelve-pound internal air would blow a man through the hatch opening, killing or severely injuring him. A routine, all-day dive would always result in a buildup of pressure in the boat, but we could bleed that down quickly enough by cracking the hatch once it was clear of the water, then throw it open for Henderson and me to scramble topside. Once sure that it was "clear all around," I would call lookouts and O.O.D. to the bridge.

In our present situation, the best thing to do was to seal off the conning tower once more, lock ourselves in it, and when the boat planed up far enough to bring the upper hatch clear of the water, we would ease off on the hatch dogs. This would let the excess pressure hiss past the rubber gasket and vent to the atmosphere.

When the pressure dropped to the point I thought safe, Henderson threw open the hatch and clambered up the short ladder, with me right on his heels. Never did night air smell sweeter or more refreshing!

Our first, eyeballs-only look showed nothing close by. After a more deliberate binocular search I shouted down the hatch to those listening anxiously below, "Clear all 'round! Lookouts to the bridge!"

We had locked Creighton, Haynes, and Metzger in the conning tower with us. Responding to my order, the three men scrambled topside. Their binoculars, preset to each man's particular diopter, hung from their necks but were tucked inside their jackets to keep them from the water that splashed down the hatch and dripped heavily from the periscope shears. Without a word they climbed to their platforms and took up the search.

Now I could take deep drafts of the pure night air, while Henderson checked the 7 MC, the bridge speaker-microphone. Miraculously, it still worked.

"Good! Make ready all engines."

Except for the conning tower, all of the boat was under twelve pounds pressure. To get that down safely we started the one low-pressure turbo-blower that was operable, sucked air from the sealed boat, and blew it into the ballast tanks. As this slow process continued, word came to the bridge, "One and two main engines ready."

Clayton Rantz was in charge of the forward engine room. He loved his two big diesels. Even during depth charging he would roam the engine room looking for any sign of trouble, his hand stroking the gleaming casing as fondly as if it were the flank of a woman. He stood by his starting levers, proud that he and his oiler, Carlos Robinson, were ready to answer bells while Kelly and LaBertew were still struggling with engines 3 and 4.

"When we start up, leave the main induction closed. Run the engines off the air in the boat," I ordered. This should draw the excess pressure down quickly.

"All ahead one-third."

I look aft anxiously. In the gloom, at the water's edge, I see a smother of foam at the forward engine exhausts and hear the cough of engines starting. No. 1 sputters and dies. For almost a minute, only No. 2 gives its throaty rumble. The starboard engine coughs again, builds up slowly, and joins No. 2 in its steady, comforting throb. No longer are we dependent on what little capacity remains in our crippled batteries.

Engines No. 3 and 4 now join in, and *Halibut* moves painfully ahead, like a wounded gladiator given a reprieve.

All was going according to plan, although more slowly than I liked. I wanted more lookouts topside and as prompt a battery charge as possible. With pressure about halfway down to our normal, I ordered the main engine air induction valve opened. The result was such a roaring, prolonged blast of air and vapor that it seemed we were having an internal explosion. Recovering from that shock, we opened the lower conning tower hatch and were once more in normal submarine operating environment.

Heads ached, lungs burned, and eyes smarted from the hours trapped in stagnant, hot, foul air. As we drew fresh salt night air through the boat, our vitality returned. We were back in the world of the living, and aside from a few cuts and bruises, no one was injured. As inspection and repair proceeded, new damage was discovered, but we were on the surface, charging batteries, proceeding slowly westward, steering by the stars.

By the time we surfaced, Guy plotted our dead reckoning position and estimated in what direction we might find *Haddock* or *Tuna*. Our gyro repeaters were useless, since the master gyro was not working, so the only way to hold a more or less steady course was to steer by a star. But helmsman LeRoy Fry, at the wheel in the conning tower, could not see the stars. At our latitude, near 20° north, Polaris was quite low in the sky and was too nearly abeam to make a good reference point. We chose Capella, which was bright and reasonably close to the direction we wanted. Joe Galligan had the O.O.D. watch. Calling down through the hatch, he coached Fry to come right or left as needed to hold a fairly steady course.

As we proceeded in the direction we hoped to find *Haddock* or *Tuna*, the radar antenna started to rotate. Soon Welley's matter-of-fact voice called up the hatch, "Radar operating." The word spread quickly throughout the ship. Most of our men had never served in a ship without a radar. Without it they felt naked and vulnerable. Now we would at least have warning of anyone else slinking through the dark night. Little did we guess the week before how important would be *Haddock*'s gift of the modulation network.

"Search all around. Then watch for interference ahead. We should pick up our other boats."

Long before we could get a return pip on a submarine, we should detect on our radar scope the familiar, swirling pattern of interference from a radar of identical frequency transmitting in our direction.

Two hours farther along our erratic course, the telltale signal appeared. We closed cautiously on what we judged to be the *Haddock*. She came slowly toward us as we communicated by keying our radar emissions. Our radios were wrecked, so this was the only way, slow though it was, that we could transmit information at a reasonable range, twelve miles or so.

Within our wolf pack, to gain some additional security and speed, it was our practice to use each skipper's nickname when communicating. Believing our contact to be *Haddock*, I told chief O'Brien to send, "Beetle, this is Pete. Need help."

From the transmissions we exchanged as the two boats warily closed on each other, it was apparent that our contact took us to be *Haddock*. Not until we approached to megaphone range about 2130 could we clear up the confusion. Our contact was *Pintado*, skippered by Comdr. Bernard A. (Chick) Clarey. His wolf pack, called "Clarey's Crushers," included *Jallao* and *Atule*, and was assigned the area just north of "Roach's Raiders." Chick and I were close friends. We had been in the same submarine division at prewar Pearl Harbor, Chick in *Nautilus*, myself in *Argonaut*.

"Chick, we're pretty well beat up. Made a torpedo attack and got a bad depth charging. No radio. No compass. I want to head for Saipan. Will you set the course? I'll follow. I'll let you know when we can make it on our own."

"Sure thing, Pete. Is there anything you need now?"

"No, thanks. Just guard the radio traffic for us, and I'll give you a message in a little while."

Reports from below confirmed that *Halibut* was far too badly mauled to continue on patrol. Closing *Pintado* once more, we megaphoned a concise report of our battle damage, to be encoded and sent to ComSubPac. We reported that we were heading for Saipan and asked that *Haddock* be informed. Twelve hours later *Pintado* relayed to us by Aldis lamp ComSubPac's reply. We had sent a matter-of-fact report of damage sustained, but it must have greatly perturbed headquarters. Their message closed rather emotionally: "Galantin, our hopes and prayers are with you."

ComSubPac directed *Pintado* to escort us all the way to Saipan, some 1,500 miles. This was a chore which Chick welcomed. It would permit him to replenish fuel and torpedoes and to extend an already successful patrol.

By this time we had things pretty well in hand. All compartments had been carefully inspected and damage listed. Officers and chiefs supervised the cleanup and repairs. Wallace and Phillips collected all the broken material and straightened out officers' country as best they could. We had restored most of *Halibut*'s systems enough to be able to make a test dive. We were well within range of Japanese air bases and I wanted to know that we could dive and surface safely should we be forced down during the long run to Saipan.

While *Pintado* stood guard, *Halibut* eased down to periscope depth. Clearly she was hurting. We could hear strange groans and squeaks, and she handled sluggishly, not like her former silent, smooth, swift self. However, she was tough, and our repairs had been adequate. We came back to the surface and proceeded with confidence. It was *Halibut*'s last dive. Never again would she respond to the hoarse diving alarm and feel the sea enfolding her.

Four hours later we sighted a twin-engine Japanese patrol plane on an opposite course. We slowed to one-third to reduce the amount of spray we were throwing, and watched for any move toward us. He apparently did not see us, for he passed about six miles abeam, heading for Formosa.

In the twenty-four hours after the depth charging all officers and men had been very subdued. It was not that all hands were fully occupied, either on watch or assisting in the cleanup and repair. There seemed to be a universal introspection, a contemplation of what might have been. Or maybe they were musing on an illusion, a fantasy of being safe in *Halibut*'s womb.

Normal sailor talk returned gradually. Small jokes were tried. Men wanted to know how Skeeter behaved. Norman Thomas, who had risen from fireman second to ship's cook second in his five patrols, was Skeeter's best friend. "Skeeter growled each time that sound passed overhead. He must've known somethin' we didn't. When the big bang came he whimpered and peed on the deck."

"Hell! He wasn't scared like I was," said Creighton. "They all thought that was a saltwater leak I was standin' in."

Guy had the reassurance, unusual for a submarine navigator, of exchanging position reports with his opposite number in *Pintado*. They showed that we were making good twelve knots on our course to Saipan. The important part that island, 3,700 miles farther forward than Pearl Harbor, was playing in our submarine campaign was evident. We sighted and exchanged signals with four boats, all heading westward to positions on the noose that was tightening around Japan. They were *Besugo*, *Pampanito*, *Searaven*, and *Sealion*.

Each day our list of repairs required grew longer. It would take up five closely typed pages of our patrol report. Most of the damage was to the hull, its fittings, and auxiliary machinery. Because they were farther removed from the explosions, the main engines and main motors were relatively unscathed, as was the after battery. However, after Jack and Chief Braun crawled through the forward battery well and found over 100 cracked jars in addition to the 10 that had already drained dry, we decided to jump out the 10 and use the rest only for auxiliary power.

I was no longer angry with the workmen of Bethlehem Steel. I wrote in my report, "The beating the ship took and survived brings our admiration and respect to the men who designed her, the people who built *Halibut*, and those who recently overhauled her at Bethlehem Steel Co."

At noon on November 19 we entered Tanapag Harbor. *Pintado* moored first alongside *Fulton*; then we moored outboard of *Pintado*. It was twenty-nine days since we had sailed from this same spot.

The time in port before *Pintado* resumed her interrupted patrol gave me the chance to compare notes with Clarey to try to find out what had hit us so suddenly and devastatingly. The buzzing noises we had heard before the explosions were still a mystery; they had never been reported by another boat, although a section of each sub's patrol report was devoted to enemy antisubmarine measures encountered. Had we been the target of a mysterious, new antisubmarine weapon? Comparison of our log with *Pintado*'s led to the answer.

The high speed we had made as we closed our target meant we could take very few and only very brief periscope looks. Intent on solving the convoy's zig plan and getting as close as possible, I had not searched the sky carefully and had sighted no planes. On the other hand, Clarey, submerged a few miles north of us, noted through his scope unusually heavy air activity in our direction. His log recorded the sound of heavy, distant explosions, their time correlating with our own. At her distance from the scene, not under attack, *Pintado* could calmly record a total of fourteen explosions, including a group of eight. Unbeknownst to her, these were the ones that hurt *Halibut*.

Forty minutes after we had fired on our targets, Chick saw their tops, but could get no closer than twelve miles. The entry in *Pintado*'s patrol report left little doubt as to the sudden retaliation our torpedo attack had triggered:

This is undoubtedly the heaviest cover we have observed over a convoy to date. From the plane contacts there was evidently a distant screen covering 20 to 30 miles ahead and on the bows of the convoy, an inner screen covering the immediate waters through which the convoy was passing and a screen astern and on the quarter to prevent end-around runs.

With this lead to go on, the answer was found. From experienced submarine officers in the squadron staff, men who had taken part in airborne ASW tests in the Atlantic, I learned that at periscope depth it is possible to hear a plane pass overhead if it is large and very low. Adding this to *Pintado*'s sighting of large flying boats, it was clear that we had been the victim of *jikitanchiki*, the Japanese version of magnetic airborne detection, or *MAD*. The anomaly in the earth's magnetic field caused by a submarine could be detected by suitable instrumentation in an ASW plane flying low over the water if the sub was not deep. That is what we had heard passing overhead—a MAD-equipped plane. Her pinpointing of our location had led to the nearly fatal depth charging by the surface escorts.

20

Out of Action

At Saipan inspection and repair parties came and went for three days, but *Halibut* needed more than a tender at an advance base could provide. The more the experts explored and tested, the more they shook their heads. We should not dive again, I was told. In the region where the heaviest blows had been felt, the pressure hull was dished-in two inches between its successive circular frames. The protruding ridges gave our battered hull the look of an emaciated cow. Even more indicative of the enormous pounding our ship had survived was the buckling of the heavy, "pressure proof" bulkhead between the forward battery and the torpedo room.

It was possible that the obsolescent 4″ gun mounted on deck forward had saved us. A depth charge must have exploded right on it; its paint was burned off; the heavy, bronze breech cover was split; its trunnions were sprung apart; and its sights were wrecked. Directly beneath the mount the most severe hull deformation occurred. Perhaps it was the few extra feet of standoff provided by the gun mount that meant the hull bent but didn't break. And it was this great hull deformation that caused the rupture of the high-pressure air lines and the splitting of the cells in the forward battery.

While the work to put us in shape for the long voyage to Pearl continued, we stretched our legs on the tender and ashore. It was the rainy season; continuous downpour added to the quagmire of ankle-deep mud. Nevertheless we could see that much progress had been made since our outbound visit. The broad paved highway running south to Isely Field (named for my classmate Robert H. Isely, shot down during the fight for the island) compared favorably with Kamehameha Highway on Oahu. Even more indicative of the advancing tide of Western culture, the Officer's Club now boasted an orchestra. Over a cool drink we watched army nurses and American Red Cross girls dancing with their perspiring escorts, and we were brought up-to-date on island happenings.

With Isely Field completed, B-29 bombing raids on Japan were to have started before this. Storms and generally poor flying weather had caused daily postponements for a full week. This was unfortunate, assuring a hotter reception for the bombers when they arrived. It was quite probable that Japanese still at large in Saipan's hills and jungle valleys had portable radio transmitters with which to report the size and timing of raids. Not at all pleased by their idleness, Army Air Force pilots derisively referred to their planes as the "Silver Statues" standing on the runways with rain drumming on their hulls.

More exciting by far were accounts of the so-called, sardonically named "Turkey Shoots" which the U.S. Marines were conducting to round up or eliminate the fanatic remnants of the Japanese garrison who had taken to the hills. At night, some would sneak down to the shore supply dumps, and sometimes succeed in stealing food, clothing, or munitions. In three days 150 stragglers had been killed or captured, but at the cost of an almost equal number of marines killed or wounded. Though the Japanese military generally chose to fight to the death, a few civilian employees were rounded up, among them two women members of the Japanese Army's "Comfort Corps." One of these girls had attended Oregon State University. When captured and searched, she strenuously resisted giving up her little black book. Her profession had thrived on a cash basis, but as the submarine blockade of the Marianas became almost complete, cash flow suffered. She had patriotically extended credit, listing in her book the dates, names, and services rendered.

All *Fulton* could do was to put us in shape for return to Pearl on the surface, where more detailed inspection would decide our fate. On November 22 we shoved off once more on the lonely transit to Pearl Harbor that we had sailed so often. No voyage seemed longer or more tedious than this one. Once out of enemy waters the homeward bound days of any patrol always dragged, their speed retarded by the trailing grass of boredom, by many weeks' encrustations of long hopes. We longed for mail; news from home; deep, quiet sleep; a change in food and drink. This time, to the ordinary monotony of repetitious days of sea and sky, we added our impatience to learn what our future would be.

Compounded of these feelings and abetted by days of constant beating into seas driven by a brisk, easterly wind that brought forth all our ship's newly acquired squeaks and groans, there was a slight, well-controlled but perceptible irritability in the boat. This could be seen in countless little ways: in the curt, peevish remarks at table in wardroom or crew's mess, in short-tempered response to unintentional collisions in the unsteady passageway, in furious reactions to bumps and bruises meted out by ship and sea, hard knocks once considered the routine lot of submariners.

"Why don't you look where you're going?" growls Allison when Black bumps into him.

"Why don't you go where you're looking?" snarls Black.

Normally even-tempered machinist Lane Logsdon from Iowa explodes, "When's this goddam ocean gonna settle down?"

At dinner in the wardroom Jack erupts peevishly, "For cripes sake, Jim, keep your elbow out of my ribs."

Morale is high, but we lack the activity and tension of patrol in enemy waters to speed the time and to absorb our thoughts off watch. We try to replace them by that age-old seaman's panacea—repeated little tasks about the ship, the work of keeping her clean and efficient, interspersed with games of acey-deucey, cribbage, pinochle, checkers, or chess.

Though we're out of the high risk area, our lookouts are still vital to our safety. They have to be first to spot a plane, a ship, or a periscope. On the bridge Joe Galligan hears port lookout Harper talk to aft lookout Riel. "Knock off the frigging around! No talking up there!" If one word could describe the chief submarine virtue, it must be *vigilance*.

We can now use our showers; we've eaten up the food stored there. Our fresh water tanks were filled from the tender and we can run our distillers almost constantly. The atmosphere in the boat seems like pure mountain air compared to the smog and stench we endured earlier.

The beards grown by so many have been washed, combed, and lovingly trimmed. They'll be a badge of honor ashore, identifying a truly seagoing, fighting sailor. They're admired and envied by our sailors who are too young to grow proper beards. As for myself, I've confined my ornamentation to a mustache.

Helping on this patrol was the movie projector that sailed with us for the first time. It gave us the use of some excellent navy training films, and a much appreciated addition to our recreation library. Unfortunately the movie exchange in Pearl would issue us only five feature-length films. In Hollywood parlance, they were all "turkeys."

Apparently no first-rate movies were entrusted to submarines. After all, they'd keep them for sixty days or perhaps not even come back. There was a far larger, more influential audience to be reached in the shore-based headquarters which, of course, had to entertain visiting VIPs and politicians. Nevertheless, there was added excitement to any submarine rendezvous at sea—perhaps we could "trade up," swap one of our low-rated films for one slightly more entertaining.

Lacking that, the frequent repetition of movies was made enjoyable by turning off the sound track and assigning roles to the more articulate members of our crew. Clayt Rantz, Silvio Gardella, and Red Creighton were our chief box office draws. We were short on sopranos, but in the dim, flickering light of crew's mess or forward torpedo room inhibitions faded and a reasonable facsimile of the original dialogue came from the voice of machinist's mate, fire controlman, or seaman. The obscene ad libs were often an improvement on the scriptwriter's work.

As Guy's successive "fixes" nibbled at the 3,933 miles of our assigned track, we came again to the international date line, the demarcation of eastern and western hemispheres, some 50 miles west of Midway. On a westward passage clocks would be advanced twenty-four hours, in effect skipping one day on the calendar. To those encountering this event for the first time, it was a mystifying rite. By many thousands of GIs and sailors who entered the imaginary Realm of the Golden Dragon, it would be remembered as a modest highlight of many days at sea. For submariners based at Pearl or Midway it was a routine event as we shuttled back and forth across the line. And to those who reasoned out the simple celestial mechanics responsible or leafed through the navigator's copy of *Dutton* for a fuller explanation, it was a way to have fun with less inquisitive shipmates.

John Phillips, our tall, good-looking, young steward's mate from New York's Harlem, was on his first patrol. He was puzzled by the loss of a day. When we crossed the line on October 12 we had skipped the next day, which happened to be Friday. Old hands assured John that submariners always skipped Friday the Thirteenth. Remembering John's concern and wonder on that occasion, this time officers and men collaborated to pull his leg. We let it be known by posted bulletin and announcement over the intercom that the day we would repeat as we went east would be the "lost" day we had skipped going west.

When Phillips brought my morning cup of coffee, I saw the puzzled frown on his face, and asked what was troubling him. "Oh, they're all trying to goof me. I know it can be Friday the Thirteenth, but when they say it's October, there's somethin' wrong. I don't see how it can be another month."

The days went by. We steamed steadily along our track, keeping within the few miles of deviation allowed. All the way across the Pacific we had been following ComSubPac's nightly messages and the shortwave radio news broadcasts. We knew it was hardly likely that at this stage of the war Japanese warships would be approaching the Hawaiian Islands, but it was best not to give any trigger-happy air patrol an excuse to bomb us by mistake.

As we closed on the island of Oahu during what we knew would be the last night together for some of us, there was in the boat a noticeable mood of expectancy and subdued excitement. Men lingered in the messroom longer than usual, recalling shoreside escapades with shipmates or retelling highlights of war patrols. It was a way to hide the discomfort of uncertainty as to what was in store for *Halibut* and crew, the dismay at soon losing shipmates with whom they had shared so much.

Up at dawn, all hands turned to with a will to make our ship as neat and clean as possible in spite of her wounds. Shortly after 1000 on December 1, 1944, we passed the sea buoy marking the channel leading into Pearl Harbor, and I went to the bridge dressed in the one set of clean khaki I'd kept for this day. I had entered this channel countless times during my four years duty in *Argonaut*, based here from 1936 to 1940. I knew every course to steer as we passed channel buoys in turn and took bearings on familiar landmarks. War's greedy appetite for land had consumed vast pineapple fields and had pushed the cultivation of lush sugar cane farther up the hillsides. But unchanged were the Waianae Mountains to the westward and the green slopes of the Koolau Range dead ahead. They still kept their vigil over the great harbor.

It was Admiral Lockwood's policy to relieve skippers after they had made four or five patrols, and I was due. If I had to leave, I wanted a new-construction submarine to which I could take as many of my crew as possible. But if *Halibut* was to go in the yard once more to repair battle damage, perhaps they would leave me where I was, and most of us could go on patrol together again. These thoughts ran through my mind as we passed Hospital Point, rounded Ten Ten Dock, and made our final turn to No. 4 pier at the sub base.

Jim Conant had the deck. I had only to keep a watchful eye and careful ear to his orders as he skillfully conned our ship alongside. When our bullnose passed the end of the pier, ComSubPac's band assembled on the dock sounded off with "The Stars and Stripes Forever." The waiting boarding party was larger and more senior than usual, no doubt drawn by the reports of our damage sent ahead from Saipan. All were eager to see and hear firsthand what had befallen us. Outwardly we seemed the same as any rust-streaked, weather-beaten boat returning from weeks at sea. It took a close look at our deformed hull and damaged machinery to guess what *Halibut* had endured.

As soon as the brow was slid over from the pier, and even as mooring lines were being doubled-up, Admiral Lockwood strode aboard, saluted the colors, and gave me a warm handclasp. Descending to the wardroom and the inevitable cup of coffee, freshly brewed by Strauther Wallace, I gave a brief summary of our patrol. But the admiral wanted most of all to see the effects of the depth charges. While I escorted him through the ship and pointed out the chief problem areas, his staff experts were examining and evaluating.

News of submarine actions, particularly of the outcome of enemy ASW measures, was closely held, but we learned with wry pleasure that a garbled version of our last attack had leaked to San Francisco. Lefty O'Doul's Tavern had held a solemn minute of silence in memory of *Halibut* friends "lost at sea." And the girls of The Forbidden City no doubt blinked back almond-eyed tears as they gazed at *Hao-lee-but's* vacant table.

The survey of *Halibut's* damage was thorough, its report more pessimistic than we had expected. Our ship was unsafe to dive, her repair too costly and time consuming; it was better to build a new ship. She would be sent back to New London to serve as an alongside school ship, a floating training aid for familiarization in shipboard equipments and layouts.

It was a sad end for a fighting ship. *Halibut* had fought a longer, harder war than any of us. Since her first arrival in Pearl in 1942 she had sailed on ten war patrols, steamed over 110,000 miles, endured countless depth charges, bombs, and even gunfire. We who manned her had given her a record that was not the best, but by no means the poorest. She had sunk twelve ships, damaged at least nine others, used her gun effectively. She earned seven battle stars, the Navy Unit Commendation, and the Philippine Republic Presidential Unit Citation.

Halibut had responded to our every demand, and had brought us safely home. She was a proud unit of a force that had lost 22 percent of the people it sent on war patrol, a percentage higher than in any other branch of our armed forces.

21

Farewell

I had now completed six consecutive war patrols, and it came as no surprise that ComSubPac had other plans for me. On December 5, 1944, Guy Gugliotta relieved me as C.O. of our battered ship. *Halibut* had been given the minimum repairs needed for surface operation, and was being sent to San Francisco for more extensive work.

As *Halibut* sounded a long blast on her whistle and backed clear of Pier 4, all hands topside waved or saluted as I stood on the pier. Silently and sadly I watched till she rounded Ten Ten Dock and was lost to view. For the first time in sixteen months I felt alone; I was without ship or shipmates.

I wasted no time. That same day I headed back to the war zone, flying westward to Guam where I would be Operations and Gunnery Officer on the staff of Capt. George L. Russell, ComSubRon 10.

Hardly had I settled in my new duties and become accustomed to the luxury of living in a commodious stateroom near my operations office on board *Sperry* when Admiral Lockwood informed Captain Russell that I was being ordered to Chungking, China, for temporary duty. I would be Submarine Liaison Officer on the staff of Commodore M. E. Miles in SACO (Sino American Cooperative Organization) in relief of Comdr. Walter G. Ebert, who had been sent out in 1944 to establish that position.

The mission of the Submarine Liaison Officer was two-fold: (1) to sift and pass on all intelligence that could be of benefit to our subs in either offense or defense; and (2) to assist the air commands, specifically the Fourteenth Air Force and the Twentieth Bomber Command, by providing submarine rescue services for airmen downed at sea.

The first of these—intelligence—meant the screening of countless messages coming to headquarters in Happy Valley outside Chungking from coast-watchers, from many other Chinese intelligence sources, and from 14th Air Force headquarters in Kunming. The naval intelligence originated by Chinese sources—coastwatchers, spies, or simple informants—initially gave me much trouble and loss of sleep. The ancient Chinese culture did not match advanced western civilization's variety and richness of expression concerning tools for death and destruction. I was startled by the frequency with which battleships were sighted, and in what unlikely waters. To a Chinese guerrilla or farmer a "battleship" was any ship, even a boat, mounting a gun. I quickly gained cartographic familiarity with China's long coastline as I plotted ship sightings, trying to validate the information reported.

By the spring of 1945 there was little movement of Japanese shipping that would warrant attack by our submarines. Small shallow-draft sampans slunk along the coast in waters inaccessible to our boats. Our air forces were well established in the Philippines and Okinawa, and their air searches covered all the sea routes converging on Japan. Aircraft could detect and attack most traffic more quickly than could our submarines. Clandestine sources were providing almost no intelligence of use to our subs. My work had devolved chiefly into assisting the recovery of airmen shot down or crashed over China in the vicinity of our coastwatchers or network of guerrilla camps. For this, no submarine officer was required.

In May, 1945, I recommended to Commodore Miles that my billet be discontinued and that I be returned to the fleet. He concurred, and after approval by ComSubPac and CinCPac I closed up shop and headed for Guam.

It was a long, roundabout journey, but the best that could be done by the transport aircraft of the day. From Chungking I went to Kunming, then back over the Hump to Calcutta. Next came Colombo, followed by the flight to Perth. At 3,400 miles it was the world's longest overwater flight. Flying on via Melbourne, Brisbane, Finschafen, Biak, and Samar, I came again to Guam.

Islands which were once firmly in the grip of the Japanese were now U.S. stepping stones on the road to Tokyo. In January Admiral Nimitz had moved the planning and operational sections of his CinCPac staff to Guam from Pearl Harbor. ComSubPac followed suit and moved his operations headquarters and a small staff from Pearl to Guam, setting up shop on board the submarine tender *Holland*, which had moved down from Saipan.

After I reported "mission accomplished" to CinCPac, I was returned to the submarine force and promptly ordered to Saipan. There I would be operations officer of Task Group 17.2, which was two squadrons of submarines under my early *Argonaut* shipmate, Capt. Willis A. (Pilly) Lent.

The seas approaching Japan now seemed crowded. In waters that only submarines once dared, there now appeared our surface ships, and both U.S. Navy and Army Air Force planes passed overhead. We had to deploy and route our boats most carefully to keep them clear of each other, and to keep them apprised of all friendly forces in their vicinity. A tragic example of what could happen had been given in January when our submarine *Guardfish* came across the U.S. salvage tug *Extractor* and sank her with two torpedo hits, mistaking her for a Japanese I-class sub.

It was increasingly a war waged by air. How drastically the war against shipping had changed is shown by the figures for sinkings in the summer of 1945. In June submarines sank 46 cargo ships totaling 91,339 tons. In July they accounted for only 14 ships of 29,477 tons. On the other hand, in June, aircraft, or mines laid by aircraft, accounted for 70 ships of 154,591 tons; and in July the same agents harvested 129 ships of 280,425 tons, most in waters not accessible to submarines. Clearly, once in position and properly supported, naval and land-based aircraft could produce a rate of sinkings exceeding that by submarines.

The battle for Leyte Gulf had virtually eliminated Japan's navy as a military factor. Our return to the Philippines and the seizure of Okinawa and Iwo Jima meant that the next major use of ground forces would be in the invasion of Japan's home islands, Operation Olympic. In the meanwhile, the Twenty-first Bomber Command and the Twentieth Air Force, flying from their new bases on Saipan, Tinian, and Guam, rained firebombs and demolition bombs on Japan. It was apparent that her antiair defenses were as inadequate as were her antisubmarine measures, but we guarded our submarine lifeguard stations with nothing but admiration and respect for the men who flew the 2,800-mile roundtrip missions.

It was an unforgettable experience to be in a darkened control tower on Saipan at dusk watching the launching of a strike against Japan. Long lines of four-motor B-17s and B-29s moved slowly to takeoff. Hundreds of engines combined their throbbing roar to overwhelm our senses. The universe seemed to pulsate with their power; the deadly bomb loads clutched in the dark bomb bays seemed incidental. Plane after plane taxied into position, opened its throttles wide, and roared into the darkness. When each dropped out of sight at the end of the runway as if it had fallen into the sea, we waited anxiously for the blue glow of exhausts to reappear as it began the long, gradual climb to cruising altitude.

On the morning of August 7 we received the news that an atomic bomb had been dropped on Hiroshima the day before, delivered by the *Enola Gay,* a B-29 from the neighboring island of Tinian. We had had no advance knowledge; not even Admiral Lockwood was informed of the readiness of the new weapon and its imminent use. From sketchy information as to the nature of nuclear explosions, we could only speculate as to their influence on the course of the war. And none of us could foresee that this release of the energy of the atom portended for the submarine a more profound extension of capabilities than for any other arm of the services.

It did seem clear that victory was assured without use of the atomic bomb, but invasion of Japan's home islands, planned for March of 1946, seemed necessary. In the bitter and protracted fighting that would ensue, it was estimated that up to 500,000 men would be killed on both sides and perhaps a million more maimed. This was apparently a compelling factor in President Truman's decision to use the bomb. Two days later the second atomic bomb was dropped, this time on Nagasaki, and events moved rapidly to Japan's unconditional surrender on August 14. Prior to the ceasefire ordered on that day, the last two ships to be sunk by submarine, two small coast defense frigates, were torpedoed by *Torsk* in the Sea of Japan.

Political pressures to "get the boys home by Christmas" hastened demobilization. As a first step, all submarines were divided between the Atlantic and Pacific submarine forces, and assigned ports for leave and recreation while postwar planning continued. Our two squadrons were ordered to Tompkinsville, Staten Island, New York. Our sub tender, the *Orion,* shepherded her flock on the 11,000-mile voyage via Pearl and Panama. It was a pleasure cruise for the fourteen boats in company as well as for those of us who rode *Orion,* but gone was the majestic unity of sea and sky that we had felt part of in our months of blacked-out, solitary cruising. The great array of ships we saw by day and the lights surrounding us each night destroyed the cosmic unity we were once part of and identified us as intruders.

I was home in New London for Thanksgiving, and drove out to the base to find *Halibut*. At one of the long rows of finger piers she rode forlornly, out of commission in her role as an alongside training aid. Her wrinkled hull and battered fitting looked indecent among the sleek, new boats nearby.

As I sat in my old place at the head of the wardroom table, I could hear Jack Hinchey teasing Alex, Joe Galligan describing Boston politics, Bill Kidwell praising California, Ray Stewart quiet (was he thinking of the girl he'd left in San Francisco?), then Guy telling me he had a good "fix" from evening stars as he slipped into his seat next to mine. And Jim, where was Jim Conant? Oh, yes, he had the deck.

Gone was the bunk where Willard Ffrench had lain painfully for 7,000 miles. No loud chatter filled the messroom. The galley where Chief Terry, Norm Thomas, and Mr. Mosley held forth was cold and dark. The torpedo rooms were dank and cavernous; Chief Soulis and his men were gone. The engine rooms were still; Rantz and Schwieso no longer coaxed full power from their pampered machines. The conning tower was empty; gone were its periscopes and the TDC Gardella tended so lovingly.

I went topside and hurried away. I would be glad when *Halibut* was decently put out of her misery, sunk as a target by a sister submarine, or lowered to the bottom for underwater tests.

In December, 1946, five years after she was launched, *Halibut* was sold for scrap. The U.S. Treasury received a check for $23,123.

Appendix I

U.S.S. Halibut (SS 232)
Sailing List
10th War Patrol—8 October 1944

Alexander, Robert John	Ens.	Kelly, Richard Edwin	MoMM1c
Allan, Robert Duncan	EM3c	Kidwell, William N.	Ens.
Allison, Jack Cameron	MoMM1c	LaBertew, Maxwell Curtiss	MoMM3c
Austin, William McMorris	F1c	Lawrence, Kelsie Earl	CRM
Bertheau, Edwin John	TM2c	Logsdon, Lowell Lane	MoMM3c
Bice, Donald Graham	RM3c	Marr, Charles Leslie	RM2c
Black, Robert Joseph	MoMM2c	Marsh, Joseph Staunton	MoMM3c
Bosch, Harry William	S1c	Martin, Lee Efton	MoMM2c
Braun, Allan Ernest	CEM	McCracken, Hugh Ellsworth	S1c
Burgess, Woodrow Hamilton	Y1c	Metzger, Harry Otto	TM3c
Burns, Richard Howard	RT1c	Miller, Everette Owen	S1c
Chalfant, Robert Linley, Jr.	CMoMM	Mitchell, Edwin Foster	EM2c
Conant, James Richards	Lt.(jg)	Noonan Donald Calvin	TM3c
Creighton, Adolph Rennyvaann	S1c	Novakowski, Raymond (n)	F1c
Cummings, Edwin Tucker	TM2c	Oakey, Eugene Snyder	F1c
Davis, Tudor Fred	TM3c	O'Brien, John Thomas	CQM
Dowling, James Harold	TM3c	O'Connell, John Patrick	TM3c
Easterling, Warren Wilson	MoMM1c	Ostrom, Gordon Peter	EM3c
Else, David Charles	EM1c	Perkins, John Marshall, Jr.	TM1c
Emett, James Stirling	MoMM1c	Phillips, John Joseph	StM1c
Eurich, Paul (n)	MoMM2c	Price, Lyle Bertram	F2c
Flaherty, Francis Patrick	MoMM2c	Rantz, Clayton Henry	MoMM1c
Fry, LeRoy Hart	GM1c	Riel, Harold Jerome	TM3c
Galantin, Ignatius Joseph	Comdr.	Rindfuss, Frederick (n), Jr.	SM2c
Galligan, Joseph G.	Lt.	Roberson, David Lee	CMoMM
Gardella, Silvio Joseph	FCS2c	Robinson, Carlos F., Jr.	MoMM3c
Goud, Harold Irving	MoMM3c	Schoenlaub, Richard James	S1c
Griffen, Jesse Ernest	CPhM	Schwieso, Albert August	CMoMM
Grisanti, Arthur Innocence	EM1c	Soulis, James (n)	CTM
Gugliotta, Guy Frank	Lt.Comdr.	Stewart, Raymond E.	Lt. (jg)
Hall, Theodore Thomas	S1c	Sturgeon, Ernest Albert	MoMM2c
Hanson, Wilfred Peter	EM2c	Terry, Allen Raymond	CCS
Harper, James John	S2c	Thomas, James (n)	F2c
Harris, Frederick Vincent	S2c	Thomas, Norman "O"	SC2c
Harris, Rupert William	F1c	Trowbridge, John McLain, Jr.	EM3c
Haynes, Harold William, Jr.	S1c	Vogel, Daniel Frank	S1c
Henderson, William Robert	QM2c	Wallace, Strauther	OS3c
Hinchey, John Joseph	Lt.	Webb, Clyde Leeroy, Jr.	EM3c
Janus, Joseph (n)	RM2c	Welley, Raymond C.	CETM
Jarzencska, Eugene Edward	SM3c	Whittaker, Harold Franklin, Jr.	CEM
Johnson, Darrel Eugene	EM2c		

Appendix II

The Secretary of the Navy takes pleasure in commending the

UNITED STATES SHIP HALIBUT

for service as follows:

"For outstanding heroism in action against enemy Japanese shipping and a combatant unit during her Tenth War Patrol in the Luzon Strait Area from October 8 to December 1, 1944. Brilliantly intercepting an enemy task force retreating from the Battle for Leyte Gulf, the U.S.S. HALIBUT fearlessly penetrated the vigilant screen's inner defenses, and while withstanding severe anti-submarine measures, destroyed with six perfectly directed torpedoes a 10,000 ton heavy cruiser. Later, after tracking a large hostile convoy heavily protected by air and surface escorts, she daringly pressed home the attack and, although extensively damaged by merciless depth charging, valiantly carried on to demolish a medium freighter. A seaworthy and gallant ship, the HALIBUT escaped destruction only by the heroic performance of duty of her courageous officers and men and succeeded in achieving a notable combat record, in keeping with the highest traditions of the United States Naval Service."

All personnel attached to and serving on board the U.S.S. HALIBUT during the above mentioned period are hereby authorized to wear the NAVY UNIT COMMENDATION Ribbon.

James Forrestal

Secretary of the Navy